THEY NEVER HEARD THE FINAL SHOT

PALMETTO
PUBLISHING
Charleston, SC
www.PalmettoPublishing.com

Copyright © 2024 by T. Starr

All rights reserved
No portion of this book may be reproduced, stored in a retrieval system, or transmitted in any form by any means–electronic, mechanical, photocopy, recording, or other–except for brief quotations in printed reviews, without prior permission of the author.

Hardcover ISBN: 9798822963313
Paperback ISBN: 9798822963320
eBook ISBN: 9798822963337
Audiobook ISBN: 9798822963344

THEY NEVER HEARD THE FINAL SHOT

After 50 Years – The Truth About Vietnam

T STARR

DEDICATED TO THE 58,220

Contents

PROLOGUE	i
CHAPTER I: *Uncle Sam Wants Me?*	1
CHAPTER II: *Call to Duty*	13
CHAPTER III: *The Making of a Soldier*	20
CHAPTER IV: *Calm Before the Storm*	58
CHAPTER V: *Preparing for War*	69
CHAPTER VI: *Destination: Uncertainty*	75
CHAPTER VII: *The Vietnam Conflict – 101*	88
CHAPTER VIII: *A War-Ravaged Country Becomes Home*	103
CHAPTER IX: *I Could Tell You, But Then I Would Have To....*	134
CHAPTER X: *The Grim Reaper Strikes out*	157
CHAPTER XI: *Victory at Hand, But Washington Falters*	176
CHAPTER XII: *Promotion Commotion*	208
CHAPTER XIII: *Paradise Found*	214
CHAPTER XIV: *A Case of Abduction*	221
CHAPTER XV: *"Highway" Through Hell*	234
CHAPTER XVI: *Paranormal Encounter*	241
CHAPTER XVII: *The Final Countdown*	256
CHAPTER XVIII: *My Farewell to Arms*	267
CHAPTER XIX: *Vietnam: Good Intentions, Bad Decisions*	277
CHAPTER XX: *Sorrowful Statistics*	294
CHAPTER XXI: *The Search for Normalcy*	297
ACKNOWLEDGMENTS	310
ABOUT THE AUTHOR	312

Illustration by CARTER

PROLOGUE

No other war in United States history has caused as much controversy, consternation, and condemnation as the Vietnam conflict. I have yet to read what I believe to be a thorough and accurate account of what happened in the warfare in Southeast Asia. My purpose is to do so in as concise a manner as possible, or at least try to give the reader a better understanding of what transpired in that far-off land, while also taking the reader along on a personal journey during my tour of duty there.

Older Americans remember the war; younger citizens have hopefully at least heard of it; and many people know someone who participated in it. I had a front row seat. Assigned a Top Secret Crypto clearance during my time in the country, I was privy to information that few others had. I can now share some of that data.

This is but one person's treatise, but my goal is to be as objective and honest as possible in this presentation. It's not an entirely somber work; you will come across some jocularity, mystery, terrifying moments, and even a bit of the supernatural. Suffice it to say I did have my share of interesting occurrences during my military assignment.

Please set aside any belief system you might have regarding this armed conflict. It would be my sincerest hope that you keep an open mind, and in the least, read it with a neutral perspective. Take a second look at the war. Perhaps this will offer the reader a better understanding of what a Vietnam Veteran experienced.

The title of this book is an analogy for the method that game officials once used to signify the end of a football game when one of them would shoot a blank pistol. Many vets from the Indochina theater feel that timid politicians fostered an inglorious situation, and that the American military was not engaged to fire the last shot, thus, there was no true "ending."

There was a stigma that they had "lost a war." The fact of the matter is that there were no American combat troops in South Vietnam for three years before it fell. The U.S. never lost one major engagement during its time in Vietnam and dominated on the battlefield against communist forces.

Still metaphorically speaking, the final shot was never heard by a lot of the returning Vets in a psychological way. Many have forever had torturous memories of their time in the rice paddies and jungles of the faraway battleground, as they re-live the hell on earth they had endured with the sounds of combat forever ingrained in their brains. They are still fighting the war in the deep recesses of their minds. There is never that "final" shot.

And, of course, to those who gave their all, many fell on distant fields in the contentious armed conflict without hearing the fatal discharge of the enemy's weapon that cast their fate. They, too, never heard the final shot.

Concerning the Vietnam War, it would be folly to go into detail over a judgement regarding the wisdom or lack thereof of our nation's presence in that historical military action. I simply won't debate the merits of it either way; that serves no purpose. I have tried making it a point to avoid playing the game of "what if?" my entire life. It is a wasted emotion; I've never learned how to go back in time to rewrite history. Simply put, the war happened.

The U.S. was obligated to assist the South Vietnamese as one of the signatories of the SEATO (Southeast Asia Collective Defense Treaty Organization) Pact, which was signed in 1954 after the Geneva Agreement was completed, separating Vietnam into North and South self-governing nations.

Whatever your view, if you are an American, I hope that you believe that despite some mistakes and bumps and bruises along the way, the basis for your country's involvement was for a noble cause; trying to help keep a people of a sovereign nation free from a totalitarian dictatorship. It was a moral commitment after signing an international agreement to do so.

I wish to make one thing abundantly clear: I hate war. I detest everything about it with every fiber of my being. It is mankind's worst and most grotesque creation. It causes nothing but misery and ruin, and in every major war, scores of innocent civilians, including children and the elderly, die for simply being in the wrong place at the wrong time. Millions of others are displaced and become homeless refugees.

Combat is nothing but a human meat grinder. Countless numbers of soldiers on both sides, if not killed in action, are maimed and/or horribly disfigured for life. Families who have lost loved ones are forever devastated. Beautiful cities and historical architecture are demolished. War is hideous in every aspect of the word and can – and often does – bring out the very worst in human beings.

Having said that, am I anti-war? From a practical standpoint, I am not. How else do you rid the world of scourges like cruel dictators, terrorists, or other evil-doers? What are the alternatives when one nation or entity harasses, invades or tries to steal the land of a sovereign state, or even attempts a takeover of that country?

For those reasons, I want the United States of America to always have the most powerful military in the world. Unfortunately, it's a fact that wickedness abounds today. Negotiations with such deplorable individuals are often a waste of time; overwhelming force is often the only remedy available. The USA has always taken the lead in standing up to history's worst bullies. To quote President Ronald Reagan: "We must not be innocents abroad in a world that is not innocent."

Technically, many consider 1954 as the start of America's involvement in the Vietnam War, primarily because of the signing of the SEATO Pact. Nonetheless, commencement was really a decade later, in 1964, when war footing was ramped up with the Gulf of Tonkin Resolution. For all intents and purposes, the role of the U.S. ended in the early months of 1972 when combat units were demobilized. The so-called Paris "Peace" agreement was signed in January of 1973, but the war would go on until late spring of 1975.

If there was one thing I learned in Vietnam, it is the fact there really are Superheroes. I cannot properly convey how in awe I still am of all who served in the war: Special Forces (Green Berets, Navy Seals, Marines, Army Rangers)....land-based and carrier-based pilots from all branches (bomber, fighter, helicopter, recon, search and rescue, medevacs, etc.)....cavalry....armor....artillery....snipers....Army grunts with their CIB's (Combat Infantry Badges) "humping the boonies"....chopper door gunners....LURPS (Long Range Reconnaissance Patrols)....psyops teams....special ops units....combat engineers....Seabees....tunnel rats....top secret MACV SOG forces....radio operators....Naval and Coast Guard units who protected the waterways in-country and safeguarded operations from the sea....and the many others from all services who toiled in the heat and humidity of Vietnam.

Bravery, courage, resolve, and fearlessness do not seem to be adequate descriptions for these individuals. I will always hold them in the highest esteem. They were the proud sons of The Greatest Generation and were a credit to their memory. A total of 215 heroes would be awarded the Congressional Medal of Honor in Vietnam, our nation's highest honor. I have had the distinct privilege of meeting many of them.

I was far from being categorized with those valorous souls. I was simply a guy, like millions of others, who responded when called upon.

This is my story.

CHAPTER I
Uncle Sam Wants <u>Me</u>?

Damn! Not again! Casually gazing down at a field after just passing over one of the many rice paddies that dotted the landscape, I was sitting in my normal preferred spot on the chopper, sideways on my canvas seat directly behind the pilot with my legs dangling out in the open air of the doorless helicopter.

A loud thud quickly got my attention. We started to spiral downward with the skipper of the Huey, a warrant officer, doing his best to counter the damage caused by ground fire and trying to minimize what was sure to be a crash landing at best. This wasn't my first rodeo; I had been through this before.

Somebody's M-16 slid by me on the floor and jettisoned out, as if it was escorting us to the ground. To make matters even more ominous, my pants were on fire.

How had I found myself in such a perilous quandary in just over the course of a year when I was finishing college and making plans for a career in college athletic administration?

I was vaguely aware of our nation's involvement in a skirmish against communist guerrillas in a small country located halfway around the world when I graduated from high school in 1965. That faraway land was named Vietnam, and it wasn't among the top one thousand things that I knew about or cared about at the time, with my top two being sports and girls, not necessarily in that order.

As required by law, I had registered for the draft when I turned 18 -- but the war was still in its relatively early stages and besides, I had a 4-F college deferment. I would be heading to the University of Iowa that fall. Thus, America's newest theater of combat operations was as distant from my mind as it was on a world map.

However, when I stepped onto the Iowa City campus in the fall of that year, I learned that the Vietnam War was indeed a source of concern for college students. As I was leaving my dorm room one morning during the first week of classes, I noticed a newspaper headline taped on the outside of the room directly across from mine. The bold-faced lettering read: "U.S. Marines Beat Off 200 Viet Cong." It was meant to be a bawdy double-entendre by the joker who resided there, yet for the first time, I started to give a modicum of attention to the conflict.

Where exactly was Vietnam? I wasn't certain that I was even pronouncing it correctly, and I certainly couldn't point it out on a world map.

Although I knew very little about our country's conflict at the time, I volunteered to work at the Veteran's Hospital in Iowa City just after starting my college career, serving as a disc jockey at the facility's radio station. I certainly wasn't close to being Adrian Cronauer of "Good Morning, Vietnam" fame, but hopefully, I helped the days pass by in a more pleasant way for those unfortunate patients, to whom we owed so much.

I had to be careful not to play anything too loudly or startling to the number of shell-shocked (now termed PTSD) individuals from World War II and the Korean War who were hospitalized. The record inventory at the medical center was woefully insufficient, forcing me to utilize my own personal album collection. I also had the duty of reading the news and sports headlines.

The chief of staff of the hospital sent me a cordial letter that stated: "Your sincere interest in the welfare of our veterans is deeply appreciated; we are grateful for the unselfish day-to-day assistance you are providing."

Coming to the end of my freshman year, I was sitting in my dentist's office and noticed the April 8, 1966, edition of *Life Magazine*, which featured a photo of Pete Dawkins on the cover. I was instantly intrigued.

***

Dawkins was a Heisman Trophy winner and consensus all-American halfback at West Point before graduating from the academy in 1958. He was also the team captain, president of his class, and first captain of the entire cadet brigade. He would go on to become a Rhodes Scholar at the University of Oxford in England and earn a PhD from Princeton. He accomplished all this despite having been treated for polio when he was 11 years of age.

At the time of the *Life* article, Pete Dawkins was in that still mysterious (at least to me) place called Vietnam. Recently named a general, he was sent to the country to serve as an advisor to the 1st Vietnamese Airborne Division. Being an advisor did not keep him out of the heat of the action and he soon found himself engaged in three major battles. He would be awarded three Gallantry Crosses (from the South Vietnamese government), and two Bronze Stars from the United States.

The article further prompted my curiosity about military action in the Far East. Soon I would learn that the U.S. had committed 185,000 troops to aid our allies in South Vietnam. Nonetheless, it still didn't really affect my life, due to my college deferment, and I was still in my freshman year.

During that semester, I stopped at a little ma and pa type convenience store a few blocks away from the campus to pick up a soda. The old gentleman who was perched on a stool behind the register asked me if I was a student, and I told him that indeed, I was. He then asked me where I was from, and where my parents had grown up. I informed him that I was from Newton, Iowa but my dad was born in Winterset and my mom hailed from Albia, which were both in the same state as my hometown.

His eyes opened wide and he grinned as he anxiously exclaimed: "I'm from Albia!" It's a good thing that I didn't have a class to attend for a couple of hours because he kept grilling me about relatives who remained in that small Iowa town.

When I mentioned the last name "Karso," he became even more animated and said: "One of my best friends when I was growing up was Andy Karso!" He then inquired: "How is ol' Andy?"

I was taken aback, because Andy was my uncle, and he had been killed at the Battle of the Bulge in WWII. I really didn't know him because I wasn't born until after the war. It saddened my new friend when I had to inform him of Andy's demise.

Following that first year as a Hawkeye, I took a summer job working for a company, Laverty Sprayers, which contracted its services out to the state of Iowa for the purpose of containing vegetation along the roadsides of the main highways in all 99 counties. I would work for that firm for the three summer breaks separating my college years.

Two-men crews, made up primarily of college students like me, were stationed throughout the state, driving Ford trucks featuring 1,000-gallon tanks and a 33-foot boom. One person would drive slowly while the other would operate the boom to saturate the ditches with weed spray.

The chemicals that we used, mixed with water in a huge round cylinder container on the bed of the vehicle, were referred to as 2,4-D and 2,4,5-T. The official titles of the two weed killers, made by the Dow and Monsanto companies, were 2,4-Dichlorophenoxyacetic acid and 2,4-5-Trichlorophenoxyacetic acid, a mixture of two herbicides.

I would one day be associated with them again under a different designation: Agent Orange.

In 1961, President John Kennedy started a program termed "Operation Ranch Hand," which was the aerial spraying of Agent Orange by helicopters and C-123 aircraft over areas of Vietnam for the purpose of destroying thick jungle and forestry that would conceal communist forces.

When the U.S. eventually became more involved in the war, many of our soldiers developed severe health problems from the spray. Studies would show that much of the 2,4-D and 2,4-5-T utilized in Nam was likely contaminated and became toxic.

While spraying the weeds beside the roadsides back in Iowa, Lavery Sprayers would sometimes hear from an irate farmer voicing his concerns over the herbicides' effects on his livestock.

On one occasion, just to ease the mind of such a countryside citizen, I witnessed a partner take a glass and fill it with the chemical-water mixture straight out of the tank, and then proceed to drink its entire contents in front of the wide-eyed man! Apparently, my fellow "Vegetation Control Engineer" (as we called ourselves when trying to catch the eye of a local beauty) never suffered any consequences from that less-than-brilliant demonstration.

In December of '66, China claimed that American jets bombed that country's embassy in Hanoi, Vietnam, although it was never verified, and the U.S. denied any bombing of North Vietnam's capital. It was learned that any damage was most likely caused by flak from the North Vietnamese Army (also known as PAVN – People's Army of Vietnam) anti-aircraft units.

The Chinese issued a statement that it would "redouble punishment to the United States." (Is that similar to being under double secret probation, as implemented by Dean Wormer in the movie *"Animal House?"*)

The next couple of years sped by and other than witnessing some minor on-campus protests and reading about other such gatherings throughout the country, plus reports in the news from the battlefield regarding clashes between the U.S. and the communists. Vietnam still wasn't directly in my sights.

However, it became front and center on January 30, 1968, when all hell broke loose. The People's Army of Vietnam (PAVN), better known to the allies as simply the North Vietnamese Army, and its guerilla movement in the south, the National Liberation Front (NLF), commonly termed the Viet Cong, launched a massive surprise attack throughout South Vietnam. Every major civilian hamlet and military installation of the U.S. Armed Forces and their Allies were hit, including those of the South Vietnamese Army (ARVN – Army of the Republic of Vietnam).

It was a total shock; both sides had always honored a truce during the annual TET (New Year's) holiday. The communist forces hoped to catch the Americans and their Allies by surprise, which they accomplished. The initial reports on the newscasts were not positive. The onslaught became known as the TET Offensive and was arguably the most famous military action of the war.

I was particularly worried about a boyhood friend of mine named Vern Dalton. I knew that he had been there for a few months, so I dropped him a note to check on his status. Here was his reply:

1 March 1968
11:30 A.M. Friday

"Dear Tom,

I received your most welcome letter yesterday and was very glad to hear from you. I am now up in Da Nang, attached to a Marine unit. We came in on an LST (Landing Ship Tank) from Saigon to here. We are supposed to be moving up within miles of the DMZ soon.

This shit just gets worse instead of better. I don't know! I now have ½ my time in and 176 days to go! I can't wait to get home!"

The correspondence made me even more concerned about my friend. If he was only going to be seven miles from the de-militarized zone between the two countries, he would be in the thick of things when the North Vietnamese forces pulled back from their massive, and what would be ill-fated, attack throughout South Vietnam.

I was relieved when Vern returned home months later, but he was a different person for a while, as were many others returning from Vietnam. I would learn that a total of 20 members of my Newton (Iowa) High School class served in the war, and several others were stationed on U.S. Navy ships in the South China Sea, just off the coast of 'Nam, including close friend Dale "Pinky" Myers on the USS Chanticleer, a submarine rescue craft. Another friend, Ron Williams, was a member of the crew on the USS Kitty Hawk, an aircraft carrier that played a vital role in the war effort.

I entered my senior year as a Hawkeye in the fall of 1968, knowing that my 4-F college deferment status was good for only one more year. There was one major change in my life; I married a wonderful girl I had been dating for two years, Nancy Nearmyer, in August of '68.

I was fully expecting to hear from the government at any time. It finally happened on April 8, 1969, when I received an SSS Form 223 "Order to Report for Armed

Forces Physical Examination" from the Selective Service Board in Johnson County (in which Iowa City is located). I submitted a written request to have a change of venue to my hometown of Newton, Iowa in Jasper County. My appeal was granted.

It would take two months before I heard from the Jasper County Draft Board. On June 24, I received an order to report to the Selective Service office in that county on July 2 at 3:45 p.m.

Official paperwork could be submitted to the Board allowing a potential draftee to have a physical exam conducted by a third-party doctor, and if approved, he could go that route. It was well-known at the time that there was a doctor in Iowa City who, for $400, would fill out the official papers specifying that you had a condition or problem that would preclude you from military service.

That never entered my mind. I don't judge any individuals for what they thought was appropriate for their actions, but I simply couldn't have done that. Many of my family members had served (and died) for their country, and I vowed to do the same if called upon. I knew that I would have to look in the mirror every day for the rest of my life, not to mention eventually gazing into the eyes of my children and grandchildren.

I reported for my appointment in Newton on July 2, and from there, we took a 45-minute bus ride to Fort Des Moines located in, surprise, Des Moines!

Our testing at the base lasted for two days, and it was rather comical. First, before the physical exams, we were asked a series of questions about our medical history. "Have you ever had a broken leg; have you ever had heart problems; have you been institutionalized for mental issues; etc." The list of questions was long and covered the gamut of human ailments.

While I was waiting in line, I overheard the responses from the potential draftee in front of me. He replied "yes" to every conceivable malady known to man! I swear that if they had asked him if he had gone through menopause, he would have answered in the affirmative. That poor chap really did not want to be a soldier!

On the second day, July 3, after all testing had been completed, I was handed a Statement of Acceptability. It read: "The qualifications of the above-named recipient have been considered in accordance with the current regulation governing acceptance of Selective Service registration and he has, on this date: Found fully acceptable for induction into the Armed Forces."

Translation: "He has a pulse."

Nonethless, you pretty much had to have all of your working parts. I had a friend from Newton named Bob Skow, who was a year younger than me, included in the group that met at our hometown Selective Service Board offices. He was hobbling along with a cane and had a noticeable limp.

I inquired as to the nature of his injury. He replied that his wife was being attacked by a strange ferocious dog in their back yard, so he grabbed his shotgun. While running out the back door, he tripped, and his weapon of choice discharged, blowing off part of his foot.

I said: "What the heck are you doing here, you can hardly walk?" He replied that it wasn't that bad, and he was sure he would be drafted. I just shook my head and grinned with that "c'mon, man" look. He told me that he would attend my graduation from basic training if he didn't have to go, which was fairly obvious that he wouldn't.

The sobering reality of being drafted and going to Vietnam was now uppermost in my thoughts. Though I started the 1969 fall semester and still needed six more hours to graduate, my four-year college postponement from military duty had expired. I knew it was probably just a matter of time before I received my notification letter from Uncle Sam.

On October 29, I perused a front-page article in my hometown newspaper, the *Newton Daily News*, where I learned that another high school classmate and friend, John Wallace, had been awarded the Bronze Star for heroism in the ongoing war.

John, a 1st Lieutenant and an Airborne Ranger, was cited for action while serving as a platoon leader with Company C, 1st Battalion, 6th Infantry. His unit came under hostile fire while securing a key bridge near Tam Ky. Wallace maneuvered through the heavy barrage and made it to a point to stand on the bridge where he could direct and control the fire of his men in securing the important structure. In addition to the Bronze Star, John added another Purple Heart Medal to one he had already garnered in previous action.

(John and I would run into each other in Vietnam on a Saigon street the following year, which gave us a chance to catch up over a beer, or possibly two....maybe three.)

It was hard for me to imagine that my boyhood friends like John Wallac Vern Dalton, and several others were now in the serious and brutal business of war. It seemed that it was just yesterday that our most pressing issues were trying to get dates for the weekend, scrounging up enough money for gas, and deciding where to eat and hang out after high school classes were adjourned for the day.

Fate was about to send me in the same direction as my buddies. It was Monday, November 3 in that year of 1969. The weather was pleasant and following a morning class, I headed to the home where my bride of one year, Nancy, and I resided. We had planned to meet for lunch in downtown Iowa City, across the street from where she worked in the School of Engineering building, that day.

THEY NEVER HEARD THE FINAL SHOT

At 11:30, I left my abode to head for my noon date. Just as I walked out the door, I encountered the mailman, who handed me a stack of flyers, bills, magazines, and everything else that fills a mailbox on a daily basis.

After a bit of small talk about the upcoming game involving the Hawkeyes, who would be playing at Indiana that Saturday, he bid me goodbye. I hopped into my car for my short drive to the restaurant near the campus.

I leafed through the stack of mail at a stop light. And there it was; a letter from the Selective Service. I didn't have to open it to know the purpose of its contents. But, of course, I did rip into the envelope and pulled out the official form. I had, indeed, been drafted and was given 30 days to report for duty. It was not a surprise in the least.

> *Gather 'round, cat, and I'll you a story*
> *About how to become an all-American boy;*
> *....One day my Uncle Sam said: 'Here I am!'*
> *Uncle Sam needs you, boy*
> *I'm a gonna cut your hair,*
> *Uhhh, take that rifle, kid!*

■   All-American Boy
       --Bill Parsons

I found a parking place and hurried to meet Nancy at a small diner close to her office where she served as a secretary in the Engineering Department. Breaking the news to my wife of only 15 months was not going to be easy.

Spotting her already sitting at a small table, I was all smiles and kept everything light as I kissed her on the forehead and proceeded to take a seat across from her. She gave me a terrified stare and blurted out: "What's wrong?" How DID she do that? I thought I had done a pretty good job of acting. Obviously, I had to tell her the truth. She was devastated.

I tried to get an extension from the draft board to allow me to finish out the current semester, but I was rebuffed, with the news coming in a reply from the Selective Service on November 13.

My life was about to be forever changed.

CHAPTER II
Call to Duty

*"In sixty-nine I was twenty-one
And I called the road my own;
I don't know when that road
Turned into the road I'm on."*

■ Running on Empty
--Jackson Browne

The day of my reporting for military duty had arrived, and after saying all my good-byes to family and friends, I checked in at the Newton Post Office, site of our town's draft board.

The date was December 3, 1969, and once again I found myself on a bus headed to Fort Des Moines. The woman who served as the head of the Newton Selective Service Board sat beside me. She asked me: "Do you know what your draft number was under the new system?" I replied: "No."

On December 1, 1969, the United States commenced a military lottery draft based on one's birthday. One blue capsule for each day of the year was placed in a large glass container. There was a drawing at the Selective

Service National Headquarters in Washington D.C. and the event was broadcast live nationally on television.

All U.S. males born between January 1, 1944 and December 31, 1950 were affected. Based on the drawings, individuals were drafted according to their lottery numbers until a specified amount of manpower had been met. For example, September 14 was the first day drawn. Thus, persons with that birthday would be the first to be drafted, they were #1. The draft would then progress until the needed quota was achieved. (Australia had a similar lottery and Aussies termed it the "Lottery of Death.")

I didn't bother watching, wanting to spend my last two days at home with my family because it was too late for me, no matter what my number was; I had already been drafted. My seat mate on the bus continued: "I can look it up if you wish." I gave her the go-ahead. She took out her list and following a quick perusal, turned to me with a somewhat sympathetic look and informed me that my number was #346. That was just 19 from the very last number selected!

All I could do was chuckle. I never would have been drafted under the new system. The Selective Service stopped taking new recruits after #195. Two days separated the lottery draft and my order to report for duty. They got me in just under the gun; I'm pretty sure that's why I didn't get my request for an extension to stay in school until the end of the current semester, which ended just one month later. "Missed it by that much," as Agent 86 Maxwell Smart would say.

By the way, the reader might be interested to know that President Donald Trump's number was #356; President George W. Bush's was #327, and President Bill Clinton's was #311. Some others of prominence: David Letterman with my same #346; Sly Stallone, #327; Rudy Guiliani, #308; O.J. Simpson, #277; Jay Leno, #223; Stephen King and Bill Murray, #204; Bruce Springsteen, #119; and Al Gore, #030. President Joe Biden was too old for the draft in 1969; thus, his name was not entered into the lottery.

Contrary to what many believe, only 10% of my generation would serve in the Vietnam War.

We arrived at the base in Des Moines and if memory serves me correctly, approximately 400 of us were immediately gathered in a large hall, seated on folding chairs in perfectly aligned rows. Standing in front of the assemblage was an Army officer who called out four names to report to a side room. Guess who was on that short list?

I got up and headed for the designated area. When I entered with the other three selected individuals, we were met by a sharply dressed Marine gunnery sergeant. He simply said: "Welcome to the U.S. Marine Corps, gentlemen!" What? He was eyeing all of us up one side and down the other and after looking at me, with a commanding voice, inquired: "Is that a wedding ring?" I answered him in the affirmative, and he pointed to the big room from whence I came and bellowed: "Get back out there in the Army!"

I have no idea what that was about. Were the Marines now recruiting, or were they low on their needed allocation and pilfering potential troops from the Army? Were they trying to hold down the number of married men in their ranks? All I know is that I was going to be a member of the United States Army.

Yes sir, I was in "this here man's Army," as the saying goes. I was fine with that; it was my time to serve and as trite as it sounds, I thought it was a small price to pay for living in what I believe to be the greatest country in the world.

Besides, I felt an obligation to my family. My brother, Dick, had served in an armor unit in the Army, and my relatives had sacrificed a lot in WWII. Simply put, it was my turn.

As previously mentioned, I lost one uncle, Andy Karso, in the German build-up to the Battle of the Bulge in WWII. While serving with the 95th Infantry Division, 379th Infantry Regiment, Andy, a Private First Class (PFC), was killed in action (KIA) on November 19, 1944, in the Ardennes-Alsace area of France near the Belgium border (and not far from the Siegfried Line).

He was initially listed as missing in action (MIA) for an extended period amid all the confusion of the surprise Nazi onslaught, which caused immense consternation among my aunt, Zoe, and her close relatives, including her sister, who was my mother (I had not yet been born). Andy, who had enlisted just 16 months prior to his untimely death, is buried in the Lorraine American Cemetery in Saint-Avold, France, along with 10,488 other American soldiers.

While Uncle Andy fought and lost his life in Europe engaging the Germans, I had a first cousin, Paul "Bubby" Flattery, who was badly wounded while fighting the Japanese on the island of Ie-Shiema (currently known as Iejima) off the Northwest corner of Okinawa, in the Pacific Campaign. Bubby served with the 77th Infantry Division, 305th Infantry Regiment. On April 18, 1945, on a hellish parcel of land known as "Bloody Ridge," he and his platoon walked directly into a hidden and well-concealed Japanese machine gun nest, which opened up on the Americans from just 15 yards away.

Bubby lost many of his fellow squad members, and he, himself, received numerous serious wounds, including having part of his hand blown off. It was routine for Japanese Imperial forces to bayonet bodies strewn across the battlefield to make certain they were dead, but fortuitously they walked over Bubby, who lay completely still face down despite being in intense pain. His ruse worked as the enemy soldiers thought he was already deceased and did not administer the deadly coup de grace. Killed in the same operation on that day was famed war correspondent Ernie Pyle, who was near Bubby and his unit when he was also raked by machine gun fire during the brutal engagement.

I had another uncle, Davy Smith, who was a Naval hero in that same war. As part of Task Force 22.3, Davy and his mates aboard the destroyer Chatelain captured a German Submarine – the U-505 – off the coast of Africa on June 4, 1944, just two days before the storming of the beaches at Normandy, France by the Allies. The confiscation was kept top secret, and the codebooks, spy machinery, and other materials found on the captive enemy sub, part of the Nazi's dreaded "Wolfpack" strategy, proved invaluable to U.S. codebreakers. Davy's task force was later awarded a Presidential Unit Citation. The U-505 has been on display in front of the Museum of Science and Industry in Chicago since 1954.

Mom's family had certainly done its share in contributing to the "Greatest Generation," a term coined by newsman and author Tom Brokaw (a fellow Hawkeye) to describe the American population – particularly the Veterans – who endured so much during that period of our nation's history. Both of my uncles, Andy and Davy, were married to sisters of my mother, while cousin Bubby was the son of still another sister of hers.

Mom told me that she had taken my brother, Dick, who was eight years old at the time, to a late afternoon movie on a day when a catastrophic event ushered in America's involvement into the war. The date was December 7, 1941. The manager of the theater stopped the film halfway through the showing and informed the audience that our country had been attacked, explaining that the Japanese had bombed an unknown place called Pearl Harbor in Hawaii. Mom said she had a foreboding feeling at that time about what was to come.

I had always remembered this quote by Heisman Trophy winner Nile Kinnick, the great football player from my alma mater, the University of Iowa, who later joined the Navy as an aviator: "Every man whom I've admired

17

in history has willingly and courageously served in his country's armed forces in times of danger. It is not only a duty but an honor to follow their example the best I know how. May God give me the courage and ability to so conduct myself in every situation that my country, my family, and my friends will be proud of me."

Kinnick had been a basketball star for the Hawkeyes as well as being one of the top college football players in the nation, finishing as the second-leading scorer on the Iowa team. He was named the Associated Press Male Athlete of the Year over baseball's Joe DiMaggio, golf's Byron Nelson, and boxing's Joe Louis in 1939.

The grandson of a former Iowa governor, Nile graduated cum laude, was president of his class, and gave the commencement speech at graduation.

Forgoing a professional football career and after attending law school for just one year, Kinnick decided it was time to serve his country, and joined the Naval Air Reserve just three days before the Pearl Harbor attack. Tragically, flying off the aircraft carrier USS Lexington on June 2, 1943, his Grumman F4F Wildcat developed mechanical difficulties and crashed into the sea, killing the young aviator. The Iowa football stadium is now named in his honor.

(Iowa's first-ever all-American football player met a similarly grievous fate years earlier in WWI. Fred Becker was one of the nation's top linemen in 1916, but then dropped out of school when the war broke out and joined the Marine Corps. Becker was killed in action in July of 1918 at the battle of Chateau-Thierry in France. He was posthumously awarded the Distinguished Service Cross, the U.S.'s second highest combat award, and the Croix de Guerre, France's top honor for heroism.)

On the day that I became a soldier, a crowd of 300,000 was participating in an anti-war demonstration in the nation's capital. That is what makes our country the great beacon of freedom that it is; they did what they felt they had to do, and my fellow inductees and I did what we believed was the proper course of action.

During the length of the Vietnam conflict, some 170,000 draft-eligible American men received conscientious objector status, primarily for religious reasons, which kept them from military duty. The most famous was boxing champion Muhammad Ali, due to his Muslim faith. Others simply burned their draft cards and refused to be inducted, with some of them going to jail. Anywhere from 35,000 to 75,000 anti-war protestors of draft age fled to the sanctuary of Canada, with possibly as many as half of them going to Toronto. (In true irony, there were over 30,000 Canadians who volunteered to fight with U.S. forces in Vietnam.) A reported 700 other Americans fled to Sweden, where they were protected against prosecution by the United States.

After a short stay at Fort Des Moines, we were dispersed to different basic training bases. I was assigned to Fort Lewis in the state of Washington. Some of us were whisked off to the airport and placed on a United Airlines flight which would take us to Sea-Tac Airport, located halfway between Seattle and Tacoma.

It would be the furthest I had ever been away from home.

CHAPTER III
The Making of a Soldier

My journey to the northwest was my first trip on a commercial jet, and I loved the experience. As young, red-blooded boys, my fellow draftees and I were in awe of the beautiful mini-skirted "stewardesses," which helped take our minds off the torture that lay in store for us. (I certainly didn't know at the time that a similarly-gorgeous stewardess – now of course referred to as flight attendants – would someday become my beloved soulmate.)

Upon landing at Sea-Tac, we were bussed to Fort Lewis, which was to be my new "home" for a while. I was now officially Private Thomas Ray Starr, 1st Platoon, Company A, 4th Battalion, 1st BCT Brigade.

I was mildly surprised that I had been sent halfway across the country for basic training; most of my buddies from Newton were assigned to Fort Leonard Wood on the southern border of Missouri, which was much closer to our hometown, for their boot camp.

Fort Lewis was named after Meriwether Lewis of the famed Lewis and Clark Expedition and is located roughly 40 miles from Seattle and 11 miles from Tacoma. McChord Air Force Base adjoined Fort Lewis

Our first order off the busses was to line up in an assorted mess that didn't even resemble a formation, and of course we were yelled at and told that we were "lower than whale shit."

We Iowa boys were joined by recruits from the likes of California, Nevada and other Western states, including about a dozen Native-Americans from Utah. We would eventually all become friends and literally comrades-in-arms.

It was a hectic first day of finding our barracks, getting our ill-fitted Army clothing, and quickly putting on our new garb. After dressing in my fatigues and admiring my new look in a latrine mirror, I thought: "Hey, I look just like those little green toy plastic soldiers I used to play with....only bigger."

We were given fatigue shirts and pants, the famous Army Peacoats, long underwear, boxers, socks, boots, stretchable blousing bands (for use in tucking in the bottom of the pants), glove liners, leather gloves, helmets with steel liners, and baseball-style caps. At a later date we received our dress greens, dress shirts and ties, dress caps, and garrison caps (known by a crude name among G.I.'s).

I did have a tinge of pride the first time I put on my Army fatigues, knowing how many great Americans had done the same thing. It's probably akin to the first time a baseball player first puts on the New York Yankee pinstripes or an Alabama football player initially dons the crimson jersey.

Next up, we had to get our haircuts. It was simply an assembly line of a "barber" going down the line and cutting off all of our hair; I believe the average haircut was 19 seconds or something of that nature. The technique involved the hair cutter starting at the front of the face and zipping over the top and down the back with an electric razor. Some of the California surfer dudes who reported with long, blond locks looked entirely different minus their manes.

We were lined up back into formation, in a downpour of rain, as the company commanding officer, a captain, addressed us on a central parade ground flanked by our billeting (barracks). And then….we met our drill sergeant. For our purposes here, I'll call him Drill Sergeant Scary (which rhymes with his actual last name).

We quickly learned that a drill sergeant is definitely not your new Mother. He is mean, rude, crude, calls everyone terrible names, and is a jerk. That was pretty much his job. (Well, at least it was back in those days.) One of the primary purposes of boot camp was to break you down as individuals and build you back up as a unit. It is magnified during a time of war.

My brother, Dick, told me a story regarding the calculated absurdity of basic training when he served in the 1950's. His unit was told to take all of the white stones in front of its barracks and paint half of them red and the other half green. When the recruits had finally finished the long, tedious job, the unit's drill sergeant came out to inspect the work that the trainees had done and proclaimed: "You painted the wrong ones red and the wrong ones green!" Thus, they had to go back and paint the red rocks green, and the green ones red.

Drill Sergeant Scary told us what every drill instructor throughout history has told his new inductees: We were the sorriest lot he had ever seen. How in the world could he take this bunch of losers and make them soldiers? The Army was asking the impossible of him.

And then, of course, there was one of the oldest, worn-out but seemingly obligatory questions to be directed at a selected trainee. The drill sergeant looked at a recruit and asked him where he was from. "Nevada, Drill Sergeant!" the new soldier answered. And then Scary sneered: "Nevada? I heard that all they had in Nevada was steers and queers and I don't see any cows around here....what does that make you, boy?" That was the refrain no matter which state was named. (I'm pretty sure they can't do that anymore!)

A job for Sergeant Scary on that day was to pass out our dog tags. He would call out a name and that person was supposed to report front and center to receive his tags. Scary would toss them to him and purposely aim low so that the metal pieces would land in the biggest puddle of rainwater or mud that he could find. The trainee would then have to fish them out. (I had to always listen closely to Scary, who – let's just say wasn't a member of Mensa – would always mis-pronounce my name "Stare" instead of "Star.")

The harassment was constant. This was the old Army, and it was intense. There was no political correctness; drill sergeants didn't have to worry about saying the wrong thing, or for that matter, doing the wrong thing. Watch the movie, *Full Metal Jacket*, and even though that film depicted a Marine boot camp, you will get a taste of what we were forced to endure.

> *"We came in spastic, like tameless horses;*
> *We left in plastic, as numbered corpses;*
> *And we learned fast, to travel light;*
> *Our arms were heavy, but our bellies were tight...."*
>
> ■ Goodnight Saigon
> --Billy Joel

One of the first things that we were taught was how to properly salute an officer. You would never salute a non-commissioned officer, including your drill sergeant. "I work for a living, don't ever salute me," would be the common retort from a drill sergeant if a recruit ever made that mistake.

We were presented with *The Soldier's BCT Handbook*, which covered everything from teaching a recruit how to drill correctly; a tutorial on treating wounds; the proper way to safely handle all weapons; knowledge of land navigation, camouflage, and bivouacking; how to treat prisoners in one's care, and other rudimentary details.

We were also eventually given a U.S. Military Code of Conduct card; an *Infantry Marksmanship Progress Booklet*; a card outlining proper procedures when confronted with a nuclear, biological, or chemical attack; a book on the *Operation and Preventive Maintenance of the M16A1 Rifle*; a booklet regarding our combat boots, and checkout cards for our rifle, bayonet, and gas mask.

Bunk assignments were allocated; I was given a top one. We were in one big room which facilitated dozens of trainees who resided there; I can't remember the exact number. The sets of top-and-bottom beds were arranged in two parallel lines with a large tile floor space in the middle. Mine was located about halfway down the left side as you entered the room. At one end was another row of bunks placed vertically to the two long rows of the other beds. At the opposite end, next to the "front door," were latrines and showers. Each soldier had a footlocker beside his bed located underneath windows which spanned the room.

We learned that every night we would be assigned two types of guard duty, roving and fire. Lights were out at 10:00 p.m. and roving guard duty, which was an hour, might be from midnight to 1:00 a.m., and fire guard duty, requiring a half-hour, could conceivably be from 3:00 to 3:30. The two never ran consecutively; simply more of the purposeful basic training annoyance. With reveille at 5:00 a.m., it's easy to see that you were never allowed sound sleep for an extended time. One's guard times were changed every night.

 The fire guard duty was easy; you simply stayed in your barracks and walked around to make certain everything was copesetic. The roving guard duty took place outside, using a pre-determined route to check that all was well around the base.

We were told that there had been rare instances when a carload of girls would somehow get by the front gate (a near impossibility) and try to convince a roving guard to hop into the car for perverse purposes. I'm pretty certain that was just a ploy to make us think that something exciting might happen because frankly, it was a pretty boring job.

We were forced to sleep with all windows open on those frosty Northwestern nights – and they were COLD -- due to the fact that meningitis had been detected at other boot camps, both Army and Marines, at the time. Evidently, the U.S. Army preferred pneumonia over meningitis.

Fortunately, we had those vintage green wool blankets that all older G.I.'s remember well. They were a tad bit scratchy. I'm pretty certain they were made from the same material as that of SOS or Brillo pads. In my mind one possible use for the bedspread might be to cut one up into little squares and use them as sandpaper or for scrubbing pots and pans. Sleeping under a thorny rose bush would have been less irritating than this wool covering, but at least they provided warmth.

Your assigned small footlocker included the proper storing of socks, underwear, t-shirts and hygiene supplies. Everything had to be stacked, placed, and rolled up perfectly or you risked the chance of the drill sergeant or one of his aides opening your locker at any time.

If one little thing was found out of place, he would overturn it with everything falling on the floor. He would then yell in the ear of the wrongdoer until he had placed everything back in its proper position in the locker in a designated time, which was just a few seconds long.

You also had to become an expert on "making your bed." The requirement was to have perfect 45 degree "hospital corners" and the sheet and cover pulled so tight that a quarter would bounce high if flipped on it. Again, if that housekeeping duty did not meet standards, the drill sergeant or aide would rip off the miscreant's mattress, sheets, blanket, and pillow – throwing them all on the floor -- and would scream at him until he quickly corrected the problem. We were always in danger of unannounced surprise inspections.

There was a requirement to "spit shine" your boots, using cotton balls, water, and shoe polish. We learned that if you could find some nylon hosiery, it would give your boots a sheen that you could use for a mirror; the problem was that nobody seemed to have any hose in the barracks for some reason! That piece of advice did come in handy after basic training, however, and there were probably a lot of wives wondering why their husbands took pairs of panty hose, discarded because of "runs," out of the trash can after they had been thrown away!

A recruit's "gig line" was important, too, making certain that the middle line of the buttoned-down fatigue shirt matched the zipper line of the trousers. Those things stay with you: I still make certain my gig line is straight and I continue to use my wife's discarded pantyhose to shine my dress shoes!

Following 5:00 a.m. reveille, we would have to jump up and completely clean the barracks every day, scrubbing down the latrines, waxing the tile floors, and assuring streak-free windows in the sleeping area. We would then proceed to breakfast, standing in line, taking one proper step at a time until inside the dining hall, going through the buffet, and finishing your meal within three minutes. If you did not succeed in the allotted time, your tray was taken from you and dumped in the trash. (I remain a fast eater to this day because of that!)

Finally, the training began. I felt confident because I was in excellent shape both from having minored in P.E. at the University of Iowa, and also because I worked out and had a running routine which I implemented after getting my draft notice. I did not want to be in poor physical condition when I considered what was to come.

Nonetheless, it was torturous and grueling. Rain was our constant companion, as anyone who has spent extensive time in Seattle might have guessed. It was a cold winter in the Pacific Northwest, with the temperature often dropping below freezing; the wind chill factor made it even more miserable. When it is that cold, a driving rain hitting your skin really stings.

Fortunately, our steel pots (helmets) helped keep the raindrops out of our eyes. We all prayed that the pounding rain would turn to slow-falling snow, but it never did. I'm no meteorologist, so I can't explain that.

We wore wool glove liners with leather outer gloves, but it didn't seem to matter; my hands still became painful and numb.

On rare occasions on the coldest days, deuce-and-a-half trucks would bring out vats of hot coffee to us in the field. I would stealthily pour out the water from my canteen and fill it with coffee, using it for a hand warmer when I could sneak in a chance to do so.

Obviously, physical training was our first priority. This included extensive calisthenics, running, and navigating obstacle courses. It was rigorous and exhaustive. I was thankful that I had the foresight to get into the best possible shape before reporting.

We did have a couple of overweight guys in our unit who really struggled, and we all helped them as much as we could, assisting them over obstacles when the drill sergeant wasn't looking. Actually, he might have pretended not to see because one purpose of boot camp was to build up camaraderie among the recruits, and this was but one way to do so.

Drill Sergeant Scary was ruthless to us, so three revenge-minded enterprising lads were able to dish out a small measure of what was payback in their minds.

Every morning our entire unit was required to "police the grounds," meaning we had to walk around the entire base and pick up all litter, no matter how small. The three amigos asked us to give any candy bar or cigarette wrappers to them.

I learned later that they knew where Scary parked his car every day, and one of them – with the other two serving as lookouts – would sneak off and stuff all the trash down into his gas tank.

We would stand in formation first thing after breakfast. In our second week, the captain stood before us and told us that we would be inoculated that day. When he departed, Drill Sergeant Scary said: "You heard the captain, you're going to be inbob….inob….inclated…." The word was either foreign to him or he was tongue-tied, so in anger, he yelled: "You're gonna get some fuckin' shots today!"

And that we did: Tetanus, influenza, oral polio, plague and typhoid. It was the first of many, many inoculations that we were to get within the next year. On that particular day, we were simply in another assembly line, a doctor on each side with one administering a shot in your right arm while at the same time another physician was giving you one in your left.

One trainee near the front of the line fainted dead away just as he was starting to go down the gauntlet; the Army's gigantic needles petrified him.

We were improving at having properly spaced formations. Simply extending your right arm until it touched the left shoulder of the soldier next to you with your outstretched fingertips provided the correct distance. Protocol mandated that you stand at attention when the captain or any officer was in front of the formation.

We learned the meanings of "Parade Rest," holding your left wrist with your right hand behind your back and slightly spreading your legs; and "At Ease," which indicated that you didn't have to stand at attention anymore. And, of course, there was the old Army "smoke 'em if you got 'em" line when we were at ease (although it was a joke because nobody was allowed to have cigarettes in basic training).

Morning formations were also a time for punishment. One of our poor mates didn't shave one day, and he sported a heavy "5:00 shadow." He was ordered to retrieve his razor and bring it back to where we stood. While we grimmaced, he was forced to dry shave. Neither water nor shaving cream was allowed. By the time he finished, he appeared to be auditioning for a horror movie, with his face being a bloody mess.

One of the Utah Native Americans in our unit was named Dreaming Bear, and that is exactly what it said on the name tag sewed above the pocket on his green fatigue shirt. It was pretty obvious that Dreaming Bear did not want to be there. He went AWOL (absent without leave) on numerous occasions.

When the sergeants would learn that Dreaming Bear had once again "gone over the hill" in military slang, we would be called out in formation, usually around 1:00 or 2:00 in the morning, and forced to stand out in the freezing rain clad only in our underwear until Dreaming Bear had been caught....and he was always eventually nabbed. The Army believed in mass punishment for the actions of one.

We were expected to correct the problem ourselves; one tried and true method through the years in the Army was putting bars of soap or other small hard objects into pillowcases and pummeling the guy in his bed while others held him down. That didn't happen; we just weren't those types of individuals. We liked Dreaming Bear and perhaps felt sorry for his plight, but that doesn't mean we didn't get mad as hell at the guy! We did certainly punish him verbally. He finally got the message that he was really hurting all of us, and he finally quit running away. Dreaming Bear had also learned that attempting to escape from the basic training area of Ft. Lewis was futile.

(Another known Army form of "group therapy" involved the use of wire boot brushes on a trainee who refused to bath. He was thrown into the shower and scrubbed down until he was raw. I was told that this happened involving a platoon in the building next to ours.)

Marching filled our hours. "And the Army goes rolling along" isn't just a song. It's a way of living. Forced marches were the rule of the day, and going 30 miles was not uncommon, sometimes with up to 80 pounds of equipment on our back. The worst part of Fort Lewis at that time was the huge rock surface that covered much of the base. They were large white granite rocks the size of softballs. They were hard to march on, especially when the drill sergeant yelled "double-time!"

We were physically drained much of the time with the constant marching, running and workouts. I would get my inspiration from beautiful, majestic snow-covered Mt. Rainier, which rose to almost 15,000 feet at its summit. Located some 50 miles from Ft. Lewis, it was always visible as it towered above the horizon. For whatever reason, it provided serenity. I would purposely gaze at it during particularly agonizing times, seeking the calming influence that it never failed to give me.

Over the years the Army had developed several marching songs to help overcome the boredom of marching hours-on-end. It's safe to say that the songs we sang are no longer in vogue in today's Army, with its expanded female role.

Another purpose of the songs was to keep proper marching cadence to assure a uniform pace and to make certain that we were in unison in our left or right steps. The drill sergeant would sing a frame and the unit would repeat it. Here is an example:

Drill Sergeant (DS): "Ain't no use in looking down"
    Platoon (all repeating): "*Ain't no use in looking down*"
DS: "Ain't no discharge on the ground"
    Platoon: "*Ain't no discharge on the ground*"
DS: "Sound off, one, two, sound off, three, four
    Bring it on down"
All together: "*One, two, three, four, one, two....*
        THREE, FOUR!"

Jody was the Army's name for the cad back home who was going to steal your girlfriend or wife, so a cadence song would go like this:

DS: "When I get a three-day pass"
    Platoon: "*When I get a three-day pass*"
DS: "I'm gonna kick ol' Jody's ass"
    Platoon: "*I'm gonna kick ol' Jody's ass*"
    DS: Sound off, one, two.... (repeat same countdown as above)

Many songs were geared towards assuring that you were stepping off either on your right foot or left foot at the proper time:

DS: "You had a good home when you <u>left</u>"
    Platoon: "*You're <u>right</u>!*"
DS: "Jody was home when you <u>left</u>"
    Platoon: "*You're <u>right</u>!*"
DS: "You'll never get home on your <u>left</u>"
    Platoon: "*You're <u>right</u>!*"
DS: Sound off, one two....(repeat countdown)

There was this gung-ho number:

DS: "I want to be an Airborne Ranger"
    Platoon: *"I want to be an Airborne Ranger"*
DS: "I want to live the life of danger:
    Platoon: *"I want to live the life of danger"*
DS: "I want to go to Vietnam:
    Platoon: *"I want to go to Vietnam"*
DS: "I want to fight the Viet Cong"
    Platoon: *"I want to fight the Viet Cong"*
DS: Sound off, one, two….(repeat countdown)

The marching song that is probably the most familiar with every Army veteran (at least in the "old" Army) was this ballad (for the sake of brevity, each line to the song will be listed just once; normal procedure is the same as above with the Drill Sergeant soloing first followed by the Platoon echoing his words):

"The prettiest girl,
    I ever saw,
Was drinking bourbon,
    through a straw;
The prettiest girl,
    I ever saw,
Was drinking bourbon…. through a straw.
I walked right up,
    I sat right down,
I ordered up,
    another round;
I placed my hand,
    upon her knee,
She said 'GI,'
    you're teasing me!
I placed my hand,
    upon her thigh,
She said 'GI,'
    that's way too high!
I picked her up,

I laid her down,
　Her long blond hair,
　　lay all around;
The wedding was,
　　a formal one,
Her daddy had,
　　a white shotgun;
And now I've got,
　　a mother-in-law,
And 14 kids,
　　who call me pa.
The morale of,
　　this story's clear,
Instead of bourbon....stick with beer!"

We were also forced to sing these two lewd and crude numbers about the female anatomy:

DS: "If I die on a Russian front"
　Platoon: *"If I die on a Russian front"*
DS: "Bury me in a Russian c**t"
　Platoon: *"Bury me in a Russian c**t"*
DS: Sound off, one, two....(repeat countdown)

And there was this one:

DS: "I don't know but I've been told,"
　Platoon: *"I don't know but I've been told,"*
DS: "Eskimo p***y's mighty cold!"
　Platoon: *"Eskimo p***y's mighty cold!"*
DS: "Sound off, one, two....(repeat countdown)

To all the moms out there, I'm sorry to tell you that your little angels lost much of their purity while going through the rigors of boot camp, which included the obscene marching cadence shown above.

"Remember when the days were long, and rolled beneath a deep blue sky,
Didn't have a care in the world, with Mommy and Daddy standin' by;
Who knows how long this will last, now we've come so far, so fast,
But somewhere back there in the dust that same small town in each of us,
I used to remember this....but this is the end....
This is the end of the innocence."

■ The End of the Innocence
--Don Henley

The publicity slogan for the Vietnam movie, *Platoon*, put it even more succinctly and would have more meaning to me and many of my boot camp buddies within a few short months: "The First Casualty of War is Innocence."

Sometimes we would march with no singing, it would simply be "*left, right, left....left, right left, go to your left....left....left, right, left....left....left....left, right, left....go to your left....left....left, right, left*" ad infinitum. (Find an old Army vet and he will explain the marching cadence and even sing the aforementioned songs for you!)

We learned how to march in precision and how to march in a parade honoring high-ranking officials, complete with the "Eyes....RIGHT" command. We also learned how to drill with our rifle; how to stand at attention with a weapon; and the proper procedures when receiving orders for right shoulder and left shoulder arms; order arms; port arms; present arms; and inspection arms.

Finally, we were able to enjoy a welcome change by participating in a fun – but literally deadly serious – part of our training: Our first trip to the firing range.

Our initial weapons (never, ever call your rifle a "gun" in the Army) were older M14's, mainly because there was a shortage of the main combat rifle utilized in Vietnam, the M16. All M16's off the production line were immediately rushed to the war zone. The M14 "battle" rifle had been an American standard since the late 1950's.

(The first M16's utilized in combat were in 1965, but it wasn't until my first year in the service, 1969, that the M16 fully replaced the M14 as the U.S. military's standard service rifle in Vietnam.)

On the infantry range, we would line up on a horizontal line, with a guard tower stationed at mid-center. Each soldier had his personal space, and when everyone was set, blaring from the loudspeaker came a booming voice ordering everyone to "lock and load." That was followed by: "Ready on the left? Ready on the right? Commence firing!"

We would shoot downrange (250 meters at the longest) -- from standing, sitting, and prone positions. We directed our fire at a stationary target which was a life-size waist-up silhouette of a person in headgear the shape of a pointed conical pith helmet, which I'm certain was meant to resemble a Viet Cong guerilla. Factors such as wind and distance influenced where we would aim our shots. This was one time when the instructors treated us like humans, calmly helping us and giving us hints instead of yelling at us so that we would stay composed. Obviously, excelling in marksmanship is a desired asset of a soldier.

At the end of the exercise, there would be a call to "cease fire" from the tower. We would then mark our accuracy results in a 4" x 5" light blue publication entitled *U.S. Army Training Center Infantry Fort Lewis, Washington Progress Booklet*, and then we would head back to our billeting.

After three weeks of rigorous training, we received a humongous and most welcomed surprise; we were going to get a few days off for a Christmas break!

Nancy had accepted an invitation from my sister, Diana Vogel, and her husband, Don (better known to all as "Vogue") to stay with them and their boys, Scott and Jim, in their Avon-by-the-Sea, New Jersey home while I was in basic training. Nancy took a job in Asbury Park working for the power and light company.

With my unexpected holiday pass, my plan was to join her there for my short break. I wanted to surprise her and asked Diana and Vogue not to tell her when I was finally allowed to use a phone at the last minute. I hurriedly got a ticket on United Airlines that would fly me transcontinental from Sea-Tac Airport to Newark, N.J. on a direct flight.

As I boarded the plane in my dress greens (allowing me to get a discounted round-trip ticket for a grand sum of $74.55), I was embarrassed because only one service ribbon adorned my uniform; the National Defense Medal, which every member of the military initially receives.

I sat back into that wonderfully comfortable seat (compared to the agony of the past month) and let out a big sigh of relief. I sat next to a window and for the entire five-hour flight, on that crystal-clear night, I was thoroughly at peace as a enjoyed my heavenly view of the beautiful Christmas lights dotting the landscape of our country.

Quite literally, I was going "from the mountains, to the prairies, to the oceans, white with foam." To this day, those breath-taking sights on that tranquel night are forever etched into my memory bank. I can close my eyes and still see that serene setting during that special night flight.

Vogue picked me up at Newark Airport in the early morning the day before Christmas and we proceeded back to his and Diana's house in Avon. I walked in the door and Nancy was sitting at the kitchen table with her back to me.

I said: "What's for breakfast?" Nancy was momentarily stunned as she spun around to see me. She looked at me as if she had seen an apparition, momentarily standing open-mouthed before running to me and hugging me like there was no tomorrow. It was the first time she had seen my stylish Army haircut. It was also the first time she had seen me in uniform.

We spent a major part of my Christmas pass lounging around or shopping at the butcher shop, bakery, and candy shop dotting Avon-by-the-Sea's quaint main street. Nancy and I also took walks on the boardwalk just a few blocks from where we were staying, although the wind was bitterly cold coming off the ocean. I didn't care, for a few days, I was a normal person again. On our last night together we all attended a New Year's Eve Party at the city's civic center.

All good things must end, and on New Year's Day I boarded a plane in Newark headed back to Sea-Tac Airport. It was bittersweet; I hated to leave, yet I was anxious to finish boot camp.

When I returned to Fort Lewis, I found that I had received a very special Christmas card; it was signed by the entire University of Iowa athletic department brain trust: Athletic Director Forest Evashevski, Basketball Coach Ralph Miller, Football Coach Ray Nagel, Baseball (and future basketball) Coach Dick Schutz (who would eventually become the executive director of the NCAA), Track and Field Coach Francis X. Cretzmeyer, Wrestling Coach David McCuskey, and Associate Head Basketball Coach Lanny Van Eman. (I had been a sports announcer and sportswriter while going to school, and that's when I had built up my relationships with them.) That gesture meant more to me than any of them could have imagined.

My Journalism School classmates surprised me the same way by sending me a card full of their signatures, as well as containing the signatures of Malcolm MacLean, Director of the UI School of Mass Communications, and Charles Cremer, News Director of WSUI Radio and my academic advisor.

On the card, Mr. Cremer wrote: "*Your 19:180 project is superb and outstanding. Grade 'A' to go along with your 10:138 grade, also 'A.' Best of wishes.*"

That was a relief because those were the last two classes that I would ever take from the University of Iowa, and it was especially gratifying because I had to miss the last three weeks of the semester due to my mandatory induction into the Army. (I had turned in the projects prior to my departure.) Thank you, Mr. Cremer. I now only had three hours of foreign language remaining to receive my BA degree.

We commenced our grueling pace immediately upon reporting back to our base. In fact, our training intensified. We started to "play" Army in earnest, learning essential military tactics.

I don't know about the other guys, but I listened intently to the instructors, knowing it could someday save my life. No stones were unturned; for instance, we were told that it would take half-an-hour to get our night vision in the jungle (we did not have infra-red goggles during that time).

We were given another plague shot the first week that we were back in camp. And, one day while in formation, the drill sergeant read a statement: "These men have volunteered to give blood today." Of course, there was no volunteering; it was a direct order, and my name was called. It was another mass assembly line and the Army used needles that were bigger in circumference than those used in civilian life to hurry along the process of draining my O positive contribution. That made it a little painful, but at least I got some orange juice and a chocolate chip cookie out of the deal!

We started to drill mano a mano, first embarking in pugil stick training. A pugil stick is a pole with heavy padding on each end. The purpose is to train an individual for close-in fighting with his rifle and/or bayonet. Our exercises were similar to the bull-in-the-ring drills that football teams utilize (or at least used to). The purpose was to knock your opponent out of the circle.

By nature, I am not a physically aggressive person. I never got into fights when I was a kid mainly because I didn't like pain. However, when it came to such things as dodge ball, fencing (which I took in college), and now pugil training, I thought the best defense was a good offense, so I really went after my opponents.

My fencing background of parry, thrust....parry, thrust really came in handy as I kept my opponents on their heels. Unfortunately, I inadvertently badly wounded one rival in our one-on-one battle, breaking his hand quite severely in several places. That, of course, knocked him out of basic training.

Obviously, I did not do it on purpose, and I felt terrible, but perhaps I did this draftee a favor because it did end his military career right then and there. (Later, I heard that he was from a wealthy family and his incensed father notified a U.S. Senator friend of his, inquiring as to whether or not boot camp was too rough.)

By this time, our unit had already lost 10 of our original 53 trainees; he was number 11. We were down by 20%. Two of those were in the hospital for meningitis; three others were in the hospital for various injuries they had suffered; the soldier in the bunk next to mine got a discharge because he kept fainting on our road marches; one was sent home because of a serious groin injury; two others were discharged for reasons unknown; and one was sent to a "fat farm" to lose weight.

Next up was karate training. We probably learned just enough to be dangerous….to ourselves! We were told that we needed to learn the defensive maneuvers in case we found ourselves in a surprise hand-to-hand ambush in Vietnam.

Sure, me against an Asian guy in a martial arts life and death struggle. Yeah….that ain't gonna happen. That would be like Barney Fife taking on Bruce Lee. If I ever found myself in such a predicament, I'm pretty sure that I could have broken many of Usain Bolt's sprinting records. (Run, Forest, run!)

We have all seen war movies which included GI's throwing hand grenades at the bad guys. I was shocked when I initially saw the destructive power of those tangerine-sized projectiles the first time we partook in those exercises. Despite what you might have seen on the screen while viewing a Vietnam War flick, we did not use the World War II "pineapple" grenades, nor did we throw them side-arm as is often depicted.

The Vietnam-era grenades were round, smaller, and weighed just over a pound. I was cocky regarding how far I could throw one because I could easily throw a baseball from center field to home plate. I was stunned at the drag the grenades had when flying through the air; they didn't sail nearly as far as I thought they would.

The hand grenade training range consisted of a long thick cement slab marked off for each trainee to stand upon, side-by-side. It tilted downward in front of us. On command, we would pull the pin out of a grenade, firmly holding the handle (or "spoon") tight against the dangerous orb. Next, we waited for the following required step as we momentarily held it up to throw, and finally complied with instructions to toss the portable bomb over a thick protective cement and steel wall standing approximately five feet high, which didn't seem that far from us. The wall, of course, protected us from the blast of the grenade (with a shorter one directly in front of us in case the thrown object didn't clear the larger wall.)

Seemingly out of a movie script, a soldier who was on the other side of the G.I. next to me dropped his explosive device after pulling the pin, and it bounced around on the ground. Out of nowhere, one of the instructors ran up and went into a slide like a baseball player going into second base, kicking the live grenade down the slope in front of our launching area.

The thick structure was built to withstand such a concussion, with the projectile rolling down the tilted front and then back under where we were standing, with another cement and steel reinforced barrier, this time a floor, protecting us from the detonation. We, of course, could hear the loud eruption underneath us.

I wish I knew the name of that trainer, who was a young sergeant; his fast reaction most likely saved my life and the lives of many others within striking distance.

Our forced marches continued, getting longer and more strenuous all the time. On one particular day, we stopped at a checkpoint and were loaded onto deuce and-a-half trucks to deliver us to the base of one of Washington state's many elevated peaks. I don't believe it was Mt. Ranier, but one of a similar nature.

We hiked up the mountain side and when nightfall came, we bivouacked out in the open in "pup tents," with two occupants each carrying a half to be connected to make a full tent. Before settling in for the night, our drill sergeant told us to beware of bears, especially those of us who were situated on the perimeter, which I was.

It was a bitterly cold, rainy night and the elevation – with snow on the ground -- exacerbated the miserable elements. (How did our troops in Korea and WWII Europe survive night after night in these conditions? I can't tell you how much respect I have for those guys.) There simply was no way to get comfortable on that frozen tundra. However, it had been an exhausting day, so I was able to doze off fairly quickly. While finally achieving a deep sleep, I was abruptly awakened by a terrifying growling noise. I was petrified because of the warning regarding bears. I looked over at my slumbering tent-mate to warn him and realized the source of the snarling; it was him. He apparently was having a nightmare.

We were finally able to exchange our M14 weapons for M16A1 models, thanks to a speed up in production of that rifle. That was a relief for us, because it was a lighter weapon for our long, forced marches. The M14 weighed 12 lbs. while the M16 checked in four pounds lighter at just under eight lbs. The M16 was also five inches shorter in length, which made it much less cumbersome, and had a convenient carrying handle.

In addition, the M14 was only semiautomatic, unlike the M16, at that time made by the Colt Manufacturing Company. (In 1965, the introduction of the M16 to American, Allied, and Army of the Republic of Vietnam troops in Vietnam made it a great equalizer and a fairer fight against standard communist AK-47 armaments.)

The M14, which is the primary ceremonial rifle of many honor guards today, is made of wood and steel. It is piston operated and has a somewhat strong re-coil. The M14 was sometimes still being used in Vietnam at the time, primarily as a sniper rifle if needed for multiple targets.

The M16 – made of aluminum, steel, chrome, and plastic is gas operated, has very little re-coil, and has better accuracy. The rounds for the M14 are 7.62 mm caliber while the cartridges for the M16 are 5.56 mm, both NATO standard. The 5.56 is lighter and faster.

(I pilfered both sizes of bullets and hid them both in rafters in our barracks that I could reach while standing on my top bunk. I wanted to keep them as souvenirs. The same was true with the ring of the first hand grenade that I threw. It wouldn't have been a pretty sight if I had been caught with them. The last thing I did after graduating and packing up for home was to reach up and grab those items and secretly stash them away in my duffel bag.)

When the M16 was first introduced in Vietnam in 1965, it had a three-prong flash suppressor at the end of the barrel. Our soldiers soon learned that the prongs could snag on the undergrowth in the jungle and become bent, with the potential of a damaged weapon exploding in the hands of an infantryman when he tried to fire it. That was corrected by simply placing a permanent ring around the ends of the three prongs.

The M16 jammed quite often when it was first introduced in 'Nam. One solution was to make proper changes to the "innards" of the rounds. Instructing troops to clean the weapons more often than they had been doing also greatly helped reduce the problem.

One thing that I found humorous, in a dark sort of way, was the fact that the Mattel Toy Company made the stock for the M16! The toy trucks in my hands that I had played with a few years back were made by the same company that helped construct the deadly weapon of war that I now held in those very same hands.

I remember our first visual instruction regarding the M16. Trainers shot rounds into a barrel of sand and then showed us the results. Where the bullet entered, there was but a small hole; but when you looked at the back of the barrel, there was a huge crater. It is a devastating but effective piece for an infantryman; the bullet tumbles inside of whatever it hits (termed cavitation), causing maximum damage. That's ugly and harsh, but so is war.

On the first day on the infantry range after we had exchanged the M14 for the M16, I learned that – at least for the two weapons I had – the trigger was more sensitive on the M16. Laying prone in the wet sand in the constant rain, my cold and wet right index finger accidentally fired off a round before we had received the "commence firing" command. Thank goodness my M16 was already pointed downrange. I was very upset with myself, but I was relieved and grateful that I hadn't accidentally shot someone; I would have never forgiven myself. Yes, I did take my share of verbal abuse from the instructors….deservedly so. (In a humorous vein, the bullet hit the target.)

The M16 was not utilized as a machine gun which is often depicted in movies or on television. We were taught that proper usage was to employ short bursts or use it as a single-shot weapon. (The barrel was susceptible to melt down with prolonged salvos; long after the war, the M16 was changed to limit the shooter to just three rapid-fire rounds.)

We were trained to differentiate the sound of short bursts from the M16 as opposed to those coming from the Russian-made AK-47, the favored weapon of the North Vietnamese Army and the Viet Cong. This was important to a soldier finding himself in the often-close quarter jungle terrain of Vietnam to know if there was friend or foe in the area.

The M16 could fire more rounds per second and had a more effective range, but the AK-47 was considered much sturdier and more reliable under adverse conditions.

In no uncertain terms, we were told that from now on, our M16 was our best friend. Expertise in knowing how to disassemble the weapon and the ability to put it back together in short order were requirements. We would often have to take apart our M16 and lay out the various parts – I believe we broke it down into 15 pieces – on our bunk. Upon command, we had a limited time to reassemble the rifle, clean it thoroughly, and line up for inspection by the drill sergeant and his aides.

While inspecting my lower bunk mate's rifle on one occurrence, the drill sergeant found a thread from a cleaning patch still in the barrel, and yelled out: "What the hell is that, a granny knot?" and then vertically hurled the M16 at the trainee in front of him. (Our weapons were always on safety and without ammunition magazines at such times.)

On January 11 we were allowed time off to listen to the Super Bowl at a Fort Lewis recreational hall that was normally off-limits to trainees. The game featured Kansas City and Minnesota, with the Chiefs beating the Vikings, 23-7. The announcers for the day were Jack Buck and Pat Summerall, both of whom I would eventually get to know professionally and personally.

K.C. quarterback Len Dawson was the game's MVP, leading a talented team that included the likes of Bobby Bell, Buck Buchanan, Willie Lanier, Curly Culp and Jan Stenrud, among many others. I would later get to know Dawson, too, when he served as a local sports announcer in the city which made him famous.

Minnesota had several stars of their own, including Carl Eller, Alan Page, Paul Krause, Ron Yary and Mick Tingelhoff.

Quarterbacking the Vikings was Joe Capp. Many years later, I invited Joe to participate in one of my future college football bowl game golf tournaments in California. He sent me a note back telling me: "I shoot in the low 70's; if it's any hotter than that, I don't like to play."

The most dreaded day for me and the other boot camp trainees, at least in my mind, was the trip to the "gas chamber." To get to our destination on time, we started out early in the morning and had to march, fully loaded, in what I believe amounted to a 12-mile trek to the facility, although perhaps it wasn't quite that long. As usual, the rain was coming down in buckets. Before we started our gas training, we took time out for lunch. The "cuisine" for the day consisted of pork and beans served on metal trays. Standing in the great outdoors, we gulped down what soon became a sloppy mess with the shower turning the meal into mush.

The time was at hand. We entered a wooden building single file with our gas masks on, placing our right hand on the shoulder of the man directly in front. Containers of CN gas were made operational, and we were ordered to take off our masks. (CN gas is a strong tear gas and is the major component of Mace.)

We walked slowly around the big room in a wide circle twice before a door was finally opened and we were allowed to go back outdoors. It is undoubtedly one of most miserable experiences that a human being can endure. Wherever there is an orifice on the body, be assured that something will be draining out of it. I managed to refrain from upchucking, but most of the guys didn't have such luck (especially after just digesting that pork and beans "soup.") Your skin burns like the devil, and you actually start frothing at the mouth.

Our squad had to endure that horror house, following the same routine, two more times. It was then time to experience what a gas attack might be like in an open field. We were taken out to a large acreage, sans our gas masks, which were stored away in pouches that were strapped to our sides.

The instructors explained that dense white smoke would soon envelope us and we would not be able to see our hands in front of our faces. Eventually, CN gas would gradually be blended into the smoke and when we detected that such had happened, we were instructed to yell "*gas*," and then put on our gas masks while hitting the ground to lay down on our stomachs. The drill sergeants were adamant in their directions: "Do not stand up and do not run, or it will be much worse for you!"

Standing in the blinding smoke, I finally detected gas and yelled out as commanded (as did all the others), grabbed my gas mask as quickly as I could, covered my face, and hit the deck. At first, your inclination is that your mask is not functioning as you cough, choke and have trouble breathing. A person's natural tendency is to jump up and get out of there, but I heeded the stern lecture of our trainers. Instead, I dug a hole as deep as I could for my face and mask with my fingers, which was not easy to do on the frozen soil, hoping that I could derive oxygen from mother earth.

Others were not following orders; several jumped up and ran and because of that, I was stepped on and kicked in the sides on numerous occasions by the frightened scramblers who couldn't see anything in the heavy fog.

At long last, it was over. After what seemed like an eternity, the wind swept the bad vapors away from us and we were able to de-mask and breathe in some good ol' country air. I can't adequately explain what a relief that was. Our unit was finished with the exercise.

We were taken high atop a large hill, obviously upwind, and given a break to look down and watch the next group go through that wretched drill. It was easy to ascertain why the instructors told us not to try and escape; anyone who attempted to bug out was grabbed by a trainer who ripped off the runner's mask and held a container of CN gas right in his face, making the experience much more abhorrent than if he had simply stayed down.

Even though chemical welfare is internationally banned – thank God!! – the Army remains vigilant. In a few months, I would be issued a gas mask which I was told had prescription eye lenses in Vietnam (although I never used it so I don't know if that was true).

Our exhaustive and harrowing day wasn't quite over. We were taken to another large field where we had to navigate our way on elbows and knees under barbed wire containing concealed trip flares, which would illuminate if a soldier crawled too high and touched the wire.

Live machine gun fire blazed overhead and small (non-lethal) explosions happened at different locales on the landscape as a trainee slithered by, catching us all by surprise, during the session. The tricky part was keeping one's M16 clean at all times, cradled in your arms as you crawled. At the end of the field, we jumped up and charged the "enemy" (large stuffed pads resembling old football tackling dummies) with bayonets fixed and ready to engage the target.

Finally, we traversed the long stretch back to our barracks, double-timing the last mile or so with our wet equipment, seemingly weighing twice what it did when we started.

A couple of nights later we did a three-hour night march, going through crude replicas of Vietnamese villages and experiencing simulated air attacks (complete with bags of flour being dropped and "exploding" around us). Compared to many of the other things we had to endure, that was actually an entertaining experience.

I remember an amusing incident prior to embarking on our march. One of the trainees in our unit wasn't the brightest individual around and was predisposed to saying and doing imbecilic things. Sergeant Scary came into our barracks and passed around camouflage sticks; olive green and black grease paint (for our faces and hands) in a container that resembled a lipstick case. When he got to our mentally challenged fellow trainee, Scary looked him in the eye and before giving him his tube, said: "It ain't candy, so don't eat the shit!"

We had a half day off on Sunday, February 1, and I told my buddies to cover for me as I snuck off the basic training part of the base and searched for a pay phone to call my sister, Kathy, who I knew was going into delivery at any time. I found a phone booth and somehow got ahold of her in the hospital. It was nighttime in Iowa, and she had actually given birth to my niece, Jill, earlier that very day!

As I was talking, a sergeant tapped on the glass and told me to hang up. From my uniform, he knew that I was in boot camp and wasn't allowed to be using the phone. When I was returned to my unit, I was given KP duty that night, peeling 100 lbs. of potatoes well into the morning.

In the second week of February, it was time for more inoculations, and I received three more shots – for tetanus, typhoid, and polio.

Our training continued and everything was going along pretty smoothly; we could see that proverbial light at the end of the tunnel. I had just 10 days to go and then catastrophe struck; I severely injured my ankle.

We were double-timing back to our barracks after another night patrol and approximately one block away from our billeting, I turned my ankle on one of those infernal big rocks that covered the base.

All of us took turns carrying the first aid kit, an ammo box painted white with a red cross on the top, and this was my night. That meant that I would be running at the back of the formation. When I took my tumble, the box went flying along with everything else that was not strapped down to my body other than my M16, which I held on to for dear life.

Remarkably, neither the drill sergeant nor his assistant, running in front, saw me take a header. I watched from the ground as my unit kept on running those last few yards to the barracks. Everyone was exhausted and anxious to call it a night.

Just two guys realized what had happened and they stopped and came back to help me, but I told them that I was fine and to go ahead.

I got up and gathered all of the scattered items, unaware of the extent of damage I had sustained to my leg. We wore very thick black boots that gave us great support. It hurt as I finally limped back to the comfort of my bunk after securing my weapon and other items, but I wasn't aware of anything serious.

Falling asleep was instantaneous when I hit my pillow after gingerly climbing to my "second level" bed, but

49

it seemed that just seconds had passed when someone was shaking me to tell me that it was my turn for roving guard duty at 1:30. I swung my legs over the side of my top bunk and experienced a new level of pain. My ankle was throbbing.

I did NOT want to let anyone know that I was hurt. The worst word that you can hear in basic training is "recycle," meaning that a trainee is required go through all of this hell all over again if the situation dictated. I was afraid that with just a little over a week of boot camp left, I would not be allowed to graduate.

My first problem was to get down from my top bunk on a bad ankle without waking up my lower bunkmate. Using my best gymnastics moves utilizing my arms and one good leg, I accomplished the task. I was able to get through my roving guard and fire guard duties, switching my scheduled fire guard time with another trainee (which was against the rules) allowing me to perform both of my jobs back-to-back.

I sat through both guard chores; my 30 minutes of fire guard was easy, as I simply sat on a small chair in my barracks. There was admittedly little roaming involved in my "roving guard" stint; I simply sat down on an outdoor stairway which was in the shadows. It had a broad view of the area so I could spot any strange activity. I did get up to take an occasional stroll around the grounds, limping slowly. It was always a solitary job so I knew I wouldn't get caught sitting on the job.

My two guard stints finally ended for the night, but it was still only 3:00 a.m. I didn't want to go through the acrobatic antics of getting back up to my bed, so I simply sat on my footlocker and leaned against the wall, quickly falling asleep. Again, it seemed that I had just nodded off when I was awakened for a new day in the fun life of basic training.

After dressing, I did my best John Wayne by gritting my teeth and tying the boot on my wounded ankle as tight as I could to get maximum support, keeping my lower leg as straight as possible.

Luckily, that day we were going to be trucked to another mountainous area and "attack" a hillside. The last thing I needed was a long march. We arrived at the base of our attack point and my unit was the first to go. I must have had an angel on my shoulder because we would not be running up the hill, we would be crawling. Perfect; just what the doctor ordered (well, had he known, he probably would have ordered something far different!).

From our starting point at the bottom of the large hill, we slowly inched up the cold, wet slope, never knowing when the "enemy" (pop-up targets resembling human figures) would suddenly spring up in front of us. As we did our Army crawl, we kept our rifles clean and dry by protecting them in our bent arms.

When a bad guy popped up, we quickly stopped and fired from a prone position to bring him down. We also tossed a few fake grenades along the way. It took us a while to crawl to the top of the ridge and when we reached it, we had to stand up and do a bayonet charge, which made me wince from my discomfort.

We then walked down the other side of the "captured" hill, which was much steeper in slope. The good news was that we could get down quicker; the bad news was that I was trying to do it on a bad wheel. At least we were out of view of our sergeants.

When we reached the bottom after the charge, we took a path back around to the front of the small mountain which was the initial attack point. Still not wanting to reveal the injury, I purposely let everyone pass me, using the excuse that I was re-tying my boot laces. When I was the last straggler, I used my M16 as a crutch (safety on and without an ammo magazine, of course).

We were allowed to sit in bleachers while the next unit undertook the same exercise. While sitting on a bench, I took my boot and sock off to survey the damage.

I marveled at my rainbow-hued ankle….pretty shades of green, yellow, purple, blue, red, and black. If Ben and Jerry had seen it, they would have named a flavor after it.

It was horribly swollen. Just then, a soldier came running over to me. It was a medic. Unbeknownst to me, he was required to accompany us for this exercise. I didn't have time to cover up my ankle, he had already seen it. He looked at me in horror and said: "You're going to the hospital; just wait here." I argued that it wasn't that bad, but he just looked at me as if I was crazy and reported me to the drill sergeant.

As it turned out, two guys received leg injuries during the exercise, with one being a dislocated knee. The three of us were helped up into a deuce-and-a-half truck. My two wounded partners and I were dropped off close to the hospital and told that we would have to walk the remainder of the way (which was approximately two blocks). Evidently the truck that we were riding in was needed ASAP in another area. Thus, the three of us would have to make it on our own from there.

So there we were….three of us with serious ambulatory issues, hobbling down the path on our way to having our ailments diagnosed. The way we were walking, if we could have found a couple of drums and a piccolo, we would have resembled the famous Revolutionary War painting, "Spirit of 76," by Archibald Willard.

At the start of our short hike to Madigan General Hospital, I was able to locate three adequate-sized dead tree branches laying on the ground off the beaten path that we could use for canes and/or crutches. We finally reached our destination, and the doctors were livid that we were forced to walk, possibly further aggravating our injuries.

In Dispensary #10, I froze when I heard the verdict from my physician after he had taken a series of x-rays;

I had broken three bones in my ankle. "Snap, crackle, and pop," I muttered. Doc forced a chuckle.

I was despondent at the news. This could affect me in two ways: (1) I might have to go through the entire basic training cycle again; and (2) it ruined any chances that I had of going to Airborne Ranger School.

Although I told Nancy differently, I really wanted to be in combat arms. I figured that as long as I was in the Army, I wanted to do what the Army does best. I had passed all of the requirements to be a serious candidate for Ranger School, and though the thought of jumping out of airplanes was a bit scary for this small-town boy, I always thought it was best to face your fears (unless it involves stupid spiders).

> "Out along the edges,
> Always where I burn to be,
> The further on the edge,
> The hotter the intensity."
>
> ■ Danger Zone
> --Kenny Loggins

But my most immediate concern was being re-cycled and repeating the mental and physical anguish of boot camp; I think I would have rather jumped out of that plane....without a parachute!

The doctor signed a DA Form 3349 and sent it to my commanding officer. Under the "restrictions" section, he ordered "no crawling, no stooping, no running, no jumping, no marching, and no standing over 20 minutes." Well, those things are pretty much all you do in the Army! I pleaded with him to not put on a hard cast, and he relented, giving me a softer, more mobile support system. I would have to use crutches.

Our C.O., who had apparently read about my journalism background, called me in and told me that he needed some additional help in the office. In essence, I became the night office manager, and I enjoyed it because I was all alone. I had had my fill of being around dozens and dozens of other guys 24 hours a day. There was *never* any privacy, and that included restroom accommodation, which was just one big room with no dividers for the facilities.

As I started to get into my new "job," I looked around and found everything to be shabbily run. I cleaned up all the desks, caught up on all the correspondence that was lagging behind, and totally revamped all of the files. I did those things mainly out of boredom, but also because I can't stand sloppiness and prefer a smooth operation.

Drafting correspondence for the Army proved interesting. For one thing, one had to know the terms, because somewhere along the line the Army felt that it needed its own nomenclature.

Bathrooms are latrines; picking up trash is policing the area; camping is bivouacking; leaving the service is mustering out; food is chow; where you get your chow is the mess hall; helmet is steel pot; tucking trousers into your boots is blousing; attaching your bayonet is fixing it; rifle is weapon; ammunition container is a magazine -- loaded it's a full metal jacket; being fired upon by fellow military mates is friendly fire; shaving kit is a dopp kit; living quarters are billets; kilometers are klicks; jail is the brig; etc. etc.

That doesn't even include all the slang, acronyms, initials, and the military alphabet (i.e. Alpha, Bravo, Charlie) required for my new position. For some reason, the Army also starts some words in "e" that begin with an "i" in civilian writing (e.g. insure-ensure). And, for gosh sakes, 5:00 p.m. is 1700 hours!

One of my duties was to answer the phone, but there were very, very few callers at that time of night, and I never had visitors. I did take the opportunity to make a quick call home, which was a no-no because personal calls were impermissible, especially for a boot camp trainee.

I telephoned my wife, Nancy, which was a brief, but wonderful, reprieve. However, during our conversation, I learned that an individual who was a year behind me in high school -- and a brother of one of my classmates -- had tragically been killed in Vietnam.

Marine Lance Corporal Dan Schrader was on a search and destroy mission in Quang Nam Province just two weeks earlier, on January 19, 1970, when he met his demise. A rifleman for Company G, 2nd Battalion, 1st Marines in the 1st Marine Division, Schrader lost his life to an enemy explosive booby trap. Sadly, the father of a baby girl had only been in the country for three months.

Time seemed to drag in my office setting, probably because it was imperative for me to be pumped up with adrenaline the previous few weeks. My down time did give me an opportunity to catch up on my reading. I remember being totally disgusted and sickened over a *Newsweek* Magazine article that I was perusing regarding the recent grisly Manson family murders. My mind could not comprehend that such hideousness existed.

Since I ate breakfast on my own, I didn't have to worry about a time limit and in a letter to Nancy, I told her that my normal morning meal now consisted of two bowls of cereal, two pieces of French toast; two eggs; two pieces of wheat toast; four pieces of bacon; and three glasses of milk! I was a growing boy!

I was within three days of my basic training cycle being over, and I still did not know my fate. I was as nervous as a snowman on the equator. Would I have to go through this purgatory again?

To my very, very pleasant surprise and shock, I not only graduated, I was one of the very few in my class promoted to E2! It turned out that I had already achieved all of the physical testing requirements (one-mile run, sit-ups, push-ups, etc.) and fulfilled my requisite marksmanship numbers (grading expert) prior to my getting injured.

Even more stunning to me was a report that came from the Department of the Army, HQ, U.S. Army Training Center, Infantry, Fort Lewis Washington, showing that I had finished #1 in my basic training cycle. I saw the list when I was working in the office (and made a copy of it). It was mind-boggling to see my name listed at the top of that chart.

On graduation day, February 13 (Friday, the 13th, no less), I officially became a United States Soldier. (Bob Skow, my hometown buddy who was sure he would be headed to basic training with me despite having blown a good chunk of his foot off while saving his wife from a dog attack, didn't show up at my graduation as promised. Just yanking your chain, Bob!)

I believe the reason for my promotion was due to the chores I had undertaken for the commanding officer. He was impressed with what I had done in transforming his headquarters office into a more dynamic operation. However, I later realized it helped spell my doom as far as combat arms was concerned.

Ranger school was out because of a leg that wouldn't be in workable condition for a while. The same was true with infantry. However, I was still hoping to get into armor, which my brother had served in, or placed in artillery. I submitted those as my two MOS (Military Occupational Specialty) preferences.

But my hopes were dashed when I was informed that I had been chosen to be a Personnel Communications Information Specialist. I was crushed: Instead of becoming Rambo, I might have to be a Radar! (As I would learn, I needn't had worried; in less than a year I would find myself in some precarious and traumatic situations.)

There were three deciding factors in placing me in that MOS: (1) A college education; (2) strong journalism and writing backgrounds; and (3) what turned out to be my unwise move of transforming our base office on Fort Lewis into a smoother and more efficiently run headquarters, thereby catching the eye of the officer corps. They, by the way, were pressuring me to go to Officer Candidate School (OCS).

I tried to fight my assigned MOS and get into armor, my brother's specialty, or artillery one more time, but it was to no avail. I called Nancy and she was relieved. She was afraid that I would get infantry; I didn't tell her about my efforts to get into combat arms.

It was my understanding that for my advanced training, I could be sent to one of three bases. One was Fort Ord, which would have been good because we had high school friends stationed there, and….well, it was in Southern California, America's favorite destination at that time. The other two were Fort Gordon, Georgia, which was also fine because we had friends from college in close proximity to that base, and Fort Benjamin Harrison near Indianapolis, which was within driving distance to Iowa, where most of Nancy and my family members still resided.

I finally learned that I was going to be assigned to the U.S. Army Adjutant General School at Fort Benjamin Harrison, which was only a seven-hour drive from our hometown of Newton. This Midwest boy was headed back to the heartland, a full-fledged G.I.

"I remember when I was a barefooted boy,
Climbing a sycamore tree;
But now I'm a little older, got a rifle on my shoulder,
Some fool made a soldier of me.

■ Some Fool Made a Soldier of Me
--The Kingston Trio

CHAPTER IV
Calm Before the Storm

I packed up my gear, hopped a ride to Seattle-Tacoma International, and caught a direct flight to Weir Cook Airport in Indianapolis, where I would next be stationed. Per our orders, there was a small group of us who had flown together from Seattle, and we were congregated at the airport, waiting for a bus to take us to the base. For whatever reason, I was designated the leader of the group and when we arrived at Fort Benjamin Harrison, my job was to report to headquarters and announce our arrival.

By this time, it was late at night, and when I entered, the only soldier in the office was a young 2nd lieutenant who had his feet up on a desk, reading the *Indianapolis Star*. With proper protocol, I marched up to his desk, gave him a crisp salute, and said: "Private Starr reporting, sir; all arriving personnel from Ft. Lewis are present and accounted for."

He looked at me as if I was a nutcase. He swung his legs off the desk, never getting out of his chair, didn't say a word, and threw me a clipboard to sign for the entire group. As I completed my task, I thought to myself that the strict nature of military discipline learned in boot camp apparently didn't always apply. Of course, the fact that I was meeting with an officer who would have fit in perfectly with those on the M*A*S*H television show probably attributed to that.

> *"A brave man once requested me,*
> *To answer questions that are key,*
> *'Is it to be or not to be?'*
> *And I replied, 'Oh, why ask me?'"*

- Suicide is Painless (theme from M*A*S*H)
  --Johnny Mandel

Before commencing my official duties on February 20, we were given a couple of days off; thus, I flew back to Des Moines to be with Nancy, who by this time had returned from New Jersey. She picked me up at the airport and we drove directly to Pella, Iowa, so that I could watch a basketball game involving the hometown Central College Flying Dutchmen and Simpson College, where my brother served as head coach.

I had not seen his team play for a couple of years and I wanted to surprise him. The game was underway when Nancy and I arrived there. We had to walk across the floor just behind one of the baskets and Dick saw us, smiled, and waved. I still had my dress greens on from my flight, so I'm certain that I stood out, which was kind of embarrassing.

After a short break at home, staying with Nancy's parents, I made the seven-hour trek in our car back to Fort Harrison, named after the former President, whose hometown was Indianapolis. In addition to being the location of the U.S. Army Adjutant General School, it was also the site of the U.S. Army Finance Center.

A day on any military base starts with "Reveille," and ends – usually around 5:00 p.m. -- with the song "Retreat" and "To the Colors," followed by the National Anthem. Protocol required personnel to stop, come to attention, and salute an American flag if one was in sight, or simply face in the direction of the music. The playing of Taps was played when things got quiet on a base, usually at 9:00 p.m.

My classes were mostly clerical in nature, even learning short-hand, and I was bored to tears, although it did help greatly when Nancy joined me in mid-March. That allowed me to live off base. Nancy and I found an apartment not far from the military complex, residing at 9036 El Dorado Drive, #201, in Indianapolis.

She had only been with me for a week or so when we decided to go to H.R. Block to have our federal taxes done. During the previous three days, including that morning, Nancy had been seeking employment and had gone to several appointments.

The agent working on our taxes was a no-nonsense, head buried in paperwork milquetoast type of individual. With a monotonous drone, he ran down his list of questions.

At one point he asked me if "Nancy was permanent." Thinking that he was inquiring about her job status, I replied "No, but we're hoping she soon will be soon because she's been working on it; in fact she was with a couple of prospects just this morning before we got here."

For the first time, our bowtie and cardigan sweater adorned taxman quickly looked up, glared at me with an astonished and horrified look, eyes wide open. I quickly realized that we weren't on the same wavelength. I said: "What was your question again?"

He replied: "Is Nancy *pregnant?*" As Emily Litella (Gilda Radnor) would say on Saturday Night Live: "Oh, that's very different! Never mind!" We informed him that she wasn't. The inquirer was not basing his question on Nancy's appearance; it was simply one of his required clerical questions with his eyes glued to the forms in front of him. Nonetheless, Nancy, who was petite and had a perfect figure, was highly insulted. She was wearing a wrap-around dress and large coat; when we got home, she threw away the dress!

On March 12, 1970, just 175 miles east of where I was stationed -- a straight shot on Interstate 70 – my alma mater, the Iowa Hawkeyes were closing out a successful 1969-70 basketball campaign in Columbus, Ohio at St. John Arena, home of the hometown Ohio State Buckeyes.

No, it wasn't a Big Ten Conference game; the 7th-rated Hawks were playing 4th-ranked Jacksonville, led by 7-2 all-American Artis Gilmore, in the first round of the NCAA Tournament. Gilmore was averaging 21.9 points and an incredible 23.2 rebounds per game that season

It was a tough draw and Iowa lost a heart-breaking 104-103 game to a team that would eventually make it to the NCAA Championship game, only to lose to the mighty UCLA Bruins.

The Hawkeyes had polished off a perfect 14-0 conference record to win the Big Ten Basketball crown that year. The Hawks, 20-5 overall, averaged an extraordinary 102.9 points per game against league competition.

Nancy and I settled into a routine life in our new Indianapolis surroundings. She landed a job at the Hibbens Company, which was a distribution center. (She was finally *permanent!*) I pretty much had an 8:00 a.m. to 5:00 p.m. schedule, although quite often obligations required me to stay on base.

We made some new friends, with our closest being husband and wife Billy and Amanda Jones from Savannah, Georgia. Amanda was all Southern belle and Billy and I would jab each other about the Civil War, all in good fun. They lived in close proximity to our apartment, and Billy and I would often ride to and from the base together.

Another good friend was classmate Carmen "Chopper" Bianco, from Easton, Pennsylvania. Chopper and

I would talk football all day. He was a huge Penn State Nittany Lions fan.

For being in the Army, it was a tranquil time for this soldier. On May 16, I had the thrill of my lifetime when Nancy and I drove two hours to Cincinnati to watch my all-time favorite baseball player, Hank Aaron, and his Atlanta Braves play the Reds in a double-header. Our tickets were $3.50 apiece.

It was a special occasion, because Hammerin' Hank was due to collect his 4,000th career hit, and he did not disappoint. If memory serves me correctly, his 4,000th hit was a semi-hard "worm-burner" drive right up the middle. However, during his next at-bat, he nailed one of those towering homerun shots for which he was famous, one of his 755 career dingers.

Severe inner turmoil at my school, the University of Iowa, was tearing apart the Hawkeye athletic department. Athletic Director Forest Evashevski and Head Football Coach Ray Nagel were feuding. Loyalties were split, causing the firing of one assistant coach by Nagel with another choosing to leave on his own accord.

Two top players – starting quarterback Larry Lawrence (son of a former Hawkeye assistant coach) and regular fullback Tom Smith – transferred to the University of Miami. Rumors were rampant that Evashevski, who had great success as the Hawkeye coach in the 50's when four of his last five teams finished in the top five in the nation and won two Rose Bowl games, was trying to force Nagel out so that Evy could take over the coaching reins again. Lawrence's roommate stoked the fire by indicating that QB Lawrence sided with Evashevski and decided he couldn't play for Nagel anymore.

To add insult to injury, the state auditor's office charged Iowa football coaches, including Nagel, with padding their expense accounts. They all vehemently denied the allegations. All of this bickering was an embarrassment to the University and was drawing scrutiny from both the Big Ten Conference office and NCAA.

The UI Board in Control of Athletics decided that it was time to do something, taking the easy way out and firing both Nagel and Evashevski. Actually, Evy had written a letter of resignation the previous December and the Board acted on it retroactively, although it did pay Evashevski on the final year of his contract. Evy's bittersweet 19-year career in Iowa City was over.

Nagel took an opposite approach and did not accept the termination. He fought the charges regarding the expense accounts, and the Iowa Attorney General, Richard Turner, agreed that, indeed, no crimes had been committed.

Turner even accused Evashevski of fabricating the charges, and outspoken Iowa State Senator Bill Reichardt, an all-Big Ten fullback for Iowa in the 1940's, agreed with Turner with both insinuating that Evy had been out to get Nagel.

Several former and then-present football players came out to support Nagel, as did many top boosters. Petitions were sent to the university president and even to the state's Speaker of the House demanding Nagel's re-instatement.

A few days later, Nagel was re-hired to finish the final year of his contract. Many felt that he been bullied by Evashevski, a genius of a coach who is in the College Football Hall of Fame, but some would say too much of a demanding taskmaster who bordered on paranoia as an athletic director.

In my few dealings with Evy (in my role as a sports announcer and sports writer), I liked him. He was a gruff man, but he was very cordial to me. Evashevski was an interesting individual. He played a key role in Tom Harmon's march to the Heisman Trophy in 1940 at Michigan, serving as a blocking back for the winner of the prestigious award. Following his outstanding playing career, Evy coached the Hawkeyes to unprecedented heights in the 1950's and was highly coveted by the NFL. He did have some successes in his role of athletic director at UI, but problems in the program seemed to multiply as the years went by.

My relationship with Nagel was excellent. Maury White of the *Des Moines Register* said that the return of the Iowa coach "may rank as the most startling reversal since the discovery of the boomerang!"

The Christmas card that I had received five months earlier – signed by both Forest Evashevski and Ray Nagel – is now a treasured keepsake!

Evy was replaced by another former Wolverine, the popular Bump Elliot, a former all-America football player and head coach at Michigan. Bump, one of the nicest individuals I have ever met, would sit in the Iowa athletic director's chair for the next 21 years.

During our off time, Nancy and I would tour the countryside and go into Indianapolis on occasion. At that point, being in the Army just seemed to be like any other job. But there was still the military aspect, including being on base for reveille to start the day, and sometimes being there for taps to end it.

On Memorial Day, May 30, despite still being somewhat hampered by my damaged ankle, I participated in a soldier's ceremonial march on the parade grounds, in perfect stride past the reviewing stands. We properly acknowledged the top brass and performed in front of an audience with all the pomp and circumstance of a grand military outing.

No soldiers were allowed off base to attend the Indianapolis 500 because of the growing anti-war sentiment pervading the country, with a fear that soldiers might be in danger if they were singled out. I did, however, go to time trials in civilian clothes, with a ticket costing a whole two dollars. (Nancy had a group of relatives come to town for the actual race.)

THEY NEVER HEARD THE FINAL SHOT

To make certain that none of us would try to sneak out on race day Sunday, we were assigned to cleaning chores on base. I had KP (kitchen patrol) duty, meaning that we had to scrub down the dining room and kitchen area, which included pots and pans.

About halfway through the day, a grizzly old red-eyed sergeant (E6) came in and started yelling at all of us about the way we were performing our KP tasks for purposes we never did understand (alcohol or drug consumption on his part was obviously the problem). He screamed at the top of his lungs and made absolutely no sense....pure gibberish.

It was -- as you see at times in the military -- a guy who was lower in rank than he should have been for his time in service, probably busted down several times, and he was taking it out on us because he out-ranked us, due to our short time in service.

After he left, everyone looked puzzled; we had no idea what he wanted. Somebody asked: "What in the world did he say?" Well, I couldn't help myself: "He said...." and tried to imitate his nonsensical garbled rant the best I could.

The guys were doubled over laughing until they suddenly sobered up very quickly and had a look of fear as I could see them gazing behind me. I gave them that look that conveyed: "He's behind me, isn't he?" Yep, he had come back and entered a door to which my back was turned. He was neither happy nor impressed with my impersonation.

The result? I ended up peeling 100 pounds again, only this time it was onions, not potatoes! Did you know that you really do cry when you peel onions? I do.

My time at Fort Benjamin Harrison was coming to a close. I graduated from the U.S. Army Adjutant General School on June 12. Earlier that week, I had received orders for where I would be transferred: The destination line read "Pentagon." That was pretty heady stuff;

I would be working in the nerve center of the United States military. I was pleasantly surprised to learn that my friend, Billy, would be headed to Washington, D.C. with me.

However, on my last day of class, I was given an urgent message informing me that my orders had been changed and to report to HQ to receive my new duty assignment. When the papers were handed to me, I quickly read the destination. It read: Military Assistant Command, Vietnam (commonly referred to as MACV, pronounced Mack-Vee). MACV was a joint service command (Army, Navy, Air Force, Marines, and all special forces) and a part of the United States Pacific Command.

Billy was also notified of a change of assignment, and learned that he, too, would be headed for the same war-torn country. It was a stunning turn of events.

I had ridden to the base with Billy that day and on our ride back to our apartments after learning this significant news, we both had only one concern: How were we going to break this news to our wives? They had been so happy and relieved knowing that we were supposedly going to stay state-side.

Personally, I was placid about the change of orders. First of all, there was the sense of obligation (i.e. if other guys had to go, why not me?). Secondly, there was the natural tinge of excitement of heading to a war zone. The movie, "Patton," starring George C. Scott, was the top box office attraction at that very time and we had just attended a viewing at the base theater. Although not intentional, it served as a fitting pep talk.

But putting my selfishness aside, I, like Billy, agonized at the thought of telling our spouses that we would be leaving them for a year, going to a place where there were no guarantees that we would be coming home. I turned on the radio to ease our minds a bit, only to hear the sad refrain of an ill-timed ballad:

> *"Which way you goin', Billy*
> *Can I go too?*
> *Which way you goin', Billy*
> *Can I go with you?*
> *I'm gonna miss you, Billy,*
> *And though I'm trying,*
> *I'm hurting so bad, Billy,*
> *I can't stop crying."*

■ Which Way You Goin' Billy?
--The Poppy Family

    Of all the songs that could have been playing, fate chose this one. I looked at Billy and said: "Sorry." We both just sort of looked down and shook our heads. At least it wasn't the song "Billy and Sue" by B.J. Thomas, where Billy gets killed in combat after receiving a "Dear John" letter. Another song would come out later with the title: "Billy Don't be a Hero" by Bo Donaldson and The Heywoods, with the subject of its title also being killed in action.

    We pulled up to my apartment and I jumped out of the car. I quickly saw Nancy out on the 2nd-floor deck catching some sun on a splendid day weather-wise. She saw me as I walked at a fast pace across the grass to the quadraplex foyer where our front door was located. I hollered up and with a huge smile and waved, remarking what a gorgeous day it was.

    I climbed the outside stairs to the second level but before I could put my key in the door of Apt. 201, it swung open and Nancy, with an extremely concerned look on her face, said: "What's wrong?" That had been her exact wording when I received my draft notice.

    How *DID* she do that? Here I thought I had done my best at looking like a happy-go-lucky guy striding across the lawn on just another typical day. She read right through it and had a terrified look on her face as if she already knew what I was going to tell her. I must have a terrible "poker face." My change of orders from the Pentagon to Vietnam hit her like a ton of bricks.

The preliminaries were over. Things were about to get serious.

CHAPTER V
Preparing for War

Now that I was heading to Southeast Asia, I had to receive more inoculations, including another one for the plague. That insidious disease must have been a major concern to the military because I received a total of four shots for that malady over the course of a year.

I was given three weeks off to spend time with family and friends and to get my affairs in order before reporting to Fort Riley, Kansas for RVN-POR (Republic of Vietnam – Preparation for Overseas Replacement) Training. We stayed at Nancy's parents' house in Newton. It was good to spend time with all my loved ones, with most of my relatives still residing in Iowa.

One exception was my parents, who were temporarily living in Junction City, Kansas, while my mom was helping to set up a new telephone system there. Dad was retired by this time. Junction City just happens to be adjacent to Fort Riley. They lived in a neat little apartment on a hill with a view of Interstate 70. To get to the complex's swimming pool, which we seemed to always have to ourselves when we visited, it was necessary to climb several steps until we were overlooking the apartment buildings. I loved the setup.

Fort Riley is named after Major General Bennet C. Riley, known for leading the first Army escort over the Santa Fe Trail. Fort Riley is now the home of the Big Red One (1st Infantry) and was once home to the famed Buffalo Soldiers. The base also features Custer Hill, named after the legendary George Custer. He was sent to the post in 1866 to take over the 7th Cavalry, which would go down in history books for its hapless mission at the Battle of the Little Big Horn. (Since that time, the 7th Cav, now 158 years old, has served with distinction in WWII, Vietnam, the Gulf War, and the Global War on Terror.)

***

When I reported to Fort Riley, I learned that because of the on-going Asian conflict requiring so many trainees, there was a shortage of billeting. I seized upon that and said that I could help the situation by staying with my parents. I was pleasantly surprised when I was granted the request. Because of that, Nancy was able to join me there. The night before training began, we were able to sneak away for some Cohen's Chicken in Junction City, the very best fried chicken. Ever.

RVN-POR Training lasted one week. Staying at mom and dad's was a treat, but it lengthened an already tough schedule. Reveille on base was at 5:55 a.m., so I had to get up every morning at 4:30 to make certain I would be on time to join my unit. Our training days were approximately 12 hours long, so by the time I got back to my parents' place, it was often 9:00 p.m. or later. I had the use of my car for the round trip to the base.

Uniform for duty during the week was (as written on the training schedule): "Steel pot with liner and camouflage cover, pistol belt with first aid packet, canteen with cup and carrying case, poncho, two ammunition pouches, and M16A1 Rifle with blank adapter."

The steel pot was a helmet; really, it was two helmets. One was the one-size-fits-all outer shell, which was the steel pot, and the inner hard hat liner, which was crafted to fit the head. The steel pot could be used for many things, including a sink if necessary (hanging it on a branch by the chin strap, for example). We were accustomed to wearing them from our basic training days.

The chin strap was connected to the outer shell but there were those who said that it was best not to fasten it to the other side because the concussion effect from a nearby explosion could literally snap your head off. If left unattached, only the helmet would be blown off. That made sense, I have no idea if that was true or if it was an old wives' tale. (Frankly, I didn't know any old wives who wore combat helmets, so I didn't know who to ask.)

My ankle was healing satisfactorily (from my bad tumble five months earlier), but I would still tie my high-top combat boot as tightly as possible to give me maximum support during the week of RVN training. Luckily, I didn't have to be on my feet much during that week.

On the first day, after a Commander's Orientation, we had an Overseas Orientation; case studies of Perimeter Defense; Duties of Sentries, Ambush Patrols, Counter Ambushes, and M16A1 Training. Most of the instruction was held indoors.

On day two, following reveille, we checked out our weapons and went to the firing range, where we spent most of the day. We were required to do Zero Fire, Field Fire, and studied Record Fire/ATP (*Army Technical Publication*). We also had to go through Qualification Fire. Following that, we had a lecture on the proper care and cleaning of our weapons.

One thing I remember about that day is that when I fired the M16 from a prone position, the spent shell casings would burn my bare arms when they occasionally bounced back (we had the sleeves on our fatigues rolled up because of the summer heat). We didn't notice that small nuisance at Fort Lewis during boot camp because we were dressed for cold weather and the shells probably just ricocheted off our coats.

Day three was an intense day. Following reveille and the securing of our M16's, we were driven in deuce-and-a-half Army trucks to an area heavily lined with trees. We were going to sneak up and attack a mock-up of a Vietnamese hamlet controlled by the Viet Cong. Prior to that, we prepped for the exercise.

We separated into different units and surrounded the village. Following the "attack," we discussed the operation and talked about field and tactical problems and mistakes made. We lost three mates who were injured during the assault. (When I eventually arrived in Vietnam, I looked back and was amazed at how well the Army had replicated such an authentic looking Vietnamese village; the facsimile at Fort Riley was very realistic.)

Day four found us primarily in the classroom again, with the topics for the day being Mines and Booby Traps; Fire Control; Combat First Aid; Malaria Control; Military Sanitation; and discussion on common weapons utilized in Vietnam.

We also had a briefing on potential biological warfare by an enemy force, which is extremely horrifying. In evil hands, it would be a far more lethal method of controlling the world than even nuclear war. (The Covid scare many years later drove home the dangers of such a frightening form of attack by sinister entities.)

The fifth day was dedicated to jungle survival techniques. Next, we were taken to a huge, flat firing range where we watched demonstrations from battle tanks, which I believe were M48 Patton's. Among other displays, they were hitting and obliterating stationary wrecked cars from a very long distance. It was an eye-opener!

The final day of RVN-POR Training featured such issues as drug abuse and other potential negative aspects of serving in Vietnam. We spent the late afternoon out-processing and receiving our next orders as to our future steps for destination Southeast Asia.

I had to pack my duffel bag that night, checking off a list of items I would need as provided by Uncle Sam. I was awake the entire night, dreading the goodbyes to mom and dad and my wife the next day. Undoubtedly, that's the most gut-wrenching task any soldier faces.

At the Manhattan, Kansas airport, I remember my Dad, looking sad, saying: "Why do old men always send young men off to war?" I recall Nancy apologizing for crying on the freshly polished brass on my collar as I gave her my last farewell hug at the airport.

> *"I'm leaving on a jet plane,*
> *I don't know when I'll be back again;*
> *Oh, babe, I hate to go...."*
>
> ■ Leaving on a Jet Plane
> --Peter, Paul and Mary

That horrible chore of goodbyes completed, I boarded a Frontier Airlines prop plane in Manhattan, Kansas. I walked across the tarmac until I was at the top of the stairs, taking one more long look back and a final wave to my family before ducking my head to enter the 54-seat craft, which would take me to Denver.

From there, I would catch a United Airlines Flight to California where I would briefly be stationed at Oakland Army Base, a major transit station for those going to and coming back from 'Nam.

I wasn't in the mood for breakfast before leaving my loved ones, thus I was starting to get hungry on that first leg to Denver. Halfway through the flight, the lone flight attendant on the small plane came down the aisle with a basket of hard candy, the only food on board. I took a couple of pieces and she reprimanded me, saying: "Just one per passenger!"

I was at the rear of the half-empty plane and the basket was still quite full. I looked at her and, seeking pseudo sympathy kiddingly said: "But I'm going to Vietnam." She took a deep breath, wrinkled her forehead, looked around, took another deep breath, looked at the ceiling, sighed, and said quite sternly and somewhat disgustedly: "Okay, you can have two!" It was obviously one of the toughest decisions of her day.

I finally arrived in Oakland via my connecting flight from Denver. My four days at "the portal to Vietnam" were pretty agonizing. We had bunk beds but no lockers in the large billeting facility, and we were called out to formation three times a day. At the first gathering on each day, a list of names was read, and they were the individuals who would be catching the next plane to Vietnam. In between those formations, we were given the dirtiest, most boring, and unpleasant jobs imaginable from sunup to well past sundown.

I believe it was a psychological ploy; you lived in the hope that your name would be called at each formation so that you could get out of that place. You couldn't WAIT to go to Vietnam.

July 31, 1970, is a "date that will live in infamy." Well, okay, just for me! My time had arrived; playtime was over. A front-page blurb, complete with photo, in the *Newton Daily News* announced that I was headed for Vietnam, a little country in Southeast Asia that had been in the world spotlight for the past few years. Prior to that, it was little known to most people around the globe.

I would get to know it well.

CHAPTER VI
Destination: Uncertainty

I thought that I had been a good soldier up to this point, and I had been rewarded for that, having been promoted three times in just seven months of being in the service. I was now a Specialist 4 (or E4).

But with promotion comes responsibility. We were taken to Travis Air Force Base to catch our military charter aircraft. We sat on the cement floor (cross-legged "Indian style," as they used to say), with our gear, in a huge empty hanger. After a couple of hours, I heard someone yell out: "Spec 4 Thomas R. Starr come up front and center!"

There's one thing you learn in the military; if your name is called, chances are that it might not be for a positive reason. I was stunned but I was pretty sure I wasn't in trouble because I had kept my nose clean. (Surely I didn't have to peel anymore potatoes or onions!)

A couple of my new-found buddies that I was sitting with asked me what my order to report up front could be about, and as is my usual way of handling things, I couldn't resist making light of it.

When I was gathering my gear, I said: "Oh, I requested a change in orders for my next duty station to be changed from Vietnam to Fort DeRussy on Waikiki Beach in Hawaii; it looks like it came through! You guys have fun over there."

Obviously, I truly didn't know why I was called upon. Why does this always happen to me? As I made my way to the front, I reflected back on my time at Fort Des Moines when I was one of four names called out of a huge crowd to transition from the Army to the Marines (until the sergeant saw my wedding ring), and also the time I was in charge of the Ft. Lewis contingent checking in at Fort Benjamin Harrison.

When I reached the snarling old sergeant who had called my name, he growled at me: "Starr, you are in charge of helping to make sure everyone gets on that aircraft!" I wasn't exactly excited about the prospect of corralling those 140 or so number of guys. Isn't that a military policeman's job or something? Nonetheless, I didn't think that it would be too difficult due to the fact that we were all confined to that hanger and our plane was just outside within walking distance. The majority of the passengers were my rank or lower, with the exception of a few officers.

However, one thing I hadn't counted on was a small, fenced area just outside the building, and a few of the soldiers rushed over to give their wives and children one last kiss, or a final goodbye to parents who were there. (I have no idea how they had gotten on base.) I knew -- and they certainly knew -- that because of where we were headed, there was the very real possibility that this could be the last glimpse they would ever have of their son, brother, husband, boyfriend or father. Some of our Vietnam-bound G.I.'s were as young as 18.

A couple of the soldiers did not want to leave, and I had to verbally order them to get on the plane and even had to almost drag one of them away from his loved ones. I hated that job, and I prayed that every one of those boys/men would safely return to those mothers, fathers, siblings, wives, and kids. It weighed heavily on me; it is a responsibility that I would not wish on anybody.

Finally, everyone was aboard, and the pilots commenced the taxiing of the aircraft that was taking all of us to an unknown future and an uncertain fate. Most Americans were asleep when we lifted off; it was 1:15 in the morning, Pacific time. As we looked out the window during our ascent, our thoughts were to ourselves as we wondered if we would be fortunate enough to see that same sight upon arrival back in the U.S. a year later. It was a reflective, yet exciting, time for a group of naïve young men.

> *"Got on a plane in Frisco,*
> *And got off in Vietnam;*
> *I walked into a different world,*
> *The past forever gone.*
> *I could have gone to Canada,*
> *Or I could have stayed in school,*
> *But I was brought up differently,*
> *I couldn't break the rules."*
>
> ■   Still in Saigon
> --The Charlie Daniels Band

We settled in for a very long trip that would eventually make four stops before reaching our journey's end. I sat by a window. The soldier next to me was from Chicago, so we Midwesterners had a lot in common, especially regarding athletics, and that helped pass the time. I knew his city and its sports teams well.

Our first stopover was in Honolulu. It was simply to re-fuel, but we were allowed off the plane for a few minutes. I was able to find a couple of postcards to send to Nancy and to Mom and Dad. After "gassing up," we lifted off and as we departed, we had a view of Pearl Harbor and the Arizona Memorial.

After several hours of flying with nothing but blue water below us, we started to circle for a landing. I looked down but could not see land! I thought: "What is the pilot doing? Is something wrong with the plane? Are we going to ditch at sea?" I finally spotted a dot in the ocean but didn't think there was any possible way that we could land on that small of an area. But there it was after we had spiraled down for a few minutes more: Wake Island.

The total size of Wake Island is 2.8 square miles. It literally sits in the middle of the Pacific with no other land remotely close. We had traveled 2,298 miles from Honolulu. and it was time to again re-fuel.

Just prior to that, we hit some severe turbulence as I was returning to my seat after retrieving a soft drink to try and stay awake. Just when we felt the first jolt, my cola went flying all over a full bird Colonel's shirt as he was coming from the other direction. He blurted out: "God damn it!" I thought "uh-oh," but quickly reasoned: "What's the worst he can do? Send me to Vietnam?" (Years later I had to laugh at the scenes when the officer kept having coffee spilled on him in the movie "Top Gun"….it brought back memories!)

After a brief stay at Wake Island, we were off to our next objective, Guam. Situated some 1,500 miles west of Wake, it is a U.S. territory. The United States directed B-52 strikes in Vietnam from Guam, the largest of the Marianas Islands, and there were several of those large bombers lined up at the airport.

While walking around and getting some fresh air after landing, I snapped a couple of pictures of the 3rd Air Force Division's B-52's on the tarmac before an M.P. rushed up to me and told me that taking photos of the strategic aircraft was not allowed. (I later learned that the first B-52 ever stationed there was named after a place I would come to love. The moniker for the Stratofortress bomber was "The City of El Paso.")

After we re-boarded, we settled into our seats again and had another 2,500 miles ahead of us before reaching our last re-fueling stop on our way to Vietnam. Our one remaining opportunity to stretch our legs was in Manila, Philippines.

While we were landing, I couldn't help ribbing my Chicago buddy about his woeful favorite baseball team: "Hey, did you know that the Cubs are thinking about moving here?" He looked at me quizzically, shook his head and shrugged his shoulders as if to say: "What in the heck are you talking about?" I said: "Yeah, seriously; they're going to change their name to the Manila Folders." He thought it was kind of funny; I thought it was hilarious.

We finally got a two-hour break from the long flight as we climbed down the portable stairs which were put into place when the door was opened. We sauntered into the Manila International Airport and strolled around, used the restroom facilities, bought some candy bars, and admired the beautiful Filipino girls who were scurrying here and there to catch flights.

Too soon, we had to get back on our plane. This was it, the last leg of our journey.

> *"And it's one, two, three,*
> *What are we fighting for?*
> *Don't ask me, I don't give a damn,*
> *Next stop is Vietnam."*

> ■ I Feel Like I'm Fixin' to Die Rag
> --Country Joe and the Fish

As we climbed to our cruising altitude over the South China Sea, I reflected back to our four stops. We had hop-scotched from Honolulu, home of Pearl Harbor....

To Wake Island....to Guam.... and finally, to the Philippines. I wondered if the ghosts of WWII soldiers past were shaking their heads at the thought of more of America's young men heading off to another war. It had been a mere 25 years since they had liberated those stepping-stones at a horrible cost.

The Japanese had attacked each of those sites in December of 1941 and over the next four years, American forces had to free lands throughout the Pacific Rim inch-by-inch. At my four stops in Honolulu, Wake Island, Guam, and the Philippines alone, in total we had lost 21,512 Americans killed in action (KIA) and another 63,942 were seriously wounded, including my cousin, Paul "Bubby" Flatterey.

Countless thousands were missing in action (MIA) or captured, at which time they were placed into torturous Japanese prison camps where the survival rates were abysmal. Many were simply executed in cold blood in the most horrific ways imaginable. The treatment of the American prisoners by their captors was unfathomably cruel.

(The Japanese Imperial soldiers were tough, dedicated, ruthless and may I say, brain washed. It would be two more years from the time of the flight I was currently taking in 1970 before the last Japanese Imperial Army soldier surrendered on the island of Guam, still uncertain as to whether or not the war had ended. He lived in a cave until 1972 before being convinced that WWII was truly over. He had been hiding in the jungle for 27 years.)

Eight years prior to the flight I was aboard, on March 16, 1962, a total of 93 U.S. soldiers, 11 crew members, and three South Vietnamese were scheduled to follow the identical flight plan of Travis AFB-Honolulu-Wake Island-Guam-Manilla-Bien Hoa, Vietnam on a top-secret mission aboard a Flying Tiger Line Lockheed L01049H Super Constellation. No American combat troops were officially in Vietnam at the time. Tragically, the plane went down somewhere over the ocean between Guam and the Philippines and all 107 perished.

As we progressed on the last 1,000 miles of our journey over the South China Sea, I ascertained an anxiousness on the faces of my "band of brothers" on this flight. In the distance, I could see land and knew that we were not far from our trip's finish line.

When we finally crossed the eastern coast of Vietnam and were over land, I looked down and saw a pock-marked earth featuring deep craters, scarred from bombs, artillery or both. I told my seat mate: "Toto, I've got a feeling we're not in Kansas anymore." Cold reality set in for all my fellow passengers and me.

*"This is what we've waited for,
This is it, boys, this is war."*

■ 99 Red Balloons
--Nena

Bien Hoa (pronounced bee-in wah) Air Base, next to the city of Long Binh (Long Ben), was our final destination, and we were there within minutes of crossing the shoreline. Just before touching down, we were told that there was the threat of a possible rocket attack on the airfield and that we were to hit the ground after deplaning if there was such an occurrence.

I had heard that the Viet Cong were superstitious and always fired in rounds of three, thus giving you the chance to get up and run to the nearest protection after every third one. True or not, I had no clue.

I don't know why, but I had a strange feeling that they simply warned all newcomers of a potential offensive either as macabre humor or to get everyone's attention. Maybe not, but in the end, there was no assault from the perimeter of the airfield when we came to a stop.

As I scanned the area, I remembered reading that the first two American soldiers ever killed in the Vietnam War by enemy agents occurred right here at Bien Hoa, just 20 miles Northeast of Saigon. It took place in 1959, 11 years prior to my arrival. They were military advisors in South Vietnam before the war had even started and were shot by communist agitators while watching a movie.

(In 1956, when U.S. Air Force personnel were training South Vietnamese pilots, a drunk and disgruntled American airman shot to death his crew chief, Tech Sgt. Richard Fitzgibbon, Jr., and some consider him to be the first to die in the Vietnam conflict, although he wasn't killed by enemy forces. Sadly, Fitzgibbon's son, Lance Cpl. Richard, III, a Marine, was later killed in combat in Vietnam in 1965.)

The Fitzgibbons were one of three father-son pairs to die in 'Nam. One such family connection was Navy pilot Lt.Cmdr. Leo Hester Sr., who died when his aircraft went down in 1967, and his son, Army Warrant Officer Leo Hester, Jr., whose helicopter was shot down in 1969.

The other was Spec. 5 Fred C. Jenkins, who drowned in Vietnam in 1968 less than a year before his son, Army Warrant Officer Bert M. Jenkins, met his fate when his Huey chopper was hit by enemy fire.

During my time in the country, Bien Hoa was the site of an Allied Prisoner of War camp that held approximately 4,300 communist fighters who had been captured. It was located 18 miles from what would be my base camp.

Bien Hoa had been the target of enemy forces many times, including a November 1, 1964, attack that killed five Americans and caused the loss of five B-57 bombers, which were totally destroyed. Fifteen (15) others suffered damage as well.

After gathering our few belongings, we hustled down the stairs of the plane of what had been our living quarters for the past day (collecting our duffel bags at the bottom) and were herded on to buses which had protective wiring over the windows to deflect hand tossed explosives such as grenades. Two things smacked us in the face right away: The stifling heat, and the "unique" scent!

On the ride to Long Binh, where we would be temporarily billeted, I took in the sights and sounds of the country that would become my new home for a year. Among the main items that caught my attention were Vietnamese citizens scurrying about in their traditional conical bamboo straw hats and black clothing; several adults balancing carrying poles on their shoulders, with baskets on each end; cyclos, a form of transportation that I would soon learn; small, dilapidated buildings, some damaged by war; guard posts dotting the street; and a Buddhist Temple.

The Vietnamese were resourceful and utilized whatever they could to build small homes, as we learned when we bussed past them. The outer walls of some of these abodes were covered by flattened out soft drink and beer cans.

Military materiel such as spent artillery shells were also used in the structures. Shanty shacks built on stilts could be seen above waterways throughout the country. I admired their industriousness.

The biggest shocker for me happened when we were stopped on a busy narrow street for a few minutes. A pretty Vietnamese girl, probably in her late teens, was walking along and to my amazement, she stopped a few feet ahead and to the side of our bus, pulled down her black silk slacks under her blue flowered silk ao dai (a traditional Vietnamese dress slit up the both sides that was pronounced "ow yigh" in the south and, I was told, more like "ow zigh" in the north), and then squatted.

This native miss then proceeded to relieve herself of re-cycled liquid before getting back up, straightening her clothing, and going about her merry way as if it was as natural as could be. I'm not saying such a scenario was a common occurrence, but I certainly never saw that happen back home in Newton!

Long Binh was the largest U.S. installation in Vietnam and was well-protected. The barracks where we were dropped off were surrounded by concertina wire, to ward off any attack. However, the Viet Cong were so adept with satchel charges (for demolition purposes) that they were able to blow holes in the fencing and get through the wire within seconds if not detected. There were beer cans filled with rocks attached to the wire, which served the purpose of causing a rattling noise, alerting posted guards to possible enemy infiltration.

Any attacking V.C. attempting infiltration through the wire might have also learned about a nasty little number called a Claymore Mine, a 5" x 8" convex plastic box sitting on short scissor legs that would fire out 700 tiny steel balls when remotely detonated. The front of the Claymore actually states: "Forward Toward Enemy." That was always a wise choice.

The communists had quite an arsenal of surprise explosives of their own spread throughout the country, including the well-known and deadly "bouncing Betty," which was an explosive device hidden just beneath the soil and detonated when stepped on and triggered. During my time in-country there were 23 booby trap dog teams whose purpose was to detect such deadly devices and warn their handlers of their locations.

The North Vietnamese Army and the Viet Cong also had more crude methods of causing serious injuries or death, including the planting of pointed punji sticks protruding up in a pit that was covered by branches and grass. An unsuspecting soldier, often reacting to an ambush, would sustain horrible wounds by jumping on the hidden sharpened sticks, which were hardened by fire and were often poisonous. They could even penetrate our steel bottomed combat boots. The countryside was awash in such unsophisticated deadly devices.

It has been estimated that as many as one-third of American casualties were caused by such non-direct military contact, which affected the morale of weary troops.

I finally reached my temporary billeting and was totally exhausted as the initial excitement waned. Severe jet lag finally took its toll. I threw my stuff in a corner once I had reached my assigned interim room and hopped up onto a top bunk bed. There was a Vietnamese mama-san (housekeeper) sweeping the well-worn floor, but it didn't prevent me from starting to drift off in welcomed sleep.

Groggily, I detected someone throwing his gear on the bottom bunk, and suddenly I heard this bellowing voice from the newcomer: "Hey, got any panties on, mama-san?" Totally disgusted, sickened, and ashamed by the horribly insulting nature of the remark, especially coming from an American soldier to a woman in whose country we were a guest, the light bulb went on in my foggy head and I suddenly realized that I recognized that voice!

I peeked over the side of my bunk and said: "Well, hello there, Drill Sergeant Scary!" I purposely dragged out the last three words. He looked up at me with eyes the size of silver dollars and quickly turned pale, which was not easy due to the fact that he was African American. It was a one in a million chance that we would meet again like this.

If there is one thing that a drill sergeant does not want to see in a combat zone, it's one of the recruits that he had put through hell; he knows that retribution could be on that soldier's mind. In Vietnam, there was an interesting phenomenon called "fragging," when a disgruntled soldier would, among other methods, roll a live grenade towards an officer or NCO (Non-Commissioned Officer) – sometimes under his bunk -- whom the attacker felt had wronged him somehow.

Well, that idea never crossed my mind, of course, because (1) that wouldn't even be something I would even remotely consider, and (2) since I was on the top bunk, that probably wouldn't have been the smartest thing in the world to do!

(There was a far less lethal method of dealing with despised superiors who were career military personnel. Soldiers who knew fellow G.I.'s in the document section of a base could have them send their target's financial records to Germany, medical records sent to Korea, career military records to Italy, etc. when that individual's tour of duty was completed. It would take him months to finally track down all of his personal papers, likely costing him a couple of pay periods before getting caught up. I certainly didn't condone it, but I knew first-hand that it occurred.)

Sergeant Scary smiled and laughed nervously, acting as if I was his best friend and one of his favorites. I'm certain that with all the cycles of incoming basic training recruits he had seen, in reality he didn't remember me from Adam, but he wasn't taking any chances. He kept rambling on and on, but my personal sandman sent him off into the distance, tuning him out as I fell unconscious on my bunk from the grueling last couple of days without sleep.

The next few days were a whirlwind, with the first step being to report to the 90th Replacement Battalion in Long Binh. It was anti-climactic because I already knew that I was going to be assigned to MACV -- (Military Assistance Command, Vietnam) and its Project Hieu (pronounced "Hugh") program, based near Tan Son Nhut (Tawn-son-newt) Air Base at the MACV compound, just outside of Saigon.

As mentioned earlier, MACV was a Joint Service Command of the U.S. Department of Defense, with leadership provided by the Army. It also contained the Navy, Marines, Air Force, and Special Forces.

MACV's mission was "to assist the government of Vietnam and its Armed Forces to defeat externally directed and supported communist subversion and aggression and attain an independent South Vietnam functioning in a secure environment."

A tall task, indeed!

CHAPTER VII
The Vietnam Conflict – 101

The country of South Vietnam had approximately the same square mileage as the state of Missouri. The capital city of Saigon, now Ho Chi Minh City (but to most Vietnam Vets and older Vietnamese natives, will always remain Saigon), was located in the lower half of the country.

South Vietnam was made up of 44 Provinces and 246 districts (similar to our state and county configurations in the United States). The U.S. military had divided the country into four regions: I Corps was furthest north and extended up to the DMZ (De-Militarized Zone); II Corps encompassed the Central Highlands; III Corps included Saigon and surrounding areas; and IV Corps incorporated the Mekong Delta in the southern part of the country. (For some reason, the northernmost Corps was called "eye" Corps, for the letter "I," instead of "One" Corps, while the rest were known by their numerical phonetics. Go figure.)

Although Saigon and Gia Dinh Province were in the confines of III Corps, it was under a separate command known as the Capital Military District.

THEY NEVER HEARD THE FINAL SHOT

Some 2,500 villages and 16,000 hamlets were spread throughout the countryside with a largely agrarian setting. Nearly 80% of its citizens were farmers. By most standards it was a poor country, and 90% of its economy went to the war effort as it tried to fight off the communists. South Vietnam brought in funding by exporting such products as rubber, lacquer, palm oil, tea, and coffee.

It had been 20 years (1950) prior to my arrival in Vietnam when President Harry Truman sent U.S. military and economic aid to the French Forces in Vietnam (it was a French colony at the time). They were fighting the Viet Minh -- precursor to the Viet Cong -- in what was then often called the Indochina War. (In reality, Indochina encompassed both Cambodia and Laos in addition to all of Vietnam, North and South.)

Among other items, Truman sent transport planes and jeeps, along with 35 U.S. military advisors to aid the French. At the same time, Chinese communist leader Mao Zedong, who became dictator of his country after defeating the Nationalist government in 1949, sent his military to Vietnam to train the Viet Minh starting in 1950. He also provided weapons and ammunition to the communist forces in the small country, as did the Soviet Union.

Over 50,000 North Vietnamese and Viet Minh troops overwhelmed some 13,000 French defenders at Dien Bien Phu (on the Laotian border west of Hanoi) on May 7, 1954. The French contingent was made up of a somewhat ragtag combination of Foreign Legionnaires, mercenaries from several different countries, and even former Nazi SS troopers who had been captured by the French at the end of WWII and forced to participate in the defense of its Indochina colony.

After the victory by the Viet Minh at Dien Bien Phu, the 17th parallel in Vietnam was established by the Geneva Accords, with negotiations lasting nearly three months. Under the terms, the communists were assigned to the North, and non-communists to the South. Both agreed not to attack each other across the 17th parallel.

At the time, the size of the two Vietnams was about equal, with the North having approximately 63,360 square miles and the South having about 65,726. The populations were also almost equal in number with the total being some 32 million citizens.

The Geneva treaty spelled out that citizens would have a 300-day grace period to re-settle and move to the Vietnam (North or South) of their preference. In short order, more than a million citizens fled from the communist North to the non-communist South – with the mass exodus made up primarily of Roman Catholics, Buddhists, landowners, and intellectuals -- following the finalizing of the Geneva agreement. In part, it was due to the fact that the communists were becoming more hardline.

North Vietnam emulated China and the Soviet Union by enforcing a land reform program, simply taking land from those who owned it. Much like the case of the two communist giants, extermination of the landowners was often the most efficient way to secure the land. Upwards of 200,000 landowners were executed by the North Vietnamese communists during that period, making those who survived anxious to get to the South and out of danger.

The South had become a much more attractive destination in which to reside. Food production flourished in the South and faltered in the North. Additionally, despite North Vietnam's vastly larger industrial complex, the South's per capita gross national product was more than 50 percent higher.

The communists were alarmed (and embarrassed) by the mass exodus of its citizens to the South. Only 90,000 relocated to the North from the South – many of them pro-communist Viet Minh members and families -- as opposed to the one million plus who fled from the North to the South. Although the Geneva Accords called for complete freedom of movement, the North Vietnamese began a process of making it all but impossible for any further individuals to make the move after the initial droves of people made it below the 17th parallel to South Vietnam.

For example, under communist rule, husbands and wives were not allowed to travel together. Special transit passes were required by the North Vietnamese government, but people were under strict travel orders and couldn't get to the required location to get the passes.

The International Control Commission (its member nations being Canada, India and Poland), whose job it was to assure a smooth transition for people who wanted to move, was officed in a building surrounded by NVA (North Vietnamese Army) troops; citizens were never allowed to get close enough to the Commission to voice a complaint or request assistance.

Finally, rigidly enforced regulations pertaining to all forms of transportation were such that it became almost impossible to travel South. In essence, North Vietnam had created a Berlin Wall without concrete.

The Geneva pact also called for all French troops remaining in the North to be sent to South Vietnam (and shortly thereafter, home). Members of the Viet Minh in the South were obligated to relocate to North Vietnam, but they did not, with most going underground in the South, later to become the Viet Cong who would try to continue undermining the South Vietnamese government.

In addition, North Vietnamese troops started to illegally infiltrate South Vietnam soon after the Geneva accord was signed. An article, titled *Tour 365*, which was published by the U.S. Army years later, indicated the extent to which North Vietnam stealthily introduced its soldiers into the South during the mid-50's.

It stated: "Elaborate precautions were taken to prevent discovery of North Vietnam's support of the southern communist organization (i.e. Viet Cong). When an infiltrator arrives at the Laotian border, his North Vietnamese army uniform is exchanged for a Lao (Laos) 'neutralist' uniform. He must give up all personal effects of an incriminating nature. A local guide takes him halfway to the first of a series of way stations along the infamous Ho Chi Minh Trail. There he is met by the next guide until the process has led the infiltrator into South Vietnam."

The piece continued: "In South Vietnam he receives a black pajama-like uniform, two unmarked uniforms, rubber sandals, a sweater, a hammock, mosquito netting and waterproof sheeting. After being issued a three-to-five-day supply of food and medicine, he is assigned to a unit for operations." North Vietnam would continue the charade of saying it didn't have any of its forces in the South aiding the Viet Cong for virtually the entire war.

In 1955, President Dwight Eisenhower first sent military advisors to train a new South Vietnamese Army, which would become known as ARVN (Army of the Republic of Vietnam).

Six years later in 1961, President John Kennedy deployed 400 newly formed Army Green Berets to teach the ARVN how to fight counterinsurgency, with the threat of an imminent attack by the North on the South. It was in the spring of that year that the Viet Minh started to become known as the communistic Viet Cong, as designated by Allied forces in the South. The literal translation of Viet Cong was "Communist Traitors to the Vietnamese Nation."

The United States was obligated to assist the South Vietnamese under the SEATO pact (Southeast Asia Collective Defense Treaty Organization), which was signed in 1954 after the Geneva Agreement was completed. England, Australia, New Zealand, France, Thailand, Pakistan, and the Philippines were SEATO partners of the U.S.

Military Assistant Command, Vietnam (MACV), the joint service entity under which I would serve, commenced on February 8, 1962, with General Paul D. Harkins as its first commanding officer.

Due to the growing concern of a major assault on South Vietnam by the North and its in-country V.C. guerrilla allies, by autumn of 1963, there were more than 16,000 U.S. military advisors in South Vietnam. It was estimated at the time that the communists already controlled 50% of South Vietnam's territory. The *New York Times* had said a year earlier that "it was a struggle that the country (the U.S.) could not shirk."

Tragically, President Kennedy was assassinated on November 22, 1963, which turned over the war effort to Lyndon Johnson, who moved up from being Vice President to the Presidency of the United States. South Vietnam had suffered the same fate, as its president, Ngo Dinh Diem, was executed just 18 days before Kennedy's deplorable slaying.

With the blessing of the U.S., top South Vietnamese generals had staged a coup against Diem, who had gradually become an intolerable dictator and presented a roadblock to free elections in the South as required by the Geneva terms.

However, the American government was outraged regarding Diem's murder in a troop transport vehicle after he was told that he was being transported to a safe place and would be allowed to flee the country.

Years later, a rumor circulated that Ho Chi Minh (Ho-Chee-Men), who brought communism to Vietnam in 1945 and was serving as President of North Vietnam, had made secret overtures to South Vietnam President Diem in 1963 just prior to his assassination, to test the possibility of reaching a peaceful settlement before a major "hot" war broke out.

I cannot find any sources to verify that account, but if such a solution had been reached similar to today's two-Korea policy, it would have changed history. Supposedly the Soviets were receptive to Ho Chi Minh's peace proposal, but the more militant Chinese were not.

If war had been averted, some 3.4 to 4 million (including military from both sides in addition to civilian casualties) would never have died in the gory Vietnam conflict. If such detente was afoot between the leaders of the two countries, Diem's murder, and Ho Chi Minh's rapidly declining health that year, grievously ended what could have been a salvation to the world.

Following Ngo Dinh Diem's ouster and assassination, South Vietnam was mired in political turmoil throughout the mid-60's, with strong religious divisions, mainly the Buddhists and Catholics, providing much of the upheaval, along with student demonstrators.

(The political situation in South Vietnam during my tenure was relatively stable under President Nguyen Van Thieu, a former general, and Vice President Nguyen Cao Ky. The swash-buckling Ky was his country's version of Errol Flynn; handsome, outspoken, and a "ladies' man" until he married an Air Vietnam flight attendant. Flamboyant and brash with a bright purple scarf as his trademark, he was a brilliant and brave helicopter pilot, serving as commander of his nation's Air Force before taking over his V.P duties. American military leaders respected him and appreciated his honesty.)

On August 2, 1964, three North Vietnamese torpedo boats fired on the USS Maddox, a U.S. Destroyer, in the Gulf of Tonkin off the shores of North Vietnam, but in international waters. It was to become known as the "Gulf of Tonkin Incident." A second attack was reported on August 4, but that proved to be wrong due to an error in intelligence reports.

On August 5th, flying off the aircraft carrier USS Constellation in his A-4 Skyhawk, Everett Alvarez became the first American pilot shot down and taken prisoner in the Vietnam War. He would be held in solitary confinement in a 7' x 7' cell for much of his eight years and seven months, often enduring torture and isolation by his North Vietnamese prison guards. (I had the distinct honor of meeting Mr. Alvarez and hearing his personal account years later.)

These actions led to the Gulf of Tonkin Resolution, giving President Johnson the authorization to use conventional military force in Southeast Asia without a formal declaration of war, as required by Congress. The Gulf of Tonkin Resolution was signed on August 7, 1964. The vote in Congress was one of overwhelming approval: 416-0 in the House of Representatives and 88-2 in the Senate.

(The Resolution was not without controversy, as some accused two American warships -- the Maddox and Turner Joy -- of "baiting" the North Vietnamese Navy over a three-day period in an operation known as DESOTO.)

Troop strength in 'Nam at the end of 1964 was 23,000. By March 8, 1965, Marines from the 9th Expeditionary Force landed at Da Nang in South Vietnam, and the U.S. commenced the bombing of targets north of the 17th Parallel, better known by then as the DMZ (de-militarized zone). By year's end in '65, U.S. troop strength in the Asian nation was 184,000.

When I arrived in South Vietnam five years later, there were approximately 340,000 U.S. military personnel in the country. That was down from a high of 543,482 American forces in Vietnam at any one time, which was just 16 months earlier.

Of major concern to the United States, and perhaps the primary reason why government leaders wanted to protect the small nation of South Vietnam, was because of the so-called "domino effect" as first espoused by President Eisenhower.

The theory held that if Vietnam fell to communism, its neighboring countries would also topple one-by-one. At the time, the Cold War was just getting underway and there was tension, distrust (and probably paranoia) between communist and non-communist countries. The North Korean communist invasion of South Korea just a decade earlier in the 1950's, exacerbated the concern.

U.S. Senator John F. Kennedy agreed with Eisenhower. "Burma, Thailand, India, Japan, the Philippines, and obviously Laos and Cambodia are among those whose security would be threatened if the Red Tide of communism overflowed into Vietnam," said the future President. Indeed, the Philippines, Indonesia, and Malaya were internally battling with Maoist (communist) rebels at the time. Even Australia and New Zealand felt menaced by communist aggression.

Several countries sided with the United States and South Vietnam. Australia, Thailand, New Zealand, and Taiwan all sent troops, with the Republic of Korea (South Korea) contributing the second-largest overall total contingent of 320,000 throughout the conflict. In addition, Spain sent a small secret force, mainly serving as medical teams. For my purposes, I am taking the liberty of echoing others by calling this contingent the "Allies." Some termed them Free World Armed Forces (FWAF).

The ROK (Republic of Korea) soldiers were tough, savvy battle-tested fighters who were known for their combat skills. On one occasion during my year in Vietnam, a small contingent of the South Korean soldiers became trapped in a traditional L-shaped ambush and were badly outnumbered by the enemy; they turned sure defeat into victory by killing or capturing all of the ambushers while not suffering a single casualty.

Up to the point I arrived in country, the South Korean soldiers had registered 33,412 enemy killed in action and had confiscated 17,428 weapons. I had my photo taken with a group of ROK troops and I had on my normal silly grin, but all of them remained stone-faced, maintaining their fierce reputation.

Also aiding the U.S. and South Vietnam cause in one form or another were Afghanistan, Argentina, Belgium, Brazil, Canada, Costa Rica, Denmark, Ecuador, England, France, Germany, Greece, Guatemala, Honduras, Iran, Ireland, Israel, Italy, Japan, Liberia, Luxembourg, Malaysia, Morocco, The Netherlands, Norway, Pakistan, South Africa, Switzerland, Taiwan, Tunisia, Turkey, Uruguay, and Venezuela.

In addition to the Army of South Vietnam (ARVN), the United States had a staunch in-country Ally in the Montagnard (Moo-ton-yard) peoples who were indigenous to the Central Highlands area of South Vietnam. In total, there were approximately 700,000 Montagnard citizens, divided into some 35 tribes or clans.

Also known as Degar, the Montagnard (meaning "mountain people" in French) tribesmen were fiercely loyal to U.S. Forces and invaluable to our cause, working particularly closely with the Green Berets as well as the 1st Cavalry Division. The Montagnard's despised the Viet Cong, who had treated them as outcasts and slaves before the Americans secured their area of the country. The V.C. called them "moi," which means savage or barbarian. The Montagnard quickly sided with the Allies.

The North Vietnamese had their own comrades-in-arms, mainly the Soviet Union (Russia), which provided jet fighters, weapons; ammunition, immense technical assistance, surface-to-air (SAM) missiles, and personnel to help with such units as anti-aircraft batteries; and China, which also offered weapons, technical assistance, and an untold number of troops (some analysts have placed the number between 170,000 to 300,000).

North Korea, contributed, too, providing pilots for the North Vietnamese Air Force Russian Migs. Communist Pathet Lao guerrillas operated in their home country of Laos against government forces. Additionally, Soviet bloc countries also served as patrons to the North Vietnam government (albeit after arm-twisting from their Russian rulers).

The Viet Cong oversaw a highly protected Potemkin Village (a façade of a model hamlet) in the Mekong Delta of South Vietnam to entertain their Chinese and Russian benefactors, complete with fake modern buildings and (forced) smiling residents, early in the war.

The deceit apparently worked as diplomats from the two powerful communist military giants flew in and viewed the seemingly happy scene, giving the impression that the V.C. were controlling the South Vietnam countryside and providing for happy and satisfied subjects. The reality was something altogether different.

Truth be known, the three superpowers – the United States, Russia, and China – utilized such proxy wars as Vietnam to field test their newest weaponry and other war materiel in preparation for a potential head-to-head confrontation involving two (or all three) of the giants on the battlefield.

Such involvement in so-called "secondary" wars also allowed each of the trio of world powers to develop a conflict-savvy officer base in addition to producing combat-hardened troops for possible future engagements. In other words, an experienced military.

We referred to the main Army of North Vietnam simply as the NVA (North Vietnamese Army). Technically, the name was People's Army of Vietnam (PAVN). The official name of the Viet Cong guerrillas in the south aiding the communist cause was the National Liberation Front (NLF). To avoid confusion to the reader, I am going to utilize the terms NVA and Viet Cong (or V.C.), the names most commonly and frequently utilized for the two entities, in this work.

American troops often alluded to an enemy combatant simply as "Charlie." (Viet Cong was often shortened to V.C., and the correct military phonetic alphabet term was <u>V</u>ictor <u>C</u>harlie. Over time it was reduced to simply "Charlie.") Make no mistake, "Charlie" was tough, resolute, incredibly brave, often had extensive battle experience, and was dedicated by indoctrination to communist principles. It had been instilled in him that the U.S. troops were simply replacements for the French and were there to take over his country.

The American military struggled early in the Vietnam campaign. It was on-the-job training; our forces were experts in a conventional war setting but had never been involved in guerrilla warfare on such a large scale.

U.S. troops were well-versed and the best in the world when it came to standard combat operations and fending off human wave attacks, but there were very few of those in Vietnam. Unlike past wars involving American Forces, there were no true front lines in this one.

Errors were made. Hills were taken at great cost to life and limb that probably didn't need to be taken. Many search-and-destroy missions were ineffective and unnecessary. Pilots' lives were lost because of tactical errors and fruitless missions. The U.S. also fell into a pattern of using the same flight plans and routes, which the NVA quickly learned and exploited.

In addition, some military hardware such as battle tanks were often useless in the jungle terrain, although they did play a role in the war. Some 800 American tanks were sent to Vietnam, mostly M48 Patton's. Among other uses, they were utilized as escorts, clearing roads of IED's, and sometimes playing a prominent part in attacks. They were essential in the victory at Hue during the TET Offensive of 1968, primarily by the South Vietnamese Army.

The most notable, and perhaps the only, armored battle between the U.S. and the communists was at the

Ben Het Special Forces Camp in March of 1969. The NVA assaulted the camp with 10 PT-76 Soviet tanks facing six American armored vehicles. The North Vietnamese were driven off and lost three of their tanks, while the U.S. forces suffered damage to just one M48.

Early on we didn't concentrate enough on winning over the people. But adjustments were quickly made and that oversight was corrected. On August 31, 1970, shortly after my arrival in Vietnam, the Hamlet Evaluation System estimated that 92.8% of South Vietnam's population was under government control, up nearly 43% from just seven years earlier.

It had been a busy year on the battlefield prior to my entry into the country. Just a couple of months before I stepped foot into Vietnam, U.S. and ARVN troops launched surprise attacks on large North Vietnam Army units which had located in eastern Cambodia without the approval of newly installed Cambodian President Lon Nol.

Nol had overthrown communist sympathizer Prince Norodom Sihanouk, who served as king and prime minister, and demanded that the North Vietnamese Army and Viet Cong leave his country. President Nol welcomed the action from the Americans and South Vietnamese to help him rid his country of the NVA and V.C.

The purpose of the massive Allied assault was to break the back of the North Vietnamese Army and capture weapons and supplies. In that encounter, the U.S. reported 11,349 enemy KIA's and the capture of large caches of weapons, severely disrupting the NVA's ability to wage war.

The base where I would be stationed was located approximately an hour from the eastern border of Cambodia. Near the partition between that country and South Vietnam was an ongoing active combat area known as the "Parrot's Beak."

Just north of the Parrot's Beak was an area nicknamed "Dog's Head. A few months before my arrival in Vietnam, a major encounter took place in that region, which was unfortunately little noted at the time and was eventually called "The Anonymous Battle."

Approximately 90 men from Charlie Company, 2nd Battalion, 8th Calvary commenced a mission on March 24, 1970, to locate and engage the North Vietnam Army's 272nd Regiment. On March 26, going on little sleep while trodding through dense jungle vegetation and stifling heat, Charlie Company found that it had walked into a cluster of NVA bunkers, manned by anywhere from 400 to 700 enemy soldiers.

The situation looked hopeless as they became surrounded, sustained heavy casualties, and were running out of ammunition. Two and a half miles away, Alpha Troop, 1st Squadron, 11th Armored Calvary Regiment learned of the dire straits in which their "brothers" found themselves. Without waiting for orders from the top, they decided on their own to proceed with a rescue mission. With five Sheridan Tanks, 14 Armored Combat Attack Vehicles (ACAV's) and about 100 accompanying infantrymen, they battled through the jungle underbrush, took on the enemy, and saved the brave men of Charlie Company from certain annihilation.

It took 39 years for the men of Alpha Troop to be recognized for their heroism. After much lobbying by those who became aware of the courageous action, that outfit finally earned the Presidential Unit Citation, the highest award for valor that a military unit can receive.

The well-known Ho Chi Minh trail, which was the main supply route of enemy supplies for their operations in Cambodia and South Vietnam, ran down the eastern borders of Laos (just west of North Vietnam) and Cambodia.

It was a constant battle to try to interdict the Ho Chi Minh supply line. The communists were able to keep it open throughout the years but paid a heavy toll, as an estimated 20,000 NVA soldiers lost their lives on the lengthy transit roadway during the course of the war.

A year prior to my arrival in Vietnam, the famous battle known as "Hamburger Hill" in the A Shau Valley had transpired with another victory, albeit a very costly one, for Allied troops, which included U.S. Army and Marine forces in addition to ARVN units. A movie, *Hamburger Hill,* -- starring Dylan McDermott and Don Cheadle -- immortalized the confrontation.

Vietnam was unlike any other war in which the USA had found itself, but in the end, basically wars are all the same. And like most soldiers throughout history, our hearts hoped that this would be the last one ever.

Unfortunately, our minds knew better.

CHAPTER VIII
A War-Ravaged Country Becomes Home

The time to make my move from Long Binh to the MACV compound near Tan Son Nhut had come. I was transferred to my new permanent living quarters, and I had it pretty cushy, relatively speaking. My home base, when not traveling, would be Dodge City, a barracks for MACV personnel. It was now official; in Vietnam military jargon, I was an FNG (Fucking New Guy). My new address: HQ, MACV, AG-H, APO San Francisco 96222.

We didn't exactly receive a formal greeting from the "Welcome Wagon." On August 17, not far from my new residence, 19 citizens in the Cholon district of Saigon were seriously wounded by Viet Cong rocket attacks. (Cholon was the Chinese sector of Saigon, with over a million individuals of Chinese descent living there. I still remember the scrumptious Japanese – yes, Japanese – peanuts that were served in the restaurants there.)

Project Hieu's office was in a complex nicknamed "Pentagon East," which also included my lodging. The entire compound was surrounded on all sides by huge bunkers and a cyclone fence with barbed wire on top, plus guard towers spaced out on the perimeter.

Pentagon East had been constructed three years prior to my arrival. The story goes that Vice President Ky was reluctant to relinquish the property, located near Tan Son Nhut Airport, to the Americans. He had visions of building a luxury hotel at the site after an Allied victory, which, of course, did not happen.

My living space at Dodge City, which I shared with others, consisted of a bunk bed, complete with mosquito netting to complement the malaria pills we had to take on a daily basis. (There were 24,606 cases of malaria, causing 46 deaths, among American forces throughout the Vietnam War). We also had a small locker in which to store our clothing, hygiene products, and weapons.

Our "pets" in Dodge City were lizards, which often stayed on the ceiling. We were glad for their company because they helped keep the bugs in check. And boy, were there bugs! Vietnam has a tropical climate, and those critters grow rather large there. On one occasion after I had just arrived, I happened to be talking to a fellow soldier outside the barracks and something large hit me in the back. I told my friend, who had already been in Vietnam for a lengthy time, that a bird had just flown into my back. He said: "Think again," and pointed to the ground. It was the largest beetle that I had ever seen.

Bugs weren't the only creepy creatures. On another occasion when I was walking through a nearby jungle terrain, something came out of the bush and hit me on the right side halfway up my calf above my combat boot. I had seen it coming out of the corner of my eye and thought it was a dog chasing another dog. Wrong! It was a rat chasing another rat. If I would have had a saddle, I'm pretty sure I could have ridden one of them back to camp.

Still another time found me just north of my base and as I approached a tree, I was about to duck because of a vertically low hanging branch. As I got closer, I quickly learned that the branch was a black python snake dangling overhead. I decided to take a different route.

The animals found in Vietnam could have filled a zoo. We would often see monkeys, and although I never came across any personally, the country did have tigers, elephants, crocodiles, and bears, among many other species. A constant nuisance for American troops were leeches, which seemed to occupy every waterway in Vietnam (I had to peel off a couple of them.)

Despite the aid of our friendly lizards, I had Mom and Dad send me bug killer spray to try and stay ahead of all the roaches and stupid spiders in our living quarters. In addition, we had an infestation of mice who resided in our small personal lockers ("Varmint Cong" as Caddyshack's greenskeeper Carl Spackler might have called them.) I had to have Nancy send me mouse traps to help keep the numbers of those creatures down to as few as possible.

The Viet Cong sometimes employed native insects to help their cause. According to V.C. defectors, amateur communist entomologists utilized small penicillin bottles filled with fireflies as a night-time warning device. They would wave the bottles back and forth, which could be seen from up to 250 yards, to alert their comrades in the jungle without making a sound when Allied patrols were approaching.

V.C. members who came over to our side also told Allied officials that they had "trained" bumblebees to attack American patrols, with a trip wire setting off a small explosive charge connected to a beehive. The intended purpose was for the enraged bees to attack the U.S. soldiers when their hives blew up after an unsuspecting soldier accidentally hit the unseen wire.

Such an aggressive massive charge by the stinging bugs could reportedly bring down a water buffalo. It was a useless strategy; apparently, no such attacks were ever reported by Allied forces.

After securing my new fatigues (which were to be worn at all times in Vietnam); assorted head gear; olive drab tee-shirts, boxer shorts, wool socks, handkerchiefs; spike proof tropical combat boots; M16 and ammo belts; and a gas mask, I was ready to report for duty. Sewn on to my new fatigues was my MACV (Military Assistance Command, Vietnam) patch.

The official MACV logo was bright red and gold but of course for practical purposes we wore the more muted and camouflaged olive green and black logo patches in 'Nam (commonplace in a combat theater). If you ever view a photo of General William Westmoreland, you will likely see the patch of MACV.

(The official symbolism of the insignia states: "Yellow and red are the Vietnam colors. The red ground alludes to the infiltration and oppression from beyond the embattled wall -- i.e. the Great Wall of China. The opening in the wall through which this infiltration and oppression flow is blocked by the sword representing United States military aid and support. The Wall is arched and the sword pointed upward in reference to the offensive action pushing the aggressor back.")

Starting in 1962, MACV's mission was to engage the enemy in combat and also to provide assistance to the government of South Vietnam, helping it to maintain a free society capable of defending itself. MACV oversaw all of the United States Armed Forces in Vietnam, and I was proud to wear its patch.

In addition to the aforementioned items, we were given a series of booklets and playing card-sized instruction documents. Those included an Armed Forces of the United States Geneva Convention Identification Card (to assure proper treatment if captured, which, in the end, really didn't matter because the North Vietnamese totally ignored Convention prisoner rights for captured American POW's); a card entitled "The Enemy in Your Hands;" Nine Rules for Personnel of MACV; Combat

Fundamentals; a reusable Liberty Pass; and various publications regarding Vietnam, including useful phrases and helpful hints when in contact with the locals (Vietnamese citizens).

The currency system was interesting. Most soldiers sent part of their pay back home, but the portion that was distributed to us in Vietnam was paid in Military Payment Certificates (MPC's), sometimes called "scrip," instead of in American "greenbacks." This was to avoid causing catastrophic inflation in the host country. Merchants in South Vietnam allowed better prices if paid by U.S. dollars, because they knew they were stable; they weren't so confident in South Vietnam piasters, the name for the currency in that country.

The MPC looked just like play money (about the size of that found in the board game, Monopoly), and I believe the highest bill was $20. To avoid hoarding of the military money by those same Vietnamese merchants (thinking that they could find illegal channels to swap MPC's for U.S. dollars), every so often there would be a totally unexpected and top secret "C-Day," when American military personnel were required to exchange their existing MPC's for newer versions. That would make the older MPC's useless to any merchants contemplating stockpiling the military payment notes for later trade-off.

Shortly after my arrival, the South Vietnamese government, worried about the shaky piaster, set up new exchange rates for U.S. personnel, which meant more buying power for Americans. The official rate was 275 piasters for one U.S. Military Payment Certificate "dollar," and 320 piasters for a regular greenback dollar. Obviously, G.I.'s tried to utilize U.S. currency, when possible, although technically it was illegal. The rate had gone up from 118 to the 275 figure within my first couple of months in country, which greatly benefitted U.S. soldiers.

I ate my meals at our mess hall when I wasn't on an assignment somewhere. One of the first dinners I consumed was a vegetable stew. When I brought my spoon out of the soup, there was a leaf on it. I told my buddy that the cooks must have made the concoction outside under a tree or something. It was at that time that my compadre educated his unsophisticated friend (namely me) about bay leaves that were used in cooking. I don't think we had bay leaves in Iowa or if we did, mom never used them.

The preliminary details out of the way, it was time to go to work. Pentagon East wasn't the Pentagon that I originally thought would be my assignment, but it would have to suffice.

In essence, I learned that I would be office managing the Project Hieu program, which was an honor but again saddened me because I would have rather been in the field.

I was not alone though; 80% of the U.S. military personnel in Vietnam were not involved in fulltime combat duties. It was what Ernest Hemingway called "a false feeling of soldiering." Nonetheless, I was there to do a job, and I would do it to the best of my ability.

As I would soon learn, I need not have worried about a boring existence. Little did I know at the time what a harrowing year was in store for me, with the ingredients being action, excitement, a bit of fear, a near drowning, helicopter crashes, a kidnapping, and other bizarre circumstances.

Project Hieu had only commenced seven months prior to my arrival in Vietnam. It was the brainchild of General Creighton Abrams, Commander in Chief of U.S. Forces in Vietnam. As a parallel to efforts on the battlefield, Abrams felt that a pilot program was needed to "win the hearts of the people," and emphasized the importance of all American military members to, in simple terms, practice good public relations with the populace.

Emphasis was being put on civil affairs and PSYOPS (Psychological Operations). This included the Chieu Hoi (pronounced chew hoy) program, which encouraged Viet Cong guerrillas in South Vietnam to change sides and work with the ARVN (South Vietnamese Army) and the U.S. military. Chieu Hoi translated to "open arms" in the Vietnamese language. A defector who switched allegiance to us was called a Hoi Chanh (hoy chan).

A Hoi Chanh was indispensable because he or she knew the communist playbook, so to speak. He was often used as a "Kit Carson" scout to help lead the American and ARVN forces in action against NVA or V.C. units, since he was cognizant of the tendencies and routines of the communist units.

The Hoi Chanh conscripts had the option to receive a trade, compliments of the South Vietnamese government, or could become a farmer if so desired. Hoi Chanhs received a monetary bonus to help them get started in their new lives and were paid $200 for any enemy weapon that they turned in.

It was a successful effort, as 800 former V.C. joined the program from just one province alone (Hau Nghia) during my first full month in Vietnam. I believe somewhere in the neighborhood of 43,000 had come over to our side from the beginning of the conflict up to my arrival in the country.

Also employed was the Phoenix Program, whose purpose was to "attack and destroy the political infrastructure of the Viet Cong." Though it was viewed as a success in some quarters, in others it was controversial because there were accusations that neutral innocent South Vietnamese citizens had been captured and killed, falsely accused of being communists.

A Position Paper had never been formulated for Project Hieu, so I was the first to draft and finalize the official seven-page manifesto, which included a mission statement and a list of objectives. In essence, it was our job to prevent an anti-American resentment among the South Vietnamese citizenry.

To do so, we had two field contact teams which conducted seminars to U.S. military troops in the field. Additionally, all in-processing MACV personnel received Project Hieu briefings.

I had the opportunity to meet General Abrams on the MACV compound and I was star-struck. My personal heroes – other than my brother, Dick – aren't athletes, actors, or singers; to me, ascribing that special title to an entertainer is a misnomer. Some of those might be idols and I was a fan of many celebrities, but my "heroes" are individuals who have faced the severest of life-and-death adversity, especially in service to their country, and persevered.

Abrams certainly fit the description of a hero. At the aforementioned Battle of the Bulge in WWII, he played a major role in blocking Germany's attempts of a last-chance massive assault to blunt the offensive of the Allies, who had been on a roll since the successful Normandy Invasion.

A Lt. Colonel at the time, Abrams commanded General George Patton's Thirty-Seventh Tank Battalion of the Fourth Armored Division. Patton later said: "I'm supposed to be the best tank commander in the Army, but I have one peer; Abe Abrams."

Against all odds, Abrams broke through the German lines and met up with General Tony McAuliffe, whose 101st Airborne stubbornly held on to the Belgium city of Bastogne. Though surrounded, outnumbered, and outgunned prior to Abrams' arrival to help break the siege, McAuliffe became famous for refusing a demand from the German high command to surrender. His one word reply to the Germans who approached the Americans under white flag with the Nazi demand, was simply: "Nuts!"

General Abrams, who served as the Commander of U.S. Military Assistant Command, MACV (COMUSMACV) from 1968-1972, was pleased when I told him of the growth and success of his Project Hieu project.

(In 1980, the United States introduced its latest and most lethal main battle tank which was named in honor of Creighton Abrams. The technical designation was the M1A1/2 Abrams. The newest model is the M1A2C. It is ultra-high tech with inconceivable capabilities, seemingly straight out of a science fiction movie.)

Abrams was one of only four generals who served as overall commander of all U.S. forces in Vietnam, and I was fortunate to have met three of them. Abrams succeeded General William Westmoreland, who oversaw the American military role in Vietnam from 1964 to 1968, after which time he became Chief of Staff of the United States Army. Westmoreland had taken the reins of leadership in Nam from General Paul D. Harkins. The final commander of all forces in Vietnam, who replaced Creighton Abrams, was General Fred Weyand.

Abrams and Westmoreland were both graduates of the fabled West Point class of 1936. That graduation year produced 48 generals, including Benjamin O. Davis, Commander of the Tuskegee Airmen; John H. Michaelis, who became Commander of the United Nations Command in Korea; Jim Lampert, a future Superintendent of the U.S. Miliary Academy at West Point; Albert (AP) Clark; a future Superintendent of the U.S. Air Force Academy; and Casey Vincent, who became a brigadier general by the time he was 30 and was one of Claire Chennault's top two fighter wing commanders with the famous China-based Flying Tigers, which helped protect that country from Japanese aggression during WWII.

General Fred Weyand served as COMUSMACV in Vietnam from 1972-1973, replacing Abrams. I always thought it was odd (and somewhat comical) that unlike his three West Point Military Academy predecessors who held the top job, Weyand became an officer by going through ROTC at the University of California-Berkeley, not exactly a place where you would expect elite military leaders to receive their training! I met General Weyand, a former intelligence officer in the Pentagon, when he was the Deputy Commander of MACV prior to replacing Abrams.

An Army football game at West Point several years later provided my opportunity to be introduced to -- and have a chance to visit with -- General Westmoreland.

There were other high ranking officers of note who served in Vietnam, and two carried the namesakes of their famous fathers, General George S. Patton and General Joseph W. Stillwell, better known as "Vinegar Joe."

The younger Patton (George Patton IV), who became a brigadier general in 1970, was known to fly over combat operations and firefights in the jungles of Vietnam. He was shot down at least three times.

Patton served three tours in 'Nam and his gallantry in action earned him two Distinguished Service Crosses and a Silver Star, to go along with the Silver Star he had been awarded in the Korean War. He served the first of his three tours with MACV, and finished his third as Commander of the 11th Armored Cavalry Regiment.

Vinegar Joe's son (Joseph Warren Stillwell Jr.), a Brigadier General, was somewhat of a character, too. When General William Westmoreland, head of all U.S. forces in Vietnam, was walking through the younger Stillwell's operations office, he noticed some pictures of female "pin-ups" among the official papers attached to the office's bulletin board.

When Westmoreland mentioned that some G.I.'s may object to the pictures of the scantily clad females, General Stillwell replied: "By God, sir, you are right, we'll poll the unit and if we find somebody who objects, we'll have him transferred!"

Lieutenant Colonel William W. Brash oversaw the Project Hieu staff and was my immediate boss. Throughout my year our office consisted of Major Mark, Captain Gaines, Captain Crump, Captain Osborne, 1st Lieutenant Cau, Sergeant Reynolds, Sergeant Chargualaf, Spec 4 Jackson, Spec 4 Russo and me.

Colonel Brash was an interesting man. We clicked right off the bat, and he took me under his wing. Brash was from Sea Girt, New Jersey and near the end of my tour, he asked me if I would be interested in going back with him to his home state to dabble in politics. In all honesty, I can't think of anything in the world that I would rather do less than that.

I'll always remember the Colonel's favorite expression: "You'd better Hong Kong, Pusan, PX believe it!" If he had a fault, it was the tendency for imbibing in the spirits a bit too much. He gave me some sage advice though. He said: "The Army made you physically tough, but it's up to you to make yourself mentally tough over here."

The most fascinating member of our staff was 1st Lt. Ton That Cau. He was born in Hanoi (capital of North Vietnam) and moved to the United States to be with his brother, a member of the Vietnamese Embassy in Washington, in 1960, before the war commenced. He was 16 years old at the time. Cau became an American citizen seven years later and was drafted in 1969 after attending the University of Maryland and North Carolina State University.

Cau went to U.S. Officer Candidate School (OCS) and became an Airborne Ranger at Fort Benning, Georgia. Obviously, he was invaluable to us with his command of the language and knowledge of the country. We were lucky to have him, but we did have to sometimes share him with General Weyand as a liaison in Weyand's office when he was still the Deputy Commander of MACV (before becoming the head of all U.S. military forces in Vietnam).

Sergeant Reynolds was the crusty Army sarge that you see in the movies; he was a wise old owl who had seen it all. He had a wonderful dry sense of humor. One day I walked into our office, and he was typing, or attempting to, I should say. He was hunched over, staring down at the keyboard, punching a letter now and then. He muttered: "I'm like a Saigon whore on this thing!" I burst out in laughter and managed a "what?" He replied: "Yeah, I'm a hunt 'n pecker."

I appreciated the efforts of Captain Osborne, a West Point graduate and hard-core Army Ranger. Osborne, who had seen combat duty in previous stints in Vietnam, did his best to get me out into the field whenever possible. He sympathized with my desire to leave the confines of Pentagon East.

Project Hieu was so new that I had to work seven days a week. Sometimes I would just sleep in the office rather than go back to my bunk.

We needed a lot of materials and early in my tenure I got into an unexpected brouhaha with a supply sergeant, who was condescending and mean, saying that we didn't need any of the items I was trying to requisition.

When Colonel Brash learned of the dressing down that I had received, he angrily picked up the phone and read the riot act to the supply sergeant and I heard him scream: "Don't you ever talk to Starr like that again!"

We also didn't have a much-needed office Jeep. Checking one out of the motor pool was too much of a hassle, so we simply "borrowed" one, which seems to be the way things are done in a combat theater of operations. We found one with keys in it on another base and it became ours, at least for the year I was there!

I started to make friends outside of my unit. Did you ever notice that in war flicks the characters always seem to have tough-sounding nicknames? Well, that really happened in my case. Some of my closest buddies were Rock.... Chopper.... Rat.... Buck.... the Gipper.... and others. I became "Ringo" based on the popular Beatles drummer at the time, Ringo Starr. I believe it was Steve Gibson who first pinned that label on me.

Regarding my closest friends outside of Project Hieu, we hailed from all over the map. I represented Iowa; Gibson was from Kansas; Carmen "Chopper" Bianco, Rod Jones, and Tom McLaughlin were from Pennsylvania; Gary Nelson was from Illinois; Jim Smyth (pronounced "Smith") was from New York; Jim Phillips was from Indiana; Jerry Garrett hailed from Virginia; and "Rat" Spencer came from Mississippi. I can't remember where Steve Barchak and Al Schmiderer were from, but knowing those two jokesters, Mars would be my best guess!

Billy Jones, my friend and colleague at Fort Benjamin Harrison who was from South Carolina, arrived in Vietnam at just about the same time that I did, but we didn't see much of each other. Other former compadres and friends from my Ft. Harrison days, Jim Phillips and Ron Derwin, were stationed at Pleiku (play-coo) and Richard Silverman ended up at Da Nang. We tried to see each other when possible. I apologize for leaving out some of my friends' names; it's been a while.

Chopper and I would talk football for hours on end when we got the opportunity. He loved his Nittany Lion football and was proud of the Pennsylvania high school ball played in his hometown of Easton and in nearby Allentown.

Gary Nelson was from Calumet City (a Chicago suburb) and was a great guy. We shared a lot of laughs. When I still think of Gary I remember him admonishing anybody who complained about the chow: "Eat it, it'll put lead in your pencil!" Jim Smyth (aka "Smitty") was from Brooklyn and he, too, was always good for a laugh. He did a great imitation of Monty Hall of "Let's Make a Deal" fame.

Smitty was an outstanding basketball player who played his college ball at St. John's under its legendary coach, Lou Carnesecca. Jim shot the winning basket against my Iowa Hawkeyes in December of 1969 at the Rainbow Classic in Hawaii, edging UI by just two points, 57-55. Small world, huh? That was the Hawkeye team that went undefeated in Big Ten play and finished 7th in the nation. The 55 points was by far the lowest number of points scored by Iowa that year; the Hawks would score over 100 points in 12 of the next 18 games that they played after that loss.

Similar to the same path that my brother, Dick, had gone down several years earlier, Smyth made the all-Army team and traveled to Germany, Greece, England, Sweden, Belgium, Lebanon, and Syria following his days in 'Nam. And like my brother's Army team, Jim's squad went on to win the All-Military Championship.

In our circle we had one character known for his phrase: "$100 to the man who can tell me…." He would come back to base late at night and say something like: "$100 to the man who can tell me how I ended up drunk." Or on another foray into Saigon: "$100 to the man who can tell me how I ended up with that old gal."

And then there was the night he came back to our barracks wearing nothing but a dress. Yep, sure enough: "$100 to the man who can tell me how I ended up in this dress!"

Some of my buddies wrote so-called "death letters" that were to be released to their loved ones upon their demise. I didn't write one of those "just in case" notes because I didn't want to tempt the hand of fate!

I received my first letter from Nancy on August 13. The mail took from 7-10 days to arrive. In the letter, Nancy said: "You have been gone for only 19 days and it seems like an eternity." I didn't receive another letter for a couple of weeks, which was frustrating, and I couldn't understand why.

And then one day I received four, and next day three, etc. She had written every day, but the letters were getting held up somewhere. It was a common refrain among my friends, too. That happened throughout the course of the year.

Nancy was driving our '61 Oldsmobile and it was on its last legs (last tires?). She was working at the Jasper County Extension Service in Newton, and I was, of course, drawing my small soldier's salary; thus, we didn't have a lot of money for car repairs.

I did, however, receive combat pay, and G.I.s serving in Vietnam did not have to pay federal income taxes, so those two things helped. (By the way, in case you didn't know, G.I. stands for "Government Issue" and became a slang term for American troops starting in World War II.) As alluded to earlier, part of my pay was automatically sent home.

Nancy's letters throughout the year all started the same: "Hi, how is my number one soldier today? Safe and well, I pray." Regarding the letters I sent home, on the back of the envelope I always wrote the number of days I had remaining in my one-year tour of duty and indicated the percentage of time I had already spent in Vietnam.

My letters home would be post-marked from many different places; Denver, Indianapolis, Birmingham, and several cities on the West Coast. I never really understood that. The Army works in strange ways!

Nancy and I also exchanged cassette recording tapes throughout that year, as I did with mom and dad. I looked forward to those so much. They allowed me to close my eyes and pretend I was home for a little while.

My wife recorded all of the University of Iowa football games on cassette tapes for me. Future close friend Jim Zabel did the play-by-play and former All-American Hawkeye quarterback Randy Duncan did the color analysis on WHO Radio. I would try not to hear or see the scores of games before receiving the tapes, which wasn't hard. Not knowing the final outcome made listening more enjoyable. Unfortunately, the Hawks were pretty mediocre again, finishing 3-3-1 in the Big Ten and only 3-6-1 overall in Coach Ray Nagel's fifth season.

Dave Clement, a former star at my high school in Newton, was a starting linebacker on that Hawkeye team and was named the team's MVP at year's end. Against Oregon State in the season opener, he had a mind boggling 29 total tackles – an NCAA record that stood for decades.

Dave's brother, Bruce, was a classmate and friend of mine and was the toughest 130-lb. middle linebacker that I ever witnessed! Another Clement brother, Stan, was later instrumental in locating the Iowa (NASCAR) Motor Speedway in Newton.

I received a form letter from the Red Cross in early September, explaining its operations for military personnel in Vietnam. It outlined procedures on what to do in case there was an emergency back home involving a close loved one. The Red Cross said that it would help facilitate my course of action to return home if necessary.

Later in the year, one of my friends lost his grandmother, who had raised him, and he wanted to get back home for her services. He became frustrated at what he thought was foot-dragging and turned to the Salvation Army, which was able to get him back to the States immediately.

The Salvation Army had also been there for us when we were first inducted, giving us all a shaving (dopp) kit filled with toiletries. (I'll forever remember the scent of the lime shaving cream that was included). I didn't necessarily need the items, but many of the poorer kids did; I thought that was very thoughtful of the Salvation Army. Make no mistake about it, the Salvation Army is a very good friend to every man and woman in uniform.

To this day, I have never failed to put money into one of that great organization's red pots at Christmas time and will always do so. Our family also contributes annually to the Salvation Army's Angel Tree, which assures that thousands and thousands of underprivileged children receive Christmas presents. (Dallas Cowboys owner and General Manager Jerry Jones has been one of the Salvation Army's biggest benefactors. We discussed it at length many years later at a banquet when I was executive director of the Armed Forces Bowl college post-season football game and he was the guest speaker at our team luncheon.)

I was learning more and more about my new resident country. I ventured into Saigon for the first time on a cyclo, which was a three-wheel motorized vehicle with a two seat "couch" in the front (over two of the tires) and the driver in back. Cyclos were the taxicabs of the city. A buddy accompanied me; you never wanted to travel alone if you could help it for obvious reasons.

Even through the fog of war, you could see that Saigon was once a beautiful city. In the past it had been affectionately termed "the Pearl of the Orient."

Our cyclo driver was an elderly Vietnamese gentleman, probably approaching 70 years of age, who, soaking wet, weighed 100 lbs., had a badly wrinkled face, and displayed a tanned hide from his many years in the tropical sun. I found it humorous that he was wearing an Ohio State tee-shirt! You Buckeyes are everywhere!

***

Most of the cyclo drivers, sometimes referred to as papa-sans, and other service-oriented men in Vietnam were senior citizens; the young to middle-aged men were needed for the war effort. Many women were in the service industry, too. A striking feature of older Vietnamese women were blackened teeth from an era when it was considered beautiful. Contrary to the believe that this was done by chewing betel nuts – which only stained the teeth brown – females, mostly prior to 1945, would first stain their teeth red and then cover that with black dye.

On that first ride on a Vietnamese "chariot," I was momentarily startled when I was pelted by a thrown object from somewhere above when we had slowed down. Obviously, it was a bit unnerving to have an object tossed at you in a combat zone, but when I instantaneously looked down at the small object that landed in my lap, I quickly observed that it was only a two-inch thin empty bottle with a label written in Vietnamese.

From the flowery scent, I was certain that it was some type of perfume. Searching around for the source of the propelled item, I saw two girls giggling and waving from a second-story window peering out between colonial shutters. What a pass; the thrower led me perfectly. Brock Purdy would have been proud of her!

A cyclo passenger had to be on alert if he was wearing a wristwatch, was carrying a weapon, or had a camera; "cowboys" were young ruffians on speedy motorbikes who would drive close to the cyclo, grab anything of value, and speed off. They were experts at snatching anything not fully secured. On my maiden voyage on such a handy vehicle, a cowboy sped by and ripped the watch off my left wrist and quickly disappeared. I learned a hard lesson on my first foray into the capital city.

I heard about an instance when an American soldier once purposely booby-trapped a bag while riding on a cyclo on a lonely stretch of road, enticing a cowboy to grab it.

One such thief took the bait and unfortunately for him, when he snatched the bag, it pulled a pin from a hidden grenade. When he sped off, the G.I. demanded his driver to come to a quick stop. They watched the resulting "fireworks" display from a safe distance.

We made our way to Duong Tu Do (Freedom Street) in Saigon to do some shopping. I wanted to send something to Nancy for our two-year anniversary. Every U.S. soldier who made it to the city knew Tu Do (pronounced Two Doe) Street quite well. Such was also the case with Plantation Road. Anything that you would want to buy, and I do mean *anything*, was available on those two roadways.

On Tu Do, there was a thriving open black market and a series of restaurant-bars with no shortage of young Vietnamese women occupying them. Hint, they were hoping to land an American soldier, but it was not for the purpose of starting a long-term relationship (unless you consider 60 minutes long-term).

If a soldier passed their establishments and did not enter after much enticement, they would yell out: "You numbah 10, G.I." He was also called a "dien-cai-dao" (pronounced dinky dow), which meant he was crazy. If he set foot into the bar to join them and get a refreshment (among other things), he was "numbah one, G.I."

One particular time, after having been "in-country" for a few months, five of my compadres and I were in Saigon and visited one of the many bars on Tu Do Street to try to drink away a bad day (we had lost a buddy). A young girl came up to sit on my knee and I politely told her that I just wanted to talk to my friends.

I faked a smile and asked her to please get off my knee and to just leave us alone. She ignored my request and continued by putting her arms around my neck. Gently pushing her away, she refused to take the hint and stayed on my lap.

Giving up on my attempts to dissuade the advances of the resident bar girl, I told the guys: "Let's just go." I put my hands on her tiny waste and slowly and tenderly lifted her off my knee. Nonetheless, she slipped and lost her balance, falling awkwardly to the floor despite my assistance. I tried to help her up, but she was scowling and refused my offer.

As my mates and I were approaching the exit, one of them yelled at me: "Duck!" I did, and my spurned "new girlfriend" missed my head with a beer bottle by just a few inches. The bartender and other girls quickly grabbed her and pulled her back. They were probably concerned about M.P.'s making their bar off limits if an American G.I. was assaulted there.

If she had been successful at bashing in my skull, I could just imagine the official note from the government that would have been sent to my parents: "The Department of Defense regrets to inform you that your idiot son was killed in action by a 4'10", 80 lb. Viet Cong guerilla."

There was a depressing side to the world's oldest trade in Vietnam. A scene that greatly saddened me was watching young street walkers, some of whom couldn't have been more than 13 years old, strolling along the main thoroughfare. Many Vietnamese were destitute, and they were reluctantly forced (in their minds) to send their daughters out to try to get money from the "rich" Americans.

Speaking of children, one thing you had to avoid was allowing a growing group of smiling children to surround you. They were sometimes not what they seemed; they had razor blades and before you knew it, several would overwhelm you, slicing all the pockets of your fatigues and stealing everything you had (not to mention causing a few gashes in your flesh).

I'm glad I was informed of that because I love kids and I wouldn't have had any qualms about them gathering around me, thinking they just wanted candy or to just joke around with a soldier.

However, that was a very small percentage of the kids in the city. I certainly don't want to leave the reader with the impression that all of the Vietnamese children acted that way, and the ones who did were only doing so at the behest of adults, most likely under a threat of some type.

We also had reports that the Viet Cong, facing a shortage in their ranks after years of irreplaceable losses, were turning to kids to do their evil work. Poor children from ages 12 to 16. who were less conspicuous than their adult counterparts around American bases, were recruited with promises of money to plant explosives and perform other minor acts of terror wherever U.S. soldiers congregated.

I found a jeweler on Tu Do Street and was able to purchase a Princess ring made of topaz and sapphires to send to Nancy for our anniversary on August 31. I bartered and bartered and finally got it down to a price I could afford.

This little trip into the city allowed me to interact with the population of Vietnam. I grew to love the Vietnamese people and had (still have) the utmost respect for them. I was always treated very well by everyone with whom I came into contact.

Some of them might not have liked me at night, though. I believe it was one of every four or five Vietnamese citizens with whom you knew and worked during the day could have possibly been a Viet Cong guerrilla after the sun went down. That could include the cyclo driver, the jeweler, the mama-san who cleaned our barracks and washed our clothes, the barber who cut our hair, and anybody else who was around Allied forces. (I'm certain that our troops in Iraq and Afghanistan faced the same issues with the native populations in the years to come.)

I was picking up a little bit of the language. I clearly remember the first few words I learned: *Chao* was "hello;" *tam biet* (pronounced tam bait) was "good-bye;" *cam on* (pronounced as it appears) was "thank you;" *xin loi* (zen loy) was "sorry;" *dung lai* (pronounced dung lie) meant "stop" or "halt;" *di di mau* (dee dee mao) was "leave immediately;" *troi oi* (pronounced choy oiwee) was an exclamation, similar to "holy cow," and if you wanted to <u>really</u> emphasize something, it was *troi duc oi* (adding the "duck" in the middle); *titi* (tee-tee) meant "tiny" or "small;" and *hieu*, meant "understanding."

The Vietnamese language was not easy to learn; in fact, the language is spoken differently in various areas of the country. It is tonal in nature, some say "sing-songy." The tone or level of your voice may change the meaning of the word.

(Depending on the inflection you gave it, supposedly there was one word that could mean either "church" or "house of prostitution." Thus, if you asked for directions to one or the other, you might be quite surprised where you ended up!)

Conversations in Vietnam were often a weird combination of Vietnamese, English, and French (every soldier who served there remembers *beaucoup*, meaning "a lot"). If all else failed, the universal language of a warm smile and hand gestures would do the trick! (Contrary to popular belief, raising one's voice a couple of decibels will not magically help translate misunderstood words.)

I received a "care package" from Nancy on September 2. It contained (per my request) a jar of instant iced tea, sugar, and two types of cookies, chocolate drop and chocolate chip, individually wrapped to stay as fresh as possible. It was always "iffy" as to whether or not you would get all of your packages. If someone, somewhere along the line between Newton and Saigon, with its many stops, wanted a snack, he would pilfer it and you would never see it.

Throughout the year my favorite item to receive, in addition to the homemade cookies, were little metal pudding cups. For some reason, my maternal grandmother, "Nunny," thought I wanted little bottles of cherries. Although I like cherry flavor, I've never been a fan of eating individual cherries. But I never told her differently. I just used the cherries as bargaining chips to trade for a different goodie that somebody else might have received from home. (And no, we have no idea why we called her "Nunny!")

I had an ample amount of reading material for downtime (when was that?). My parents got me a subscription to the *Des Moines Register* for $18.50 a year (isn't that what *one* newspaper costs today?) Nancy ordered *Sports Illustrated* for me for a whopping annual fee of $6.24. (Hey, wait a minute....I don't think I ever got my free shoe phone!) Additionally, somebody sent me a subscription to *Playboy* as a going-away gift.

I was able to keep up with the athletic scene in my home state by reading the *Register*. The Sunday sports edition for that newspaper was called *The Big Peach* (with the pages colored accordingly) and was often ranked the top sports section in the country, with good reason. The paper also kept me informed as to what was going on locally and nationally. I also always enjoyed Don Kaul's *Over the Coffee* segment in the news section.

Sports Illustrated allowed me to keep up with the sports world in general. At a much later time I became acquainted with the lead writers and the photography editor for *S.I.* I marveled at the new technology that made the photos so clear, as the publication covered events throughout the globe. As I sat there staring at them, I realized that I was looking at exotic places that I would never experience or enjoy. The same could be said regarding the photos in *Playboy.*

We also received *Stars and Stripes*, an excellent military newspaper. It was another good way to keep up with what was going on back home as well as throughout Vietnam. It featured bikinied pin-up girls on the back page of each issue; I have a feeling that this tradition has gone by the wayside. The *Stars and Stripes* started operation at the outset of the Civil War in 1861.

Still another military publication that I perused as often as possible was *The Army Reporter*.

I remember reading a September 4 article in the *Des Moines Register* revealing that the great football coach, Vince Lombardi, had died at the tender age of 57. I had the opportunity to spend time with the Green Bay Packer legend at the Amana VIP Golf Tournament on one occasion. I was sad to read of his passing.

In that same issue of the *Register*, I also saw a news article and photo of pretty Cheryl Browne of Bettendorf, who had just been named Miss Iowa. It was significant because she became the first-ever black contestant to participate in the Miss America Pageant. It was unfortunate that it had taken so long (1970), but I was proud of my home state for breaking the barrier.

The Armed Forces Vietnam Network (AFVN) provided our musical entertainment, and although Adrian Cronauer, subject of the movie *Good Morning Vietnam*, was gone by the time I landed in the country, his insistence on playing the most popular current rock music endured.

Sometimes the songs would lag a little bit behind their popularity in the States, but occasionally we would see a list of top songs that occupied the top 100 hits back home. I remember reading that "Joy to the World" by Three Dog Night was a top ten song in America, and I was puzzled: "Why in the heck is a Christmas song popular out of season?"

At night, every now and then we could pick up Hanoi Hannah on our radios. She was North Vietnam's answer to World War II's Tokyo Rose in Japan and Axis Sally in Germany. Our forces also heard from Pyongyang Sally in North Korea and Baghdad Betty in Iraq in those military conflicts.

The purpose of those soft-spoken, sexy-sounding voices representing our enemy was, in each case, to convince Americans (in English) that the war was a hopeless cause for us; that our wives and girlfriends were seeing other men back home; and that their troops and capabilities were so much stronger than ours. It was always good for a laugh.

Two can play that game: Khanh Ly, a very popular female singer in South Vietnam, recorded a song, "The Lonely Sleep." The American 101st Airborne PSYOPS (Psychological Operations) team broadcast the song on loudspeakers – many times from the air -- in areas known for enemy activity. It was aimed at breaking the morale of NVA and V.C. soldiers, who were living under constant bombardment and in miserable conditions, to convince them to turn themselves in. It was a successful endeavor as thousands crossed the line and joined the Chieu Hoi program to work with U.S. and ARVN troops.

I had only been in 'Nam a few weeks when I learned that a buddy, who had already been in country for eight months, visited an orphanage when he could spare the time. I told him that I wanted to go with him when we could coordinate our schedules. A couple of weeks later I accompanied him.

When we arrived at our destination, I noticed that a very tall concrete wall, with shards of broken glass and barbed wire imbedded along the top, surrounded the building which housed the orphans.

When I entered the structure through big wooden doors, I quickly noticed how austere the setting was. Two elderly Vietnamese Catholic Nuns greeted us. I recall one being quite tiny with a very wrinkled face and a gold tooth in front, while the other was deformed (bent from the waist) when she walked. They were taking care of approximately 25 little ones, ranging in age from newborn to four years old. There were two babies who were only four days old, and a couple of others who were just two weeks of age when I first visited. Cute would not adequately describe them; they were precious.

The Nuns, dressed entirely in white, including nurses' caps, were aided by a young girl named Thuy (Twee) who was only nine years old. This solemn-faced angel had been born and raised in the orphanage and was forced to grow up before her time. She was tasked with keeping the area clean, sweeping, doing laundry, feeding the babies, dressing the toddlers, changing diapers, and any other chores required by the Sisters.

Over time, to allow her to at least find a little bit of joy in childhood, I tried to bring Thuy such items as toys and coloring books whenever possible, thanks to everyone who sent them from back home. A few months later at Christmas, I gave her a Barbie doll and miniature items for the doll including a make-up table, little hairbrushes, etc. The ecstatic smile that lit up her face – I had never seen it on her before -- replaced her normally stoic expression. She had tears in her eyes upon receiving the Barbie. My cheeks became a bit moist, too, it must have been raining on my way there.

As I looked around, the Nuns and their helper did their best to make the setting an oasis of serenity; safe from the insanity of war that was taking place outside the surrounding cement barriers.

The walls inside needed painting and all but the smallest infants slept on bamboo mats over cardboard atop the concrete floor; the youngest cherubs had crude rocking cradles. In the middle of the biggest room was a long table, where they had their meals. Many of the occupants were Amerasian, the offspring of American soldiers and Vietnamese women (with a good chance that the mothers were prostitutes).

The communist forces despised such children with their partial American DNA; thus, the reason for the broken glass and barbed wire on top of the walls to protect them as much as possible. An attack on a Buddhist orphanage by 30 uniformed North Vietnamese soldiers near An Hoa on August 30 resulted in 12 deaths and more than 50 wounded, most of them children.

(In his autobiography, *American Soldier*, General Tommy Franks pointed out the ruthlessness of the communist troops when it came to children. In a little village near Dong Tam, American medics inoculated the young boys and girls of the hamlet for measles. At night, the Viet Cong came in and mercilessly chopped off those children's arms as punishment to the villagers for allowing the vaccinations by U.S. soldiers.)

I didn't know how I could help, but I knew that I was on a mission to do whatever I could for the shelter I was visiting. That would include food, clothing, toys, and whatever else was needed. One of the first things we did was to organize a Christmas drive, which I told Nancy about in a letter (it was still September, but we had to get an early start). She and her mother organized a philanthropic effort back in my hometown and several clubs got involved. My parents and brothers and sisters also contributed greatly, as did many friends.

I visited the orphanage as much as I could during my year in-country. I wish I could have taken every one of them away from that misery, but it wasn't practical. Misery might be the wrong word; their gleeful giggles ALWAYS brightened my day. Kids are amazing; their laughter is magical, even in the most dire circumstances in their thankfully ignorant bliss.

When we would arrive during our visits, a couple of the children would run to the front door and excitedly yell "Americans, Americans" with some jumping into our arms. The 19th Century author John Ruskin once wrote: "Give a little love to a child and you get a great deal back." So true.

With my concern for the children, I tried my best to see if there was any way that we could provide security for the unprotected orphanage, but the drawdown of U.S. troops from the war did not allow the required manpower.

I was quickly learning many other things about Vietnam. For one thing, street drugs were abundant and readily available.

The Golden Triangle in the area, which stretched from the borders of Thailand, Laos, and Burma (now Myanmar), was the largest producer of heroin in the world in those days, and it was easily accessible, as were any other drugs known to mankind. That was not exactly a secret.

Some blamed China for the prevalence of the illegal narcotics, purposely targeting American troops, but the distributors were most likely drug lords from the three named countries. At first my dad worried that I would become depressed or something and fall into that horrible trap, unknowingly becoming a drug addict.

Going down that dark road did happen to some of my friends, and one of them died from an overdose. The drugs were super potent. We had one 18-year-old at our base who was leaning towards running with that crowd, but I took it upon myself to put him under my wing. I read him the riot act, telling him what a life-long mistake he would be making, adding that we would only be in 'Nam for a year and then he could resume his life back home without regret.

I kept a positive outlook that I would return to my dream of a career in intercollegiate athletic administration, and I didn't want drugs to interfere with that, or be the legacy of my year. Plus, I simply didn't have any desire to do drugs; that's just not me.

There were two guys I knew who would get high, sneak into Tan Son Nhut Airbase, and then go out and lay just past the end of the runway watching the F-4 Phantom jets lift off right before they got to the two prone stoners. They were lucky they weren't fried, and I would guess they went on to have severe hearing problems later on in life.

Sadly, it was estimated that 40,000 U.S. military members became addicted to hard drugs while serving in Vietnam.

I did have my share of alcohol in Vietnam, which was very unusual for me before and after my year there. Every time somebody was mustering out (going home), and someone was *always* going home since we were serving staggered tours of duty, we would celebrate.

Each soldier had a limit of purchasing three bottles of whiskey each month at the small base PX, and we would take turns supplying the hooch for the parties.

During one of the times when I was responsible for securing the liquor, I went to buy my three bottles and the shelves were bare. I bought the last two bottles of Seagram 7, the only kind remaining, and a bottle of whisky that was made in Vietnam.

None of the guys would touch the Vietnamese whiskey, but I grabbed it and said: "Give it to me, I'm not proud." I wish I *would* have been proud. I drank quite a bit of that Vietnamese "moonshine" that night and thought I was going to die the next day….no, it was one of those occasions when you *hope* you would die the next day. I have never been so sick. Maybe I should have gotten a hint when my first swig tasted like battery acid.

We would also drink beer, mostly when playing poker during a rare down time, but one had to have a taste for Carling Black Label, because that's the only kind we could get for a while. Rumor had it that someone along the military supply line allegedly got into trouble for running a kickback scheme, but I have no idea if that was true. Anyway, because of the intense heat, it would not be unusual to polish off several beers in a sitting and not even feel the effect of it; you'd simply sweat it out.

We had a mama-san who cleaned our areas and would do our laundry literally the old- fashioned way of beating the clothes on cement and rocks. (I learned later that mama-san was a derogatory term at one point in history, but we certainly didn't mean any disrespect. We loved our elderly mama-san!) She always had a smile (somewhat toothless) and she would actually pull pranks on us on occasion. She came as close to having a grandmother as we would have over there.

I thought that the stipend we gave her was too low, but the South Vietnamese government regulated the amount so that it would not upset the country's economy, believe it or not. I guess there were a lot of mama-sans taking care of U.S. soldiers throughout the 44 Provinces!

When I first arrived, the government control stipulated the equivalence of $8 to each mama-san per month, which went up to $12 during the end of my tour. We did not pay them directly. Nonetheless, I couldn't help but secretly slip her a few extra Vietnamese piasters every month. Maybe that's why I was her favorite.

The mama-sans would all get together for lunch and cook nuoc mam. Perhaps it is pretty good in today's Vietnamese restaurants, but I think my 'Nam mates would agree with me that the nuoc mam, a sauce made from fish which were dried (rotted?) in the sun, cooked by these gals was the most gawd-awful smelling food item ever prepared.

In his autobiography, *A Soldier Reports*, General William Westmorland said a bottle of nuoc mam broke on his private plane and the occupants almost had to put on gas masks to survive the ordeal.

The mama-sans would also brew tea as they sat crosslegged on the floor, chattering away and laughing while waving their arms to emphasize what they were saying. It always made me smile to see them having a good time; their personal lives probably weren't exceptionally cheerful with the ongoing war and the country's poverty levels.

One of the biggest military operations ongoing in mid-September was a covert incursion into Laos by MACV-SOG (Military Assistant Command, Vietnam Studies and Observation Group) consisting of U.S. Army Special Forces and Montagnard commandos.

Named Operation Tailwind, it was an effort to put pressure on occupying North Vietnamese communist forces and give aid to operations of a collaborator to our side, the Royal Lao Army. Native Hmong "Hill People" were strong Allies of the U.S. and were valuable partners in the combat operations which took place in Laos (often termed the "secret war").

Some of the action in Laos occurred in the Plain of Jars, which is a fascinating historical landmark. It measures some 500 square miles and consists of thousands of huge stone jars sticking up from the ground that some believe were used as burial urns. The origination of the "jars" is a mystery, but they are believed to have been created by people of the megalithic iron age (500 BC to 500 AD).

In just one short month, I had learned a lot about the country in which I was now a "citizen." I would learn that my education had barely started.

CHAPTER IX
I Could Tell You, But Then I Would Have To....

Shortly after my arrival in Vietnam, I was officially informed that I had a Crypto clearance. Before I received the official notice, Colonel Brash had mentioned it. When he said "Crypto," I had no earthly idea what he was talking about.

The actual truth is that the first thing to come to my mind was Kryptonite, the only thing that could neutralize Superman! I wondered if the U.S. had come up with some secret weapon similar to that substance to use in the war and I was somehow going to be part of it.

But no, that wasn't it. It was a security level, and it was at the very top. It trumped everything. If I remember correctly, the levels of security, from least secure to the most, went like this: For Your Eyes Only, although I don't think this was an "official" level; Confidential; Secret; Top Secret; and Crypto. I was allowed to see virtually everything regarding the war effort.

I didn't understand why I needed such a lofty classification status because what I was working on with Project Hieu certainly didn't require such high consideration. I would later learn that I would become involved in other matters that would require such scrutiny.

(My Grandmother Starr and a couple of my friends told me later that they had been visited by official-looking type men driving dark cars asking questions about me. The only thing I can figure is that they were FBI agents or whoever's job it was to check up on individuals, doing a background check before extending the Crypto clearance. I couldn't imagine who else it could have been.)

I didn't give the Crypto clearance much thought until one day a tall, muscular red-headed captain, complete with an equally red bushy mustache, came into the Project Hieu office. He conferred with one of our officers after entering, and after being pointed out, he walked up to me, and asked in a commanding voice: "Are you Starr?"

When I replied in the affirmative, he took his forefinger and made the "come with me" gesture and told me to follow him. We hopped into a Jeep, and he took me to a different building on base. He told me that I was to take notes of a classified meeting which required my clearance level. When we walked into the room, I saw more stars than one would see on a dark night in Texas. The room was full of generals from different U.S. branches and some from our Allied nations.

Throughout the year I was on call for this purpose. Colonel Branch was the only one on the Project Hieu staff who knew about my confidential role. When I was informed of an upcoming session requiring my presence, because a lot them pertained to military movements, I nicknamed them and would tell the Colonel that I was going to another "Immersion in Incursion" meeting.

I was not allowed to tell any of my buddies, and, of course, I was sternly threatened not to divulge the contents of any of the meetings with anyone. I took that to heart. There was nothing nefarious about the sessions, but I took my vow of silence seriously (unlike some soldiers and politicians today). I still will not talk about some things regarding my Vietnam experience.

These new duties buoyed my spirits because it gave me a new purpose and since I knew that I couldn't always be physically out in the field, I hoped that I could help those who were by taking part in meetings that pertained to the Allied effort. Once in a great while I could even insert my thoughts when on a *very* rare occasion the high-ranking attendees asked for my point of view as an enlisted man, and probably because of my age.

Some of the notes that I took ended up in communiques to President Richard Nixon and the Commander-in-Chief, Pacific Command (CINCPAC), who was Admiral John S. McCain, father of the former late Senator by the same name and a one-time POW in Vietnam.

Crypto clearance also allowed me to see enemy documents, mostly COSVN Resolutions. COSVN was the acronym for the clandestine Central Office for Vietnam, the secret communist political and military headquarters in South Vietnam. As far as I know, its primary location was never pinpointed; the NVA and Viet Cong did a great job of keeping it hidden. Many believed that the communist nerve center in South Vietnam was never a stationary site; it was constantly being re-located, sometimes even into Cambodia, which made detection by the Allies impossible.

One COSVN document that I read indicated that the NVA and V.C. were contemplating an all-out attack across South Vietnam in September to celebrate the one-year anniversary of the death of Ho Chi Minh.

The onslaught never occurred, and U.S. intelligence believed that it was due to lack of adequate ammunition, an indication that our side was doing a good job of interdicting supplies from the north.

September finally came to an end, and it had been the longest month of my life. When I looked back after my one-year tour of duty was over, I still considered

September to be the slowest month. Like every soldier, I missed home and everyone I loved.

> *"Now I'm a solider, a lonely soldier,*
> *Away from home, through no wish of my own;*
> *That's why I'm lonely, I'm Mr. Lonely,*
> *I wish that I could go back home."*

■ Mr. Lonely
--Bobby Vinton

In my final September letter from Nancy, she informed me that one of my high school classmates, Ron Current, had just returned home from Southeast Asia. His tour of duty as a helicopter pilot had concluded, and now he was back with his family after flying the unfriendly skies of Vietnam for the previous 12 months.

One of Nancy's letters a couple of weeks later did not contain such positive news. She informed me about the horrible crash of a plane involving the Wichita State football team which occurred on October 2. While traveling to play a game at Utah State, one of the university's two chartered team planes crashed into a mountain in Colorado, killing 33 of the 41 people aboard. That included the athletic director and head football coach and their wives.

It was just over a month later, on November 14, when tragedy would strike another college football team. The Marshall Thundering Herd, coming home on a DC-9 from a game at East Carolina, met the same terrible fate, smashing into a hill just short of the Tri-State Airport in Huntington, West Virginia. All 75 aboard perished in the calamitous inferno.

Jack Lengyel, who had the difficult task of walking a fine line of honoring those lost in the accident while trying to rebuild the football program as its new head coach, would later become a confidant when he served as athletic director at Fresno State, Missouri, and Navy and I was also in the field of intercollegiate athletics. Matthew McConaughey would play Lengyel in the hit movie, *We Are Marshall*, in 2006. Jack took a lot of ribbing about that; they do not exactly resemble each other!

By mid-October, I was added into the rotation for perimeter guard duty (officially termed MACV Defense Force). I would be stationed in a two-story high guard tower, with a 10' x 10' square platform deck, complete with sandbags piled five feet high on each of the four sides. Four posts on each corner held up a slanted roof (probably to both deflect enemy projectiles such as grenades and to shield us from the blazing sun and rains during monsoon season).

The guard position was accessed by a ladder that came up through the floor. The scaffolding featured iron "legs" on all four corners, slightly slanted and connected by crisscrossed steel girders.

Not far in the distance to the right I could see the trailers that housed the generals. The primary side faced a Vietnamese cemetery bordered by a high wire fence. Posted up there in that tower all alone at night with your M16, trying to stay alert, you couldn't allow your mind to play tricks on you if you saw movement, possibly by a roaming animal, in the darkened graveyard. It was usually eerily quiet for the most part, with the only sound being that of various insects performing in concert. I could sometimes see reconnaissance planes circling the skies for the purpose of taking photos to look for any enemy activity.

Our guard responsibilities were lightly regarded as a joke by a lot of the guys, who felt that our base was secure. Unfortunately, perhaps those were the same thoughts of the soldiers stationed there two years earlier when the V.C. mounted a surprise attack through that same graveyard during the TET New Year. A total of

157 were killed on or near my base and another 512 just outside of it on that occasion. That included 18 ARVN soldiers who were killed in the vicinity of the cemetery.

It was wise to stay aware. Within the first couple of weeks of October, a total of 24 Viet Cong was killed within 20 miles of my base; a helicopter was shot down just 10 miles away with the loss of four Americans; and five other G.I.'s were killed and four more wounded in action only five miles from where I was located.

I was supposed to travel up to Pleiku (play-coo), just south of the Laotian border, the first week in October, but my orders were changed at the last minute. Instead, I took my first "chopper" (helicopter) ride to Bien Hoa that week. Captain Osborne had to brief 75 pilots regarding Project Hieu, and he asked me to accompany him. I jumped at the opportunity.

We flew out of Tan Son Nhut early in the morning on a four-seat Jet Ranger, the smallest of all the helicopters used in Vietnam. The briefing was a solemn occasion; the wing that he addressed had lost seven pilots to enemy fire the previous week.

At the conclusion of Captain Osborne's presentation, one pilot stood up and said that if anyone questioned the bravery of ARVN (South Vietnamese) troops, he wanted to convey his experience on the matter. He talked about a U.S. service member and ARVN soldier who were both badly wounded when their aircraft went down due to enemy fire. The South Vietnamese trooper lost most of his left leg and was blinded in one eye. Nonetheless, he dragged the unconscious American for almost a mile to a landing zone (LZ) to be picked up by a Medivac helicopter.

The Captain and I flew out of Bien Hoa at 10:00 p.m. Before hopping aboard our ride home, a pilot standing beside us said: "You know, those Jet Rangers are great little machines, but an AK47 (the primary weapon of communist forces) can bring one of those things down pretty easily."

Well, thank you for sharing that nugget of information, big guy. We were about to fly home over some reported enemy activity in the area. We did have a couple of flares buzz by us, one red and one white, on the way home, but there wasn't any small arms fire as far as we could ascertain.

Our pilot did alter his route and it is my understanding that friendly forces on the ground had fired the warning flares to alert us that we were about to fly over territory that had been infiltrated by communist troops and was not secure.

It would be the first of many times that I would find myself on a chopper that year, most of them being Huey's. The official designation of the helicopter was UH-1, and troops just started calling it "Huey" for short.

There was a reason why Vietnam was called the helicopter war; that mode of transportation was tailor-made for the small Asian nation, serving many purposes, primarily for combat duty.

The first thing one learned when being in proximity of a Bell Iroquois UH-1 "Huey" Helicopter was to NEVER walk around the back of one due to the nearly invisible tail rotor blade. A high-ranking Allied officer -- I believe he was from Thailand -- made that mistake after landing to attend one of our meetings at Pentagon East.

The hapless visiting dignitary jumped off the copter and trotted around the rear of the aircraft and when all was said and done, he was much smaller, about a head shorter to be exact. You needed to keep your head on your shoulders when you were around those things, and he didn't, literally. In this case, the "chopper" did, indeed, deserve its nickname. The military calls it "situational awareness," and the visiting officer unfortunately didn't have it.

When I returned from Bien Hoa, a box of sugar cookies and the Iowa-Wisconsin game cassette tapes were awaiting me. I truly treasured receiving the Hawkeye game tapes; it would take me away for over three hours as I laid in my bunk and imagined that I was back in my seat in the press box at Iowa (later re-named Kinnick) Stadium, when I was a student journalist, or remembering when I would lay in a hammock and listen to the UI games in the backyard of my home during my days of growing up.

This one was special because Iowa recorded its first victory of the year with a win over the Badgers, 24-14. The Hawks were led by Tim Sullivan, who had two touchdowns, and sophomore quarterback Kyle Scogman, starting his first game. It was extra rewarding because I had told two guys from Wisconsin that I had audio recordings of the game, and they listened to the battle between our neighboring state schools with me. The Badgers were favored, and they razzed me pretty good before the contest, but I got the last laugh.

I was swamped and almost overwhelmed with various duties (both my official ones with Project Hieu and my extracurricular stealth Crypto chores) at the time. On October 6, I scribbled a quick note home: *"Nancy, sorry, no time to write. Working day and night. Please explain to everyone. Love, Tom. P.S. I am fine."*

Nonetheless, I always looked forward to mail from back home. In addition to Nancy's much-anticipated letters, I received them from all of my family members and friends. On that day when I had written that I was so busy, I did get a laugh from a note I had just received from hometown pal Doug Auten.

He informed me that his wife, Tanya, a high school classmate of both of ours, was pregnant and they were hoping the due date would be on my birthday, April 12. However, their doctor said that it would be April 8. "I don't know how he would know," wrote Doug. "He wasn't there when it happened!" He ended the correspondence by saying: "Keep your head in your helmet and keep your helmet in a safe place."

Maybe because I was now in a routine and acclimated to my surroundings, October passed much more quickly than September. There was one major difference between the two months; thunderstorms commenced in earnest. It was my understanding that the primary monsoon season happened in the spring and summer in our area of the country, but all I knew is that we were getting pelted.

It seemed like clockwork when the torrential downpours would start; Noon and 9 p.m. seemed to be the hardest hitting cloudbursts. Usually, the heavy bombardment would only last 30 minutes at the most.

On the first day of November, I received a report from the Saigon Civil Assistance Group Military Advisory Team regarding the total number of arrests in the capital city for the 1970 calendar year, which I found interesting.

There was a total of 50 categories, with some of those being counterfeiting (166 arrests); ARVN deserters (932); fake I.D.'s (1,612); Viet Cong suspects (27); illegal residents (3,535); "hooligans," the aforementioned "cowboys" (291); opium smokers (229); hippies (1,685); and prostitutes (391 – they weren't looking very hard!)

There had been some enemy activity in and around Saigon and our base. On November 2 four rockets killed six Vietnamese civilians residing in the city. On the 12th, a grenade was tossed at the front door of the USO Club but luckily there were no casualties.

During that first week in November, we received word that U.S. Secretary of State William P. Rogers wanted us to expand Project Hieu. That would require more staff members, but we never got the additional manpower, which meant that our workload would simply increase.

I had a very pleasant surprise on a November 8 Sunday afternoon when a friend of mine, who worked in the office of Ellsworth Bunker, U.S. Ambassador to South Vietnam, was able to get the emissary's personal boat for a fun afternoon.

Five or six of us went out on the Saigon River and cruised up and down the waters, staying far away from the banks. As I look back, it wasn't very smart of us because we traveled quite a distance, and we were very fortunate we didn't receive any V.C. fire from jungle foliage that lined the waterway. I took my turn at the wheel of the craft, which was a first for me.

On November 13, I perused another document from MACV Military Intelligence, authored by Major General W.G. Dolvin, Chief of Staff. It outlined the concerns about more widespread use of anti-personnel devices (i.e. mines and booby traps) by the NVA and V.C. and listed possible ways to combat them.

An Army captain came up to me after a Project Hieu briefing and asked if I was the same Tom Starr who was a sportswriter and sports announcer at the University of Iowa. I said that I was, and he told me that he attended Iowa at the same time.

While there, I served as both the sports director of WSUI radio and asst. sports editor of the *Daily Iowan*. He remembered that I had replaced Pete Taylor, who later became the voice of the Iowa State Cyclones, at WSUI.

Furthermore, he was a native Iowan from Belle Plaine and after talking at length, we learned we had a mutual friend in Keith Junge, one of my former Hawkeye roommates.

A joint service raid on the Son Tay Communist Prison Camp occurred on the night of November 20. Army Green Berets and an assault group from the Air Force staged the daring raid just 23 miles west of Hanoi, the capitol of North Vietnam. Navy pilots created a diversion in Haiphong Harbor to the east to draw the attention of North Vietnamese armed forces. The participants in the American raid had practiced at a full-size mockup of the prison camp at Elgin Air Force Base in Florida.

The surprise attack went flawlessly with the objective being to free American Prisoners of War being held. Unfortunately, all 55 of the POW's had been moved just prior to the raid, thus, none were rescued to the chagrin and disappointment of the members of the perfectly executed plan.

For the rare occasion (timewise) when we wanted some recreation, my buddies and I started to play volleyball whenever possible. However, it was definitely not your ordinary garden-variety sport. We played by "jungle" rules, which were popular among soldiers in Vietnam. Basically, there were none. If someone on the opposing team went up for a spike at the net, he was normally punched hard in the gut. Sometimes the jab was a bit lower, which usually sent that player to the sideline in agony for a bit.

Broken noses, broken arms, broken ribs, broken ankles and an assortment of other injuries could be the result of these fun (?) games as played by soldiers throughout Vietnam. I was not aware of anyone succumbing to the activity, however. That would have been a tad embarrassing:

"Hey, did you hear that Eddie was killed in 'Nam?"

"Viet Cong?"

"No, volleyball."

I listened via cassette tape to Iowa's last football game of the season, when the Hawkeye's beat Illinois, 22-16, to end the 1970 campaign. The following week, on November 28, my buddy, Chopper Bianco, and I stayed up until early in the morning to listen to the Army-Navy game, which, unfortunately (for us in the Army), ended up in an 11-7 victory for the Midshipmen. The game was broadcast live over the Armed Forces Vietnam Network

(AFVN). Thankfully, it was the only 2:00 a.m. kickoff that I have ever had to endure!

For the Thanksgiving holidays, Nancy, bless her heart, sent a huge care package that included brownies, sugar cookies, fudge, chocolate drop cookies, chocolate chip cookies and pumpkin bread for my fellow Project Hieu members and friends. The pumpkin bread was a major hit and even prompted Captain Osborne to send a very nice personal thank you note to my wife.

Thanksgiving was like any other day, although the quality of food on that holiday was much better than the normal fare, thank goodness.

The week after Thanksgiving, I was starting to feel tired and listless. All I could think of was that the heat and the workload were starting to get to me. I wrote to Nancy: "The weather just drains everything out of you here."

Back at the University of Iowa, Head Football Coach Ray Nagel finally announced his resignation at the annual Football Banquet on December 1, 1970. Numerous injuries, the lingering effect of a 1969 black boycott, the defection of key players, and the long internal struggles with Athletic Director Forrest Evashevski had worn on him, and those items and others had greatly reduced his chance to succeed.

Nagel and I had grown close commencing with my journalistic chores at Iowa. I dropped him a note from Vietnam to tell him that I hated to see him go, but certainly understood his reasoning. He responded immediately, and in a letter dated December 10, he told me: "There have been many factors that entered into my decision to leave, and I must admit there will always be a certain question in my mind about what might have been."

Ray, who would go on to serve as athletic director at both Washington State and Hawaii as well as executive director of the Hula Bowl, and I remained good friends until his death in 2015.

Early in December, I learned, much to my surprise, that I was being considered for promotion to E5, the equivalent of sergeant. I guess my superiors at Project Hieu and/or the officers that I worked with regarding my Crypto Clearance, had entered my name to upgrade me to a higher rank. I was surprised because it was my understanding that at the time, you had to be in the Army for at least two years to be considered for E5, and I had only been in the service for 12 months.

I had to appear before a MACV Review Board to be interviewed and was grilled on all aspects of Army life and the Vietnam War, including displaying a complete and full knowledge of my branch of service's regulations.

On December 12, I received a list from MACV Headquarters showing the names of all 92 finalists throughout the country who were being considered for promotion to E5 (I have no idea how many additionally appeared before the Board and were not considered). To my total shock, I had scored the highest point total and found my name at the very top of the list in order of merit, ranked #1. Somehow, I scored a 598.3 out of a possible 600 points. (I wonder where I screwed up that other 1.7?)

I received a plague shot on December 16; it was my fourth inoculation to protect me from that dreadful disease in less than a year. Once again, I thought that the malady must have certainly been a worry to those in the know.

An American G.I. was killed in an explosion at a Saigon bar on December 17. That, and a host of other incidents, forced the military to declare most of Saigon off limits to American Armed Forces personnel for a while.

Among other concerns: The U.S. Air Force said it had intelligence reports showing "a very likely possibility of increased attempts of assassination and kidnapping of U.S. servicemen." It was also learned that pre-Christmas waves of terrorist attacks in Saigon were also being planned by communist forces. There was definitely an uptick in assaults around my base.

Hostile action included two rocket attacks on the capital city, killing six, with four of them being children. One of the rockets slammed into a gas station located just 100 yards from the U.S. Embassy. In addition, a 38-lb. explosive charge went off in the lobby of a U.S. Officer's billet; three Americans were killed and 14 wounded in bomb and grenade attacks just outside Saigon; grenades were thrown into a group of Americans and Vietnamese outside of a Naval billet near Tan Son Nhut; there was a satchel (explosive) attack on a U.S. official's billet; and a South Vietnamese National Assemblyman was assassinated in his Saigon office. All these incidents occurred within 10 miles of my location.

The United States and South Vietnamese military hierarchy increased patrols in Saigon to counter the enemy activities.

Christmas away from home had come for me and the other 334,600 U.S. military personnel remaining in Vietnam. I was briefly in the field on Christmas Eve and attended a service with the back of an artillery piece serving as the "altar." Due to my circumstances, it was probably the most authentic religious ritual I had ever attended, before or since.

We hosted our holiday party for the orphanage the day before that, which was a much needed "feel good" mission. Thanks to my family, friends, and organizations back home, we had received so many toys, dolls, crayons, coloring books, storybooks, pens, pencils, writing tablets, and items of clothing that in addition to the orphans who were our primary concern, we were able to help another orphanage while also hosting a party for the children of ARVN soldiers.

There is nothing like seeing the look on the face of a child who may never have had a doll or stuffed animal before.

Mr. John Muhl from my home state (Oskaloosa, Iowa) donated 100 cases of Pepsi-Cola to the parties. I was thoroughly amused at the reaction and surprise of many of the kids who took their first-ever drink of the carbonated beverage, as the bubbles tickled their noses. To me, the laughter and giggling of children is probably my most favorite sound in the world. How can it not make a person smile?

Nancy sent me gifts, popcorn balls, holiday-decorated sugar cookies, coconut cookies, and pumpkin bread throughout the month to help keep my spirits up. She also sent me a cassette tape of a radio broadcast on KIOA radio in Des Moines, in which she had called to dedicate the song "Merry Christmas Darling" by the Carpenters. The song is about two people who are far apart during the holidays. Obviously, that tugged the heart strings.

I received a ton of very welcomed Christmas cards from relatives and friends. All had warm wishes and encouraging words. Another favorite high school bud, John Pierce, related in his card: "I wish I could speed up the grains in your hourglass." The Red Cross gave us "ditty bags" full of items such as needed stationery.

President Bill Vernon of the prominent Vernon Company in my hometown sent me a "care package" of items and a very nice personal note, which he ended with: "All of us in the Newton area are thinking of you and hoping for your safe return in the very near future."

Members of my family sent gifts as well. They were all spending Christmas at my brother Dick's house in Indianola, Iowa. Fittingly, they had snow and, while in the stifling heat that we were enduring, it was hard to fathom those big, beautiful, fluffy white flakes lazily falling, painting a truly breath-taking winter wonderland over the landscape.

> *"I'll be home for Christmas,*
> *You can plan on me,*
> *Please have snow, and mistletoe,*
> *And presents on the tree....*
> *I'll be home for Christmas,*
> *If only in my dreams."*

■ I'll be Home for Christmas
--Bing Crosby

And dreams were how we managed to get through Christmas. I won't sugar coat it; it was a rough day.

However, I do have to give credit to the Department of Defense for attempting to boost our morale with a Christmas Day dinner that any grandmother would have been proud of. Believe it or not, it consisted of shrimp cocktail, roast turkey, mashed potatoes with gravy, corn bread dressing, cranberry sauce, glazed sweet potatoes, buttered mixed vegetables, hot rolls, and pumpkin pie! Yumm! We were briefly in culinary heaven!

It is my understanding that DoD tried to assure that all U.S. service members in Vietnam had a turkey dinner that day, no matter how deeply they were entrenched in the jungle. I have no idea if it was successful or not. Quite honestly, I would doubt it. I knew from the briefings I attended that some of those guys were in extremely remote areas.

After chowing down the most scrumptious meal that I had enjoyed in over six months, I climbed up to a roof top, stripped down to my G.I. green boxers, and simply laid on a towel with my eyes closed and imagined that I was home with everyone, opening presents, having Christmas dinner, listening to holiday songs, and enjoying the closeness with family at that special time of year.

As late afternoon fell, I opened my eyes and got up to go join my buddies for a beer that we would celebrate with, or cry in. Reality hit me in the face immediately. Just as I stood, from a distance I could see dozens of paratroopers dropping from the sky. I had no idea if it was simply a drill by U.S. or ARVN forces, or if there was some hostile activity in their drop zone.

Bob Hope brought his annual USO Christmas show to Long Binh, which was approximately 12 miles from my base of operations. That year his entourage included singer and dancer Lola Falana; singer Gloria Loring; baseball star Johnny Bench; The Golddiggers from the Dean Martin Show; Miss World Jennifer Hosten; and Les Brown and his Orchestra.

I had the opportunity to join the other 22,000 guys who attended the outdoor extravaganza but chose not to. I did not want a taste of home until I could actually go home. I did appreciate Mr. Hope saying: "We don't hear about all the great things you guys are doing here with orphanages."

(On one of his annual visits to the war zone, the always flippant Hope said upon landing at Tan Son Nhut Airbase: "I received a 19-gun salute….one of them was ours.")

The Viet Cong called for a three-day truce at both Christmas and New Year's, but the United States and South Vietnamese had learned not to fall for that ruse as the V.C. were notorious for blatantly violating such cease-fires.

Instead, the U.S. and ARVN forces reported that they would observe a 24-hour suspension of hostilities commencing at 1800 hours the day prior to the actual holiday in each instance (i.e. 6:00 p.m., December 24, to 6:00 p.m., December 25, and from 6:00 p.m., December 31 to 6:00 p.m., January 1).

As usual, as I learned from my reports, the Viet Cong violated their own announced Christmas truce, with a disclosed total of 81 purposeful infractions with 26 of them aimed at American forces. Fortunately, only four

G.I.'s were reported wounded in action. One was a crewman aboard an OH56 Iowa observation helicopter shot down on Christmas afternoon near our base. A total of 17 ARVN (South Vietnamese) troops were killed while the enemy losses were put at 30 KIA during the cease-fire breaches.

Tragically, on Christmas Eve, nine American soldiers from the 101st Airborne had been killed and another nine wounded as a single errant 105mm artillery fired by a nearby U.S. battery struck their position 11 miles southwest of Hue. My heart sank for those guys and their relatives back home who would hear this devastating news at Christmas time.

Prior to the two U.S. holiday cease-fires, the Allies had increased their bombing of North Vietnamese supply routes to hamper the NVA from attempting to re-supply its troops in the South during the coming periods of truce.

Our normal routine resumed the day after Christmas and on December 29, I was ordered to report to the Fireguard, Headquarters Detachment at 1700 hours. Basically, it meant that I had to patrol the compound to keep an eye out for, well....fires! Actually, the job also entailed maintaining diligence for any other suspicious activity.

The year 1970 was ending and I couldn't be happier; the next one would see me going home. My buddies and I toasted in the New Year and went right back to work the next day.

Enter 1971, the Year of the Pig. We had survived the Year of the Dog. My workload pretty much stayed the same, but I did take a half-day off to go into Saigon with Rod Jones on Saturday, January 3.

We were walking along a city street and came across a motorcyclist lying in the middle of the road, in what we assumed was a hit-and-run accident. It was pretty bloody and absolutely nobody was going to the man's rescue as he laid beside his destroyed motorbike. Rod and I ran over to him, and we could quickly see that he had a devastating leg injury.

The Vietnamese were often reluctant to help some of their fellow citizens for fear that it might be a hoax and the man could be booby-trapped or something. In addition, there was somewhat of a "caste" system in the country, and it was obvious that this man was not among the upper classes; that also accounted for lack of action by his fellow countrymen.

To be honest, the guy was filthy, and his odor was nauseating; he must have been wearing Eau de Skunk cologne or something. Nonetheless, Rod and I had to get him out of the busy roadway. He was slight of build, so after checking him for possible explosives, I picked him up, with Rod holding his injured limb, and carried him over to the side of the avenue.

A deranged lady came over and started to pull on the man's badly injured leg, for whatever reason. I had to push her away because I knew that she was only worsening the anguish from the compound fracture that he had. You would have thought she would have taken a hint from the guttural screams emanating from the guy.

A nearby American civilian government worker saw us and rushed over to warn Rod and me to leave, or we could very well end up being responsible for the wounded man's doctor bills. He also indicated that it might be a ploy by the Viet Cong to put us in the sight of a sniper. I disgustedly told the official that I didn't think this person had purposely mangled his leg, which appeared to be pointing in three different directions, as a "ploy."

We tried to flag down some "white mice" (the term given to Saigon police who dressed in all white and had a reputation for not being overly courageous) to no avail, but finally stopped a military jeep with two young South Vietnamese (ARVN) military policemen, and after explaining the situation, they agreed to call an ambulance.

We stuck around to make certain that they complied, which they did, and I was surprised when a "meat wagon" responded fairly quickly to pick up the poor guy with the mutilated leg.

Rod and I snuck away before they could get our names. We didn't want to be involved in any reports; we simply wanted the stricken man to receive care.

When I returned back to my Dodge City residence, I received a box of chocolate chip cookies and a letter from Nancy. She informed me that the temperature back home was 40 below zero with the wind chill factor. She also said that Iowa was having its worst storm since 1941; visibility was zero and even snowplows and Highway Patrolmen were taken off the roads.

On January 5, 1971, the U.S. Congress, with Democrats holding both the Senate and House of Representatives, passed a revision of the Cooper-Church Amendment (originally adopted in June of 1970) disallowing American forces from entering enemy sanctuaries in Cambodia and Laos. It also called for ending support of ARVN (South Vietnamese) forces in those areas.

In the meantime, China and the Soviet Union were sending the communist forces, illegally staging in those neighboring countries, all the weapons and ammunition they needed. A report that I viewed stated that over 25,000 tons of arms, ammunition, and other military supplies had been illegally channeled into Cambodia over the previous three years.

An Airborne Ranger friend of mine, who was a captain, told me on the QT that his unit had recently gone against policy, sneaking across the Cambodian border a couple of miles, and unearthed a cache of Chinese military uniforms, meaning that the communist country must have also been directly supplying troops to aid the North Vietnamese in their illegal hideouts in the Cambodian nation

The North Vietnamese Army was known to have over 140,000 soldiers in Laos and Cambodia, whose border was less than a couple of hours from my base, in early January and were now free to plan their operations with impunity against South Vietnam without fear of attack or reprisal from the handcuffed Allies.

The war had changed course and our intelligence indicated that the communist forces were exploiting this Congressional action and were using their illegitimate bases in Cambodia and Laos to a much greater extent.

Our military leaders urged the president and his advisors to allow action against the North Vietnamese in the Cambodian and Laotian sanctuaries, but Lyndon Johnson's cabinet said that the threat was "overblown." The naivete or unwillingness to grasp the obvious was astounding; there was overwhelming evidence of the massive communist buildup. U.S. Ambassador to South Vietnam Ellsworth Bunker tried to stress to Johnson and Congress the recklessness of ignoring North Vietnam's escalation in the neighboring countries, but to no avail.

The NVA could now put intense pressure on South Vietnam both from the north and from the west, in addition to having their clandestine guerillas (V.C.) creating havoc throughout the South.

In other words, the communists now had troops and could stage their attacks from four countries (Laos, Cambodia, North Vietnam, and South Vietnam), while the Allies were restricted to just one (South Vietnam).

Stifling U.S. forces from entering Cambodia was one thing, but it was devastating to cut off aid to the South Vietnamese units trying to protect their borders.

Furthermore, the Cambodian and Laotian governments were friendly to South Vietnam's cause and appreciated the assistance of the U.S. and ARVN to help eradicate the unauthorized communist presence in their two nations. Unfortunately, Cambodia and Laos did not have the military strength to do it on their own and were hoping to rely on the Allies to help eliminate the unwanted occupancy. The Cooper-Church Amendment put an end to those aspirations.

Johnson and Congress indicated the primary basis for the unilateral action was to avoid widening the war! News flash: North Vietnam had ALREADY widened the war!

If our President and Congress had no intention of doing what it would take to win in Vietnam, why were we there? As the Duke of Wellington, a British hero in the victory over Napoleon at Waterloo, once told the House of Lords in England: "A great country cannot wage a little war."

Now the communists had free rein to operate from their illicit sanctuaries without fear of attack.

Fortunately for Allied Forces, Congress eventually came back to its senses a bit and the ban to prevent any U.S. air activity over Cambodia and Laos was lifted, which allowed our air power to at least harass, hamper and interdict the communist efforts in those two countries. However, no Allied ground forces were allowed to enter Cambodia, Laos, or North Vietnam, which greatly hindered the war effort.

There was action in the Mekong Delta in the southern part of South Vietnam in the first half of January, where B-52 strikes were pounding logistical points in that region. Closer to home, enemy sniper fire was detected on our compound.

The Chieu Hoi program, whereby Viet Cong members would change sides and start working with the ARVN and U.S., was experiencing increased success. Some 1,066 former V.C. members became Hoi Chanhs in the first two weeks of January.

High school classmate John Wallace was heading home from what I believe was his third tour of duty in Vietnam. As mentioned earlier, I saw him briefly on one occasion while we were both in Saigon. John, a captain, had been serving as an ARVN advisor in the often bitterly contested Parrot's Beak area near the Cambodian border. My highly decorated friend would be discarding his fatigues for good when he returned to Newton. He went on to earn a degree in Veterinary Medicine from Iowa State University and eventually started his own vet clinic in Las Vegas.

Including Wallace, several of the guys I had grown up had already served their time and returned home from the Vietnam War. We all grew up together and at the time, certainly didn't know that we would be thrown into the middle of a historical military conflict. I'm so proud to call you friends.

CHAPTER X
The Grim Reaper Strikes out

Carmen "Chopper" Bianco and I were able to get away for a couple of days to fly to Vung Tau, sometimes referred to as Cap St. Jacques, a beautiful beach setting on the South China Sea 50 miles southeast of Saigon. Supposedly early in the war it was an in-country R&R (rest and recuperation) site for both Allied troops and the Viet Cong, although I can't imagine how that was possible. Today, it is a resort.

Bianco served in the office of General Creighton Abrams, and he was able to secure a Huey for us to make the trip. The 1st Australian Logistic Support Group was located in Vung Tau and we were able to enjoy a few Foster's beers with some of the Aussie soldiers, although we couldn't drink nearly as much as they did. I think the average size of a Foster's beer can at that time was equivalent to a 55-gallon drum.

It was on this trip where I had perhaps the most frightening moment of my life, and it had nothing to do with the war. I decided to go to the beach on day two, but Chopper was preoccupied with something else. I had the section of the seashore all to myself; there was nobody else in sight. The area was secure, thanks to the Australians.

I waded out waist deep into the crystal blue water of the South China Sea, relaxing and enjoying the soothing feeling, when a strong undercurrent swept my feet from under me. I was not aware of the strong riptides there. Before I knew it, I was several yards offshore and heading further and further out into the ocean with each passing second. Land was quickly becoming a distant mirage.

It was a panic situation. At one point I had resigned myself to the fact that I was probably going to die. No, I determined that my existence wasn't going to end this way.

Somehow, someway, with inner strength that I never knew I had, I swam and paddled against the waves that were crashing against me with all the energy I could muster, for what seemed like an eternity.

I was not aware that you are supposed to swim sideways in such a situation. I know that now, it would have been handy to have had such knowledge back then. Finally, I made it back to shore, totally exhausted. I simply laid on the beach for about an hour.

Years later, I watched a movie named The End, in which the main character, played by Burt Reynolds, found himself in a similar predicament. While he was struggling in the water trying to make it back to land, he prayed: "Help me Lord, please save me and I'll be a better man. I'll be a better everything; all I ask of you is to make me a better swimmer!"

Chopper and I were seriously considering applying to become helicopter door gunners, with the thought that we could hopefully serve on the same bird. In addition to getting out into the field, we would make $55 more per month; big money to us in those days! We talked about it at length on the trip.

Unfortunately, LTC Brash found out about my plan; I had foolishly mentioned it to someone in the office when I returned, and he put a kibosh on that. He would not allow me to leave Project Hieu, and I'm sure I wouldn't have been able to get out of my Crypto duties anyway. Chopper's superiors in General Abrams' office were of the same thinking as mine; thus, our plan, forged in daydreaming, was grounded before it took off.

The Colonel wanted me to accompany him to Bangkok, Thailand on a temporary duty assignment for ten days in January. I was excited about making that trip to see another one of Asia's dynamic cities. However, I received a disappointing blow when MACOI (Military Assistance Command – Office of Information) ordered Brash to release me to that entity on temporary duty to assist with some crucial projects that were time-sensitive.

Following that assignment, MACOI tried to steal me away for good, but somehow, Brash over-ruled a couple of brigadier generals by convincing them that he needed me to help complete General Abrams' vision for Project Hieu.

Before I was released by MACOI, I was required to help find my permanent replacement and we did a thorough search for candidates at the bases in Da Nang, Hue, Pleiku, CuChi, Can Tho, Cam Ranh Bay, Nha Trang, and Chu Lai before the officers were satisfied that we had found the right person.

(By the way, to you fellow Vietnam vets, you might be interested to know that Chu Lai did not come about because of the Vietnamese language; it was the mispronunciation by the citizens of that country of the name Victor Krulak, a Lieutenant General who was the U.S. Marine Corps Commander in the Pacific. Krulak and his officers got such a kick out of it that they named the site after the improper enunciation.)

I received another letter from Nancy dated January 12, complete with a package that contained Rice Krispie treats; small cans of pudding; and some more mouse traps and Decon to help control my growing mouse problem. She said that the weather was still frigid in Iowa with the actual temperature being -10 degrees that day (-35 with the wind chill) continuing a week of below-zero weather. In my return letter, I requested that she please search for and send me two books; *I Am Third* by football great Gale Sayers and *Ball Four* by baseball pitching ace Jim Bouton.

At 7:00 a.m. on January 15, Lt. Cau from my office and I took off on a two-hour flight from Tan Son Nhut to Song Mao, just south of Cam Ranh Bay, aboard an Australian Royal Air Force de Havilland DHC-4 Caribou Transport plane. We were traveling there for the purpose of gathering some counter-insurgency materials. The landing strip at Song Mao, laid by Army Engineers, was made of steel planking and it made for a loud and bumpy taxi after we landed.

A U.S. Army Major and his driver pulled up to the plane in a Jeep just as we were disembarking from the rear walkway ramp to pick us up. All roads in the small village were simply dirt paths, and we kicked up considerable dust as we drove to the camp. Very noticeable were the numerous structures that had been peppered with small arms fire, with some of the buildings badly damaged, apparently from rockets and mortars.

Twenty-four months earlier, the elite Viet Cong 200C Special Forces Battalion hit Song Mao, which is surrounded by mountains, in a surprise attack after considerable planning and perfect execution. Song Mao was an ARVN Artillery Base Camp. The communist forces inflicted over 1,000 casualties on the shocked and unsuspecting South Vietnamese defenders. It was one of the V.C.'s rare victories of the war over the ARVN, but no U.S. forces were involved.

A major attack by three North Vietnamese battalions tried to overrun the base again just eight months prior to my trip there, but this time an ARVN regiment and the U.S. 1st Cavalry stopped the communist raiders in their tracks, suffering light casualties but killing 151 of the NVA.

There were 34 Americans stationed at Song Mao ARVN Firebase at the time of our visit, assisting the South Vietnamese Army. We interrupted a major volleyball game going on when we arrived. And yes, it featured the rough-and-tumble, anything-goes jungle rules described earlier.

I visited a Montagnard Village not far from Song Mao, and that is where I received a treasured homemade bronze bracelet from one of the natives there. The citizens in that hamlet resided in crude mud and stick huts.

The Montagnard ("mountain people") were indigenous individuals from a loose collection of several different tribes as described earlier. Sadly, they were considered outcasts by some of the Vietnamese, but they proved to be great allies of our American Special Forces. They were incredibly loyal and brave and certainly gained the respect of those who fought alongside them.

After spending the night with our three dozen fellow countrymen, we were off to our next stop, Phan Rang, the huge American air base located in the Central Highlands, just three miles inland from the South China Sea.

Lt. Cau and I hopped aboard a Huey, along with a couple of infantry "grunts" for our direct flight out of Song Mao to Phan Rang Airbase, where we would catch a ride back to Tan Son Nhut. We were "flying Hollywood" without the doors as usual, and none of the others wanted to sit by the open sides, which I preferred.

I liked to sit sideways ("side saddle") directly behind the pilot on the left side, looking down and scanning the countryside. I held on to the steel bar that separated the "back seat" from the door gunner with my left hand (wrapping my arm around it) and could quickly grab the metal frame under the cot-like canvas seat by my right hand if necessary. Some Huey configurations were different, but I would always find a way to sit in such a fashion.

Unfortunately, we had an unscheduled stop halfway through our flight. Our chopper developed engine trouble. We started to rapidly go down, and I reached back to grab the iron bar with both hands. The pilot did a skillful job of avoiding a South Vietnam cemetery, which had large tombstones similar to the above-ground monuments found in New Orleans.

It was a little nerve-wracking not knowing whether or not we would miss those pillars of the dead. I guess it would have hurt us much more than it would the buried inhabitants. But heck, I figured that if you're going to die in a crash, it might as well be in a graveyard. You avoid the middleman that way.

Our excellent pilot managed to maneuver away from those oversized gravestones and made a jarring – though upright -- landing just beyond the cemetery. If I remember correctly, the experienced flyer was a captain.

After hearing small arms fire albeit from a distance, he ordered us to set up a defensive perimeter. The two door gunners positioned their M-60 machine guns towards the nearest tree line some 200 yards away (I'm a football guy; I measure by yards, not military klicks). The rest of us had our M-16's at the ready.

We popped a red smoke grenade to pinpoint our location to a rescue helicopter. Unfortunately, Charlie would see that, too. We didn't land in a hot LZ (landing zone), but it would become one soon if we didn't get out of there. We were in the Central Highlands and there were known hard core North Vietnamese Army units in that vicinity.

Thus, we were relieved when the second Huey swooped in and extracted us in short order. Our savior flew directly to the South China Sea to avoid potential enemy ground fire and transported us safely to Phan Rang.

It was always wise to fly over waterways, mostly rivers, rather than travel over jungle or forestry areas in Vietnam, where the enemy could fire on the Huey's while staying concealed under a visually protected canopy.

Phan Rang, located in Ninh Thuan Province, was a U.S. Air Force Base, earning the nickname "Happy Valley" in some quarters. Ironically, it was originally built by Japan during its occupation of Vietnam in WWII. Though still a French colony at the time, France was forced to co-exist with the Japanese in Indochina because the war in Europe -- including Germany's occupation of its country -- demanded France's full attention.

(As a side note, Japan's occupation of Vietnam was a factor in the Japanese preemptive attack on Pearl Harbor in 1941, with that country going on the offensive to prevent any attempt by the United States to try to dislodge its Imperial Forces from Indochina by impeding U.S. military capabilities. Japan was reacting to rumors that America wanted to take steps to rid Southeast Asia of its Japanese conquerors.)

The American military had to greatly upgrade the Phan Rang airfield in 1965, primarily to make the runways compatible to facilitate high tech jet fighters and other modern aircraft.

I had another encounter with a crippled helicopter a few weeks later, with my destination again being Phan Rang. On that occasion, once more I found myself suddenly aboard a damaged chopper, only this time it was caused by ground fire from the NVA. It was the flight in which my pants caught fire.

I was sitting in my normal "side saddle" position with my feet dangling down. Suddenly, there was a loud noise, the chopper lurched, and we started to rock back and forth. I was hanging on for dear life, securing my grip and wrapping my left arm around the iron bar next to me while reaching behind with my right hand to grab the metal pipe at the top of the canvas seat.

As we were going down, somebody's camera and weapon slid on the floor straight out of the aircraft from the left side where I was sitting as it was tilting, but the jerky motion of the stricken aircraft didn't allow me to lift my legs up in time to enable me to swing around and stop the rapidly moving items. I always wondered if some poor Vietnamese rice farmer on the ground got conked on the head with the flying debris; what a strange way to get killed by an M-16.

As we were falling from the sky, I heard one of the G.I.'s on board praying aloud (and we were all probably asking for a little guidance from above in our own way). That old WWII axiom that there are no atheists in foxholes apparently also applied to those in a stricken helicopter in Vietnam.

There was something else that I soon took note of; the mid-section of the top of my fatigue pants was on fire! It might have been caused by a spark from the stricken aircraft, or it could have come from a cigarette which had flown out of a smoker's mouth at the time of the sudden jolt that we had just encountered (would that qualify as "friendly fire?").

Going down in a disabled helicopter is an attention-getter, but it kind of becomes your secondary concern when flames are coming up from your crotch area. I don't know why, and this is based on nothing, but I thought that our fatigues might at least be somewhat fire retardant. I wondered if my mama-san had slipped in some cheap locally made knockoffs in my laundry). I couldn't use my hands to try to extinguish the fire because I had to keep holding on as if my life depended on it, which it did, during our unique roller coaster ride. Luckily, the flames seemed to be somewhat dissipating on their own as we sped to the ground.

I was bracing myself, thinking that we were going to flip over and land on our side, which was frightening because the rotor blades would snap off and could be lethal if they hit one of us, that is if we survived the crash at all. Once again, one of our ace chopper pilots somehow managed to force the big bird to land upright on its skids, bouncing a couple of times.

I always heard that it is sometimes human nature to laugh when individuals find themselves in desperate situations, called gallows humor. Despite the dire straits in which we found ourselves, after a hard, jolting landing, the door gunner on my side of the Huey was getting a charge out of watching me trying to extinguish the last small flame when I could finally use my hands.

I grinned back at him and yelled: "Why are my pants on fire? I didn't lie to anyone!" Kiddingly, he retorted: "Hey, I'll put you in for a Purple Heart!" I replied: "Yeah, I would like to see how they would write up that citation!" I continued the comedy act: "If I get that Purple Heart, I'll name my first child after you; if I can still have any!" I think the other guys on our nearly doomed ride thought we had both lost our minds, wondering why we were so cheery. I suppose we were merely masking our fear.

Once again, we set up a perimeter defense and popped a smoke grenade. We heard several bursts of AK-47 fire coming from a dense jungle area, but we held off returning fire. We weren't exactly sure where we were, and we didn't want to risk hitting friendly Allied Forces who might be in the area. That was a favorite tactic of the Viet Cong; pop up and start shooting in the middle of two American units in relatively close proximity to try to start a crossfire between them, and then the V.C. would slip away undetected.

The "cavalry" -- another rescue chopper – quickly came to save the day again. We darted out of there immediately. It was amazing how fast the extrication teams worked in Vietnam. We were whisked away very quickly in both of my Huey "incidents." All I can say is thank God for our skillful and brave helicopter pilots. I marveled at their calm demeanor; they were bonafide saints to me, especially the ones who maneuvered crippled aircraft on which I was riding to safe landings, and also those who braved ground fire to swoop down and get us the hell out of harm's way.

Although having experienced it twice, going down in a chopper in 'Nam was not rare or unusual. The Vietnam Helicopter Pilots' Association reported that a total of 11,846 such aircraft (there were five different types) were shot down or crashed during the war (some were returned to service). Over 5,000 pilots, crew chiefs, and door gunners died in those incidents. I could not locate a report as to how many "passengers" on those flights were also KIA.

To this day, because of the two near-disastrous flights, the sound of whirling blades from a helicopter still brings back memories and sometimes sends shivers down my spine, although at that time, the increasingly loud rotors from the approaching recovery helicopters provided sweet music, indeed. (I always get chills when I hear the rotor blades at the beginning and ending of Billy Joel's "Goodnight Saigon.")

We finally made it to Phan Rang, again flying a good distance over the South China Sea on the rescue chopper before touching down at the air base.

Just about every plane in the United States arsenal could have been seen at Phan Rang, including F-4 fighters, B-57 bombers, and dozens and dozens of other types of aircraft. Several Tactical Fighter Wings were stationed there throughout the course of the war.

One fascinating plane that called Phan Rang home was the C-47 "Spooky" gunship. Designed and originated by fighter pilot Major Ronald W. Terry, it's call sign was Puff, which earned it the nickname "Puff the Magic Dragon."

Adapted from the civilian Douglas DC 3, it was a relatively slow-moving, lumbering plane for a combat zone, but the communist forces might have been more fearful of it than any other aircraft in the U.S. fleet. Puff had three miniguns (or gatling guns) that could lay down a round every couple of yards on a surface the size of a football field, which made it invaluable for close ground support. Charlie (i.e. Viet Cong and NVA) hated it.

C-119's and C-130's were also converted to Spooky gunships. When I was in Vietnam, there were 45 C-47's, 52 C-119's, and eight C-130's "Magic Dragons" in operation. They were all deadly and effective. Major Terry flew 56 combat missions in the C-47 and 140 missions in the C-130.

The F-4 fighter jets were sleek and powerful with their sparrow and sidewinder missiles. They were initially devoid of guns until the pilots urged that they be added, which they were in 1967. The downside was that it cut down on fuel capacity because of where they had to be placed.

I came within a whisker of realizing a dream of flying in an F-4 (nicknamed the Phantom, a moniker attributed to me when I worked in college athletics years later). A pilot friend said he could take me up in one at Tan Son Nhut Air Base for a quick spin, probably not authorized. I was going to be his GIB (guy in back). Unfortunately for me, he was called away at the last minute for a mission over Laos in February and I missed an opportunity of a lifetime. Truthfully, perhaps he found out he couldn't really do that for me, and that was his way out. I don't know.

Pilots of the A-7 Corsair were just as proud of their attack aircraft. A friend who flew that jet believed that it didn't receive enough credit or recognition due to the popularity of the F-4. I'm sure the same can probably be said of the A-4 Skyhawk, the A-1 Skyraider, and the A-6 Intruder.

Jumping off the slick (still another name for a helicopter) after we touched down in Phan Rang, I profusely thanked our rescue pilot. We were picked up in an open Jeep and as we rode to the terminal area, we followed a fully loaded petroleum semi-truck. I was hoping that the bad guys didn't have a bead on that vehicle with a Russian RPG (Rocket Propelled Grenade) or something. That would have made for a first-class fireball with us right in the thick of it.

While checking in for temporary lodging in Air Force transient billets, standing outside a small wooden building and looking through a hazy window, I heard someone say, "Starr!" I squinted and lo and behold, I ran into still another classmate of mine from Newton High School, Jerry Groom. He ran outside and gave me a hug. It always made me feel so good when I saw a familiar face; I guess it reminded me of home. Jerry told me that one of our other 20 classmates who served in the war, chopper pilot Ron Current, had been stationed there before he had gone home the previous September as Nancy had informed me at the time.

I checked into the infirmary to check on my burns, which, thank goodness, were minor. To my surprise, I saw the only two American females that I would see during my entire year-long tour. They were Red Cross Girls (aka "Doughnut Dollies").

As dusk approached, several of us sat outside enjoying a beverage. I had changed my burned-out fatigues and doctored up my slight burns by then. I watched a Cobra gunship, a lean, mean helicopter fighting machine, as it strafed a mountainside.

I asked a pilot who was sitting next to me why the Cobra was doing that, and he told me that it was "recon by fire." The helicopter was baiting some young Viet

Cong or NVA soldier to take a potshot, which would reveal his unit's hidden position.

Sure enough, some poor schmuck fired at the gunship and I'm certain he wished he could have taken it back moments later. In addition, his buddies were probably a little more than upset at his impetuous decision. At least one more Cobra joined the fray, and they unleashed a barrage of rocket fire targeting the area from where the firing was initiated. We also had ground forces in the area and a firefight ensued for a few minutes.

Nighttime had shrouded the field of action by this time and from our faraway vantagepoint, it became a tennis match of tracer rounds that were visible at night. The Allied troops fired red tracers while the communists utilized green ones. The American troops also fired grenades from an M79 launcher.

My new pilot drinking buddy told me that these skirmishes weren't all that rare. Pointing to the scene of all the action, he asked me: "Do you know what they call that?" I shook my head and he replied: "Charlie's Mountain." He told me that a force of 400 V.C. had tried to attack the base a few nights earlier but were quickly repelled.

The following day it was time to go "home" to my MACV base. I would be transported on another Australian Caribou aircraft (sometimes referred to as Wallaby flights), this time back to Tan Son Nhut.

I smiled as I walked up the rear steel grating ramp and plopped down in a seat made of netting for the 170-mile trip back to my base of operations. Over the past month an angel on my shoulder had protected me through a near drowning and two helicopter crashes.

Nice try, Diablo.

Basic Training Rookie!

Casualty of War

Camouflaged VC hideout

Mama-san and friends

THEY NEVER HEARD THE FINAL SHOT

Children of ARVN Soldiers with 1st Lt. Cau and Me

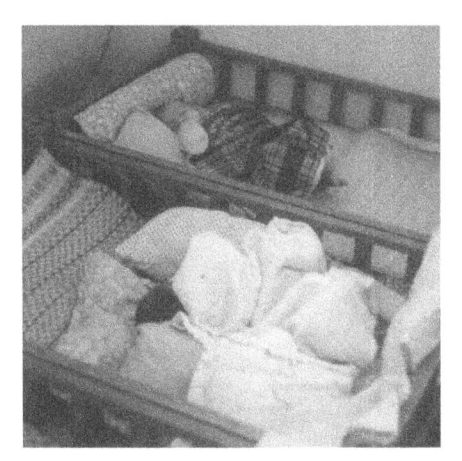

The Young Suffer Most in War

Watching over the Orphanage

Time Spent at the Orphanage

A Gathering of Angels at the Orphanage

Where am I?  *The riptides of the South China Sea*

Summoning our Rescue Chopper

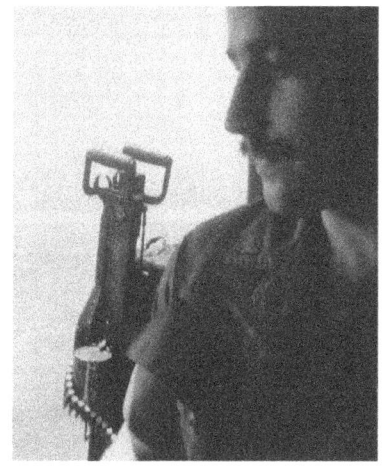

My buddy, Carmen "Chopper" Bianco 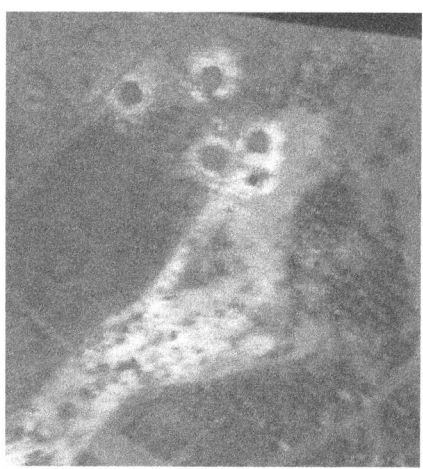 *Bombing Aftermath*

THEY NEVER HEARD THE FINAL SHOT

Our Taxi Service

Remnants of War

Strike Force

Honored to stand with Iraq Medal of Honor recipient David Bellavia

Honored to stand with Vietnam Medal of Honor recipient Harvey C. Barnum, Jr.,

Honored to stand with Everett Alvarez, first U.S. pilot shot down and held as a POW for eight years

A Welcome Sight, Indeed!

THEY NEVER HEARD THE FINAL SHOT

CHAPTER XI
Victory at Hand, But Washington Falters

Unfortunately, I did not get a chance to listen to the Super Bowl, played on January 17, because I was out in the hinterlands. In that game, the Baltimore Colts beat Dallas, 16-13, in the Cowboys' first-ever appearance in the annual contest of the NFL's best. The winning points were scored by the Colts' rookie kicker, Jim O'Brien, who booted the ball through the uprights from 32 yards out with just five seconds left in Super Bowl V. The game was satirically dubbed the "Stupor Bowl," thanks to a total of 11 turnovers and 14 penalties.

The game featured two future Hall of Fame quarterbacks, Baltimore's Johnny Unitas and Roger Staubach of the Cowboys. Unitas exited the game in the second quarter with an injury, and super-sub Earl Morrall took over to guide the Colts to the win.

Dallas Coach Tom Landry decided to go with veteran Craig Morton at QB and he played the entire game while Staubach rode the bench. Roger, a graduate of the Naval Academy, was only in his second year in the NFL after serving out his military obligation.

Staubach was no stranger to Vietnam, volunteering to serve a one-year tour of duty in the country, where he was stationed at Chu Lai before going into the NFL

Following his dormant situation in which he found himself in the 1971 Super Bowl, he would go on to be named the MVP in the big game the following year, and, of course, followed that up with an outstanding career.

There was a fragging (a tossed hand grenade) a couple of barracks down from mine on the 19th of January, which, sadly, killed a Captain. I do not know if the perpetrator was ever identified.

I was due for another smallpox inoculation and on January 22, I received one. It involved being poked with a pin on my bicep for about 10 minutes. Later, my arm swelled and was constantly draining. The lymph node under my arm also became bloated. The location of the pin pricks blistered and itched, causing a little bit of pain for a while. However, that was better than the alternative.

On January 24, I received a letter from Nancy written on the 17th in which she said she was awakened by a nightmare in the middle of the night, sometime around 1:30 a.m. She woke up startled, fearful that something bad had happened to me. Doing some fast calculating, I figured out that it was exactly the time when my helicopter had gone down on the 16th. I didn't tell her or my folks about either of my chopper crashes. Once again, I thought to myself, how *DOES* she do that?

During the Vietnam conflict, especially in its later stages, there was a holiday each year that caused anxiety, nervousness, fear and uncertainty among the citizens of South Vietnam and to all of the Allied armed forces: It was Tet Nguyen Dan, or simply "Tet" as it is more widely known.

Tet is described by *Merriam-Webster Dictionary* as "The Vietnamese New Year observed during the first several days of the lunar calendar beginning at the second new moon after the winter solstice." In 1971, the year I was in 'Nam, it commenced on January 27.

What was once a joyful and fun-filled holiday had turned into a time of apprehension because of the Viet Cong and the North Vietnamese Army.

I wish to reiterate that my purpose is not to take a stand on the complexities of the Vietnam War. It is in the history books.

> *"Remember Charlie, remember Baker;*
> *They left their childhood on every acre;*
> *And who was wrong, and who was right?*
> *It didn't matter in the thick of the fight."*

> ■ Goodnight Saigon
> --Billy Joel

I would like to believe that we did some good things for the people of South Vietnam, building wells, roads, schools, airports, bridges, canals, dispensaries, and other basic infrastructure needs. We also provided medical aid, educational and vocational training, agricultural programs, and technical assistance programs. And, for a little while at least, also protected a population that really did not want to be under the harsh thumb of communism. This became evident in the early months of 1968.

My goal here is to provide the reader with a detailed, yet hopefully understandable account, of the conflict's most prominent and defining military campaign of the entire Vietnam War – the TET Offensive of '68. I hope to do so in as succinctly as possible.

I also want to make it clear that the following account is based on my thoughts, views, and opinions after extensive research, plus personally having a familiarity of the theater of operation in which it took place. Also, of course, I had a knowledge of some things that remained confidential but which I was privy to because of my security classification. In my estimation, the TET Offensive of '68 was the most opportune time for the U.S. and its Allies to win the Vietnam War.

The two opposing foes in the Southeast Asian conflict decided early on to abide by a truce during TET -- a "gentleman's agreement" if you will -- regarded by most as the most significant holiday in Vietnamese culture. Until 1968, both for the most part adhered to the cease-fire.

Contrary to what many believed, Le Duan, not Ho Chi Minh, was the primary decision-maker in North Vietnam from the mid-1960's on.

Ho Chi Minh's health was failing and Le Duan, the General Secretary of the Central Committee of the Communist Party, took advantage of the situation and assumed control of the war effort. Over the final four years of his life before dying in 1969, Ho Chi Minh was simply a figurehead.

A staunch communist, Le Duan was aggressive and had long wanted to stage a go-for-broke major offensive against South Vietnam. He began his final planning in the fall of 1967 and to assure that there was no chance of his highly-classified plan leaking out, he sent Ho Chi Minh to China under the pretense that he needed medical attention.

Le Duan did the same to the NVA's top general, Vo Nguyen Giap, who reportedly was lukewarm to such an onslaught in the South, by sending him to Hungary, also under the guise of needed medical care. Though initially not convinced that Le Duan's invasion plans were prudent, Giap, known as the "Red Napoleon" because of his small stature, did return to eventually lead all communist forces in the military attack.

Le Duan arrested any politicians, journalists, military leaders, and any others he deemed were not loyal to him and his vision. He wanted to isolate them and eliminate any opposition. His number one concern was maintaining the element of surprise against the Allies.

TET of 1968 became Le Duan's target date for his massive invasion of the South. The operation would supposedly consist of over 84,000 North Vietnamese Army and Viet Cong fighters (later, however, the South Vietnamese government said that this number was far too low and that there were more Communist troops than that already dispersed throughout the South during the time of the raid.) In unison, the North Vietnamese Army and Viet Cong would attack 36 of the 44 provinces in South Vietnam.

The plan was kept secret by Le Duan and his closest associates until the last possible moment when the rank and file of the two communist forces were told of the bold mission. The NVA and V.C. foot soldiers were promised that the citizens of South Vietnam hated their government and would welcome the "saviors" from the North with open arms, and that the ARVN (South Vietnamese) troops would throw down their weapons, desert, and rush over to the communists' side. North Vietnam could then proclaim victory and chase out the Americans.

The North Vietnamese Army and Viet Cong forces would soon learn that they had been badly misled. The 1968 TET offensive resulted in one of the most colossal military blunders and worst miscalculations in the history of warfare. It was an abject failure for the communists.

Unfortunately, however, as strange as it may sound, though the U.S. and South Vietnam trounced the invaders in the foolhardy offensive, in a stranger-than-fiction scenario, it ended up being a major contributing factor in North Vietnam eventually securing victory in the long war, thanks primarily to disinformation distributed in our country.

To facilitate the surprise attack and cause mass confusion, many of the participating NVA and V.C. troops carried false identification papers and were dressed in civilian clothing, uniforms of the South Vietnamese Army (ARVN), or even in women's dresses to hide weapons.

When the attack materialized, the enemy troops secured other weapons that had been smuggled into South Vietnam in such unsuspecting modes of transportation as coffins and on commercial trucks. The enemy attacked across a broad front late on the night of January 30 and early in the morning of the 31st of 1968.

ARVN (South Vietnamese) troops were on leave because of the agreed-upon TET cease-fire and American forces were standing down for the same reason. Thus, by purposely violating the truce that they themselves had proposed the previous November, the communists were able to catch the Allies with their guard down.

There was much bewilderment, but miraculously, when it was clear what was occurring, units were hastily reassembled and the Americans and South Vietnamese forces, along with their other Allied partners, took the fight to the enemy and performed admirably.

Nonetheless, January 31, 1968, was the bloodiest day of the Vietnam War for American Forces. The unscrupulous surprise countrywide attack by the North Vietnamese and Viet Cong during a ceasefire did initially take advantage of our unsuspecting and unprepared forces and 246 Americans went down on that day.

Despite the unforeseen mass incursion by the communists, within a little over two weeks, their forces had been repelled and badly mauled in every area of South Vietnam other than in the City of Hue, where the NVA held out for several weeks. For the most part, the battle of Saigon was over in a week, with nearly 700 of the communist infiltrators eliminated.

In all, some 120 cities, villages, hamlets and military bases had been simultaneously hit, but the Americans and South Vietnamese, in addition to the other Allied fighting forces, were able to keep them under control.

By mid-March, the communist invasion in the country had pretty much fizzled out as mop-up operations by the Allies continued.

That was a good thing; documents accumulated from dead Viet Cong attackers indicated that they had created lists of individuals marked for immediate execution in every city.

There were several reasons for the Allied successes in those military engagements. The most pertinent of them was the fact that the South Vietnamese population did not welcome the attackers with open arms as assured by the North Vietnamese leadership.

For the previous decade, the Viet Cong had carried out a sustained and ceaseless campaign of intimidation, kidnappings, rape, torture and summary executions (an estimate of over 35,000 such murders) against the citizens of South Vietnam, going from village to village and hamlet to hamlet in its reign of terror, plus shelling the large cities which produced indiscriminate killing of men, women, and children.

Crowded trains and buses were bombed, roads destroyed, and bridges and schools burned by the V.C. It was astonishing that the communists could miscalculate the hatred that the people of South Vietnam had built up for the Viet Cong. (Over 38,000 South Vietnamese citizens would be killed by the V.C. and NVA during the TET offensive.)

The population of South Vietnam was also livid that its fellow Vietnamese from the North would stage such a hideous invasion on TET, their culture's most revered holiday, which included honoring the dead.

Other pertinent reasons for the failure of the massive communist invasion: Not one ARVN unit defected, instead, the South Vietnamese soldiers fought courageously and held their own; also, North Vietnamese leader Le Duan badly underestimated the power, the will, and especially the mobility of the American forces.

In addition, there was poor centralized planning on the part of the communists. COSVN (V.C.) and NVA Directives were complicated and confusing. The communists had spread out their forces much too thinly. Promised reinforcements never materialized for the initial raiders, who were soon encircled, outnumbered, and badly pummeled.

Prior to the commencement of the TET Offensive, the North Vietnamese Army tried to fool the Allied leadership by what many felt to be a feinting massive attack 14 miles south of the De-Militarized Zone (DMZ) at Khe Sanh (Kay-Sawn) and in surrounding hills on January 17, in hopes of luring a large contingent of the U.S. fighting force from throughout South Vietnam to that area. The thinking among communist leaders was that thinning the protection in the south by diverting a large number of U.S. forces to the DMZ would have aided them in their intended surprise sweep in the South.

There was definitely heavy activity in the Khe Sanh area, but the strategy didn't work for the North Vietnamese, who suffered a drastic number of casualties. Intelligence reports indicated that three full NVA divisions, up to 50,000 communist troops, were operating in I Corps near the DMZ.

Over the course of the next several weeks, some 5,000 American Marines plus South Vietnamese Rangers held off the large contingent of NVA regulars. It was hell on earth for the Allied defenders, who had to endure 77 days of constant bombardment. The communists used artillery, mortars and human wave attacks, but at the end of the day, the resilient Leathernecks coupled with American airpower reigned supreme.

Some, including General Creighton Abrams, believed that the NVA's objective at Khe Sanh was to try and emulate the communist successes against the French at Dien Bien Phu, which led to the victory over the

French forces. It didn't happen. The U.S. Marines did what they do best; they won.

The U.S. Army's 1st Cavalry Division and 101st Airborne were also instrumental in the successful efforts over the North Vietnamese military in the encounter, as were, of course, the brave Marine, Navy, and Air Force fighter and attack aircraft pilots.

Additionally, because of the constant bombardment of the base by the North Vietnamese regulars, American C-130 aircraft had to do "touch and goes," landing with the back ramp down to push out needed supplies before immediately lifting off again to avoid being hit. Sometimes they didn't even land and stayed just a few feet off the ground, simply pushing out their cargo with the crates, which were slowed by attached parachutes. The flight crews of these dangerous missions called themselves "mortar magnets."

The Army 5th Special Forces, with only 24 men, along with a contingent of Royal Laotian troops, Montagnard tribesmen, and a CIDG (Civilian Irregular Defense Group) element made up of South Vietnamese citizens, were stationed four miles away from Khe Sanh at Lang Vei and stood in the way of the NVA, which attacked the small detachment.

The communists, led by the NVA 304th Division, had infantry, armor, artillery, sappers, flamethrowers and anti-aircraft capability at their disposal. Though badly outmanned, the defenders put up a ferocious fight but were eventually overrun, taking heavy casualties. Seven of the 24 Americans died in the struggle, with three others being captured. Survivors had to make the 4-mile trek to Khe Sanh on February 7.

The NVA had surprised the Allied Forces at Lang Vei by using 15 PT-76 Russian tanks, one of the rare occasions when communist forces had utilized armor. The Allies knocked out seven of them before fleeing the overwhelming odds they were facing.

The primary battle for Khe Sanh lasted 11 weeks, although there was still more limited action at that location in the coming months. The North Vietnamese paid a heavy price, thanks largely to the Allied use of devastating air power, including B-52 strikes, which offered a huge advantage. Up to 15,000 NVA soldiers were killed while American losses totaled just over 200.

General William Westmoreland, the head of all U.S. forces, had an inkling that the enemy was planning a substantial offensive early in the year, although he didn't know what, when, or where for certain. Although sometimes criticized, "Westy" did a credible job of playing chess with U.S. forces, placing them in what would be advantageous positions when the TET attack commenced.

Guided by his suspicions of an attack of major proportions, Westmoreland asked South Vietnam's President, Nguyen Van Thieu, to either cancel the TET truce or at least cut it from 48 hours to 24, to make certain that ARVN troops could return to their bases after cutting their holiday short. Thieu agreed to trim it to 36 hours.

When the TET Offensive first got underway on the starting date of January 30, the South Vietnamese Capitol City of Saigon was a prime target for the North Vietnamese and the Viet Cong for obvious reasons. Over 1,000 V. C. had become secretly entrenched in the city when the surprise communist attacks throughout the country began.

Early in the morning of January 31, 1968, the V.C. coordinated attacks on the U.S. Embassy, MACV Headquarters (which would later be my base of operations), the Presidential Palace, the Joint General Staff HQ, the South Vietnamese Naval HQ, the radio station, and Tan Son Nhut Air Base, which was especially of major concern to General Westmoreland.

Up to three Viet Cong battalions (1,200 men) attacked Tan Son Nhut at 2:00 a.m. and at one point breached the perimeter, but South Vietnamese troops and the 4th U.S. Cavalry drove back the communists, killing some 325 of the enemy.

The big story of the day was the assault on the U.S. Embassy by 19 Viet Cong raiders, from the V.C.'s elite C-10 Sapper unit, at 2:47 a.m. They blew a three-foot hole in the outer wall in the southwest corner of the four-acre compound with explosive satchel charges.

When they rushed through the gap, the V.C. platoon leader and some of his men were quickly gunned down by surprised but fast-reacting U.S. Military Policemen, who in turn were killed by return fire from the surviving communist raiders.

Within less than six hours, 18 of the 19 invading Viet Cong members had been eliminated, and the wounded sole survivor was captured. Four American M.P.'s and one Marine were killed in the unexpected aggression. The Embassy building itself was never breached.

There were several heroes that day, including Private First Class (PFC) Paul Healey. A member of the 716th Military Police Battalion, Healey rushed to the scene of the attack and finding the gates to the compound padlocked, he tried to ram a jeep into the metal doors to break the chains holding them shut.

He was unsuccessful in his attempt, but he quickly jumped out and shot off the lock with his .45, charging into the compound under heavy fire. He personally killed eight of the enemy sappers with hand grenades and his M16.

Though wounded by a V.C. grenade, Healey charged after the lone remaining communist soldier into a villa on the compound, where an aide to the ambassador, retired Army Colonel George Jacobson, was located. After two attempts to root out the lone Charlie (V.C.), Healy finally lobbed a tear gas cannister into the building.

Knowing that Jacobson was trapped on the second floor, Healey ran outside and tossed his .45, two magazines of ammo, and a gas mask up to Jacobson, who was leaning out an open window. Colonel Jacobson, the ambassador's advisor, eventually shot and killed the remaining V.C. sapper, temporarily blinded by the tear gas, who was shooting wildly while running up the stairs. For his actions that day, PFC Paul Healey was awarded the Distinguished Service Cross.

Reinforcements from the Army's 101st Airborne rushed to the Embassy, landing on the roof of the chancery building by helicopter, although everything was pretty quiet by the time they arrived.

The situation was so secure that at 8:30 a.m., General Westmoreland visited the scene for a first-hand look.

Reporters who resided in nearby hotels heard the gunfire and one Associated Press writer saw the chance for a huge scoop. He quickly sent a story across the wire that the V.C. had made it into the chancery building of the U.S. Embassy, which was completely untrue. The Viet Cong sappers had barely made it past the outer wall several yards from the government building and were eliminated. Many tried to hide behind any barrier they could find, but they were flushed out and terminated in short order.

***

Unfortunately, the erroneous report that our Embassy had been captured spread like wildfire in media reports throughout the world and there was a widespread assumption that the communists had won a major engagement and took over the residency of our ambassador. Again, that was simply false. It was the furthest thing from the truth.

That was the beginning of the end for the Allies. Walter Cronkite, the grandfatherly reporter for CBS News, evidently believed the erroneous information and asked aloud on the air: "What the hell is going on? I thought we were winning the war!" Millions of Americans were loyal Cronkite watchers and hung on to every word he verbalized, as if they were gospel.

Cronkite's counterpart at NBC, Chet Huntley, announced the Viet Cong were inside the Embassy building and had chased out the defenders. Another totally fallacious account.

For the most part, the Allies routed the communists throughout South Vietnam within two weeks. The South Vietnamese capitol of Saigon was secure and out of danger within just six days. For a few days, the V.C. did occupy Phu Tho Racetrack near the Cholon district, a place I would pass by often in my days in Vietnam.

The only remaining North Vietnamese Army holdout in the TET Offensive was in Hue (pronounced "whey"), the old Imperial City, some 60 miles south of the DMZ. A communication failure disrupted a plan that would have placed more American troops in Hue.

"Although I had reported to Washington on January 22 that a multi-battalion attack might be expected at Hue, for some reason, I learned later, that information apparently failed to reach a small MACV advisory group in a little walled compound in the city (of Hue)," explained Westmoreland.

Once the attack on Hue commenced, several Army and Marine reinforcements had to rush to the scene to face the well-entrenched communist forces. The battle for Hue lasted 26 days, and it was a grueling campaign.

For the first time in history, television viewers in the United States saw war up close and personal, and millions of Americans did so nightly. It's safe to say that it gave them a queasy feeling.

It would take 11 ARVN battalions, 4 U.S. Army battalions, and 3 U.S. Marine battalions to root out the heavily fortified communist troops, which committed 16 battalions to the battle. Finally, the Allies prevailed and on March 3, the U.S. and South Vietnamese forces had won still another major encounter.

In the battle of Hue, the enemy paid an enormous price, as over 5,000 NVA soldiers were killed with some 3,000 other KIA's in nearby combat. The ARVN (South Vietnamese) lost 452 and American forces had 216 fatale casualties. (Some disputed those figures, but many did not understand the overwhelming and destructive firepower – artillery, armor, air support, and infantry – that the Allies unleased on the communist occupiers.) The South Vietnamese flag was raised over the city in victory after just over three weeks.

Unfortunately for the Allied cause, Cronkite had gone on the air on February 27 – five days *before* the impressive U.S. and ARVN victory at Hue, saying this: "It is increasingly clear to this reporter that the only rational way out (of Vietnam) will be to negotiate, not as victors...."

This, after a stunning two months when the Allies had mauled the combined communist armed forces! In football terms, the Allies had produced an ass-kicking of the highest order.

Obviously, Cronkite was a well-respected journalist, and I had an opportunity to meet him later in life. He was a nice gentleman. It just seems that it was hard for him to hide his disdain for the war, and it crept into his normally-objective reporting. Cronkite actually asked the on-air question: "Who won and who lost in the great TET Offensive? I'm not sure."

Seriously??

Even North Vietnam's brilliant General Vo Nguyen Giap, a hero in his country's defeat of the French, said that his communist forces (NVA and V.C.) were "on their knees" after TET.

Another NVA general, Tran Van Tra, said: "We did not correctly evaluate the specific balance of forces between ourselves and the enemy (Allies); in part it was an illusion based on our subjective desires."

And then there was this: A captured top secret COSVN (communist) communique said the following: "We failed to seize a number of primary objectives and to completely destroy mobile and defensive units of the enemy (Allies). We also failed to hold the occupied areas. In the political field, we failed to motivate the people to stage uprisings and break the enemy's oppressive control."

In other words....the communist forces lost, and they admitted it.

The aftermath of the battle for Hue following the communist TET invasion of 1968 was ugly and horrifying. When Allies entered the city, they learned that the North Vietnamese Army had executed up to 5,700 civilians inside its gates.

Over 2,800 hundred men, women, and children were found in three mass graves, many with their hands tied behind their backs and shot in the head or buried alive. Three German doctors, two French monks, two U.S. government workers and several Filipinos who had been in Hue during the attack had also been brutally murdered by the communists.

U.S. Information Officer Douglas Pike, in a paper entitled "The Viet Cong Strategy of Terror," said that the communists had established a policy of eliminating what they termed social negatives." Those selected for execution included intellectuals, educators, politicians, and religious leaders. (But why all the children?)

Sadly, and I'm sickened to say this, but we had our own shameful chapter just two weeks after the discovery of the slaughter at Hue by the communists. It became known as the My Lai Massacre. A task force of the Americal Division's 11th Infantry Battalion, which had suffered numerous casualties over the previous weeks, was seeking out Viet Cong troops. The unit came across the hamlet of My Lai (also referred to as Pinkville) in Quang Ngai Province, and to make a long story short, it turned into an orgy of violence perpetrated by U.S. soldiers.

There's no easy way to say it; on March 16, 1968, they slaughtered between 350 and 500 civilians -- men, women, and children. Those murdered were not enemy combatants; a total of only four rifles were found in the village. There were also allegations that girls and women had been raped.

Some back home tried to justify the killings as simply saying "that's war." No, it was mass murder. There is absolutely no reason or rationale for soldiers – no matter how much pressure they were under or how much their unit had been hit – to slaughter and rape innocent civilians, and that's exactly what they did.

It took a year before the facts became known. At that time, the Army Criminal Investigation Division (CID) brought charges against four officers and nine enlisted men. Two other officers and three enlisted men were tried, and 25 other enlisted men were implicated, but since they had already been discharged, they were beyond the Army's jurisdiction.

Twelve other officers were charged with dereliction of duty, and Secretary of the Army Stanley Resor took administrative action against two generals and eight other officers of the Americal Division for lackluster investigation and insufficient reporting of the massacre.

The after-action report by the brigade showing just four confiscated rifles should have raised a red flag to those superiors. The initial official report stated that 128 "enemy" were killed.

My Lai was one of the darkest hours in United States Army history; it remains a hideous stain. I am not naïve enough to think that atrocities never happen in war, they do, far too often, but this was beyond the pale.

There were at least two American heroes who emerged from this tragedy. One was Army Warrant Officer Hugh Thompson, Jr., a pilot who landed his observation helicopter when he saw the atrocities taking place in an open field.

***

He ordered a halt to the killings and had his door gunners aim their M-60 machine guns at their fellow Americans who were committing the savagery to prove he meant business. Thompson ran over to help those civilians who had not yet been shot and loaded them onto his chopper. He evacuated several survivors and brought to a halt the carnage.

The other standup soldier was Spec 5 Ronald Ridenhour, who was told about the barbarity and kept insisting that the grotesque incident be brought to light, which finally led to the beginning of serious investigations by the government a year later.

My heart literally sinks when I think that this bloodbath occurred and was perpetrated by American military members. Unfortunately, not everyone who wears a uniform is angelic. But I take solace in the fact that the great majority of U.S. soldiers are good and honorable men like Thompson and Ridenhour.

Following the victory at Hue and the clean sweep over the communists during the TET Offensive, the Allies were in their best position ever to press the issue and win the Vietnam War. But that golden opportunity was squandered and any hope for victory by the U.S. and South Vietnamese soon ended up in the trash bin of history.

The media has a huge influence on the American population, and the negative comments coming from Cronkite and his ilk, plus the "raw" day-to-day television coverage of what has happened in every war, but had never been seen by the public, had taken its toll. Americans simply read accounts about battles in WWII and Korea but did not witness the horrifying results of war live with their own eyes. Had they seen the bloody devastation unleashed in the Pacific Islands, across Europe, and Korea, during the two previous wars, our citizens may have demanded the return of our troops at that time, too.

It's hard to argue that there wasn't at least a subtle anti-war slant to much of the reporting on the Vietnam War at the time. (I still see that today in books, documentaries, and movies regarding the conflict.) Mark Twain once said: "Get your facts first, then you can distort them as you please."

A frustrated President Lyndon Johnson stated: "The press is lying like drunken sailors....how can we possibly win and survive and have to fight the press?

Even North Vietnamese Army General Tran Do was puzzled and pleasantly surprised at the negative reactions of U.S. citizens and journalists after American forces had thoroughly beaten his communist troops: "In all honesty, we didn't achieve our main objective (during TET), which was to spur uprisings through the south. As for making an impact in the United States, it had not been our intention, but it turned out to be a fortunate result."

Regrettably, the false narrative of a takeover of our Embassy in Saigon and misreporting of what were American successes painted a far different picture back home in America than what was actually taking place in South Vietnam.

In his book, *The TET Offensive: A Concise History* (an outstanding account), James Willbanks disclosed that, at the time of the combat, "A Harris poll reports that 60 percent of a public opinion sample believes that the TET Offensive was a standoff or defeat for the U.S. cause in

Vietnam." Unfortunately, those polled believed the inaccurate and incorrect media reports.

That is unfair to the resiliency and skill that our fighting men and pilots showed in turning the tables on a surprise communist country-wide ambush, leading the Allies to total victory in the major encounter….in less than three weeks, no less!

The ingredients for ending the Vietnam War were there in the spring of 1968. The communists had suffered catastrophic losses. Many Viet Cong units, which suffered the brunt of the lost battles, had almost been decimated, with an estimated 70% casualty rate.

The North Vietnamese Army's nose had been bloodied pretty good, too. It was estimated that the NVA had lost up to 30% of its top-ranking junior officers. The communist forces suffered over 40,000 KIA's in a 45-day period.

The NVA and Viet Cong foot soldiers were stunned and demoralized; they had just been whipped on the battlefield and the promise that they would be regarded as liberators in the South did not come to fruition.

The V.C. had suffered such heavy losses in TET that it was considered finished as an effective fighting force; in the future, almost three-fourths of their units had to be manned by North Vietnam Army regulars. Securing more manpower for both groups, because of the heavy losses, was a growing concern for them.

In addition to the calamitous loss of able-bodied fighters, an astonishing amount of communist weaponry had been confiscated by the Allies during the period between January 31 and March 3.

A U.S. Psyops (psychological operations) report showed that NVA soldiers were exhausted and discouraged after being away from home for years, often living in the wet, bug-infested jungle or in tunnels without proper food and medical care, and with little, if any, pay. They were often ill and were depressed from watching so many of their buddies killed in the war. Some of them were as young as 15.

The communist soldiers were under constant bombardment from American or ARVN artillery, as well as from the air. Many just wanted to go back home to resume being farmers or laborers. For the first time in the war, officers from the North Vietnamese Army had been surrendering. There was starting to be a strong distrust in what their leaders were telling them. Gung-ho allegiance to communist principles was waning. The staggering losses during TET were a blow to the NVA and V.C. leadership.

War, in its coldest, most hard-hearted terms, can be boiled down to two basic elements: (1) Real Estate and (2) Attrition. After TET of 1968, the Allies had both in their favor while also controlling the air and the sea. The North Vietnamese had lost over half of their most prized and sophisticated jet fighters, Soviet MIG 21's, to American pilots in the ingenious Operation Bolo a year earlier. (North Vietnam lost a total of 193 MIGs during the war.)

Intelligence reported that all airfields and fuel dumps in North Vietnam could have been destroyed within three days. Bombing raids on anti-aircraft batteries had already taken a heavy toll on that country's air defenses.

The communists were on their heels and although they were definitely not a totally defeated force, they were struggling. There's no doubt in my mind that the U.S. could have dealt them a final blow, or in the very least, end the conflict with a permanent two-nation solution similar to that on the Korean peninsula, had the U.S. pressed the attack. That would have allowed North Vietnam to maintain its independence, with the South doing the same.

The North Vietnamese weren't going to concede anything without pressure, and the Allies were in perfect position to make that pressure unbearable.

An overwhelming air and land campaign by the Allies; cutting off retreating troops to the north; intensifying the bombing campaign against SAM (surface-to-air missile) sites, airbases, and fuel dumps; blockading Haiphong Harbor to curtail Soviet arms shipments by sea; air strikes to take out the railroad bridges on the China/North Vietnam border to impede munitions shipments from the Chinese; doubling up efforts to destroy or greatly hamper the Ho Chi Minh Trail; and cleaning out the sanctuaries of the enemy along the Cambodian and Laotian borders once and for all – were needed to bring the war to a favorable conclusion.

Better yet, why didn't we subscribe to the thesis that turnabout is fair play and invade North Vietnam for the first time in the entire war, ending the ridiculous one-sided policy of not allowing Allies to take such a course of action?

It would not be a walk in the park, of course. But if tranquility and freedom were to be achieved over a determined foe, doing whatever it took, short of nuclear war, was necessary to assure victory.

A lightening-like thrust into North Vietnam for the first time in the war, a blitzkrieg if you will, would have caught the NVA military chiefs, who had never feared an assault on their country, entirely off guard. They had sent the great majority of their forces to the South, leaving the North lightly defended against ground troops raiding their own countryside.

Furthermore, the NVA had called in all reserves at their disposal for the failed TET attack in the South. At the time, North Vietnam, for the most part, was defended by old men and very young boys who were most likely ill-trained. (There were also reports of an uptick in the number of all-female cadres among the communist forces, and word spread that they were even more cruel and sadistic than their male counterparts.)

It was a perfect time for a surprise onslaught; Allied strength totaled over 1.4 million (including South Vietnamese forces) and there was ample war materiel (weapons, ammo, etc.). In addition, there were 200,000 troops being held in reserve back in the United States earmarked for Vietnam if needed.

The NVA and V.C. could only counter with just over a fourth of that many healthy soldiers (not counting an unknown number of Chinese troops, which at most totaled 300,000). They were badly crippled after the TET rout by the Allies.

A raid on the North could have been handled entirely by South Vietnamese forces, with that country's Marines and Army (ARVN) landing near Haiphong in North Vietnam, less than 60 miles from the country's capital of Hanoi. They would have been supported by the South Vietnamese Air Force and Navy, which, surprisingly, was one of the largest in the world at that time, made up mostly of French and American ships.

The United States military and its other Allies could have protected South Vietnam, keeping the NVA troops occupied, harassed, and unable to rush back to their homeland, while South Vietnam's armed forces went for victory inside the communist North.

South Vietnamese Premier and Vice President Nguyen Cao Ky was extremely disappointed that we didn't put the full court press on the staggering communists. The colorful leader said this: "The great tragedy of TET was that North Vietnamese losses were so great that I believe we might have been able to inflict serious blows had we been allowed to go over to an immediate counterattack. If only my pleas to President Johnson to let us take the offensive had been answered."

Ky, an Air Force General, added: "I wanted to send South Vietnamese troops across the border into Ho Chi Minh territory and set up a base in North Vietnam. If the communists could establish a stronghold in the

South, there was no reason why the South Vietnamese could not build a secure base in the North. With such a base we could mobilize anti-communists in the North, and become a strategic thorn to the communists, who considered North Vietnam a secure base from which to send their troops and supplies to attack us. I volunteered to parachute down into North Vietnam and command the base. Regrettably, President Johnson said 'no'."

To exacerbate the situation, Johnson ordered a drastic cut in the bombing of the north in late March of 1968, naively believing that by making such a concession, the communists would be ready to talk peace after the rout of NVA and V.C. forces in the TET Offensive.

General William Westmoreland said that a member of the International Control Commission, which was supposed to oversee the Geneva Accords, which the communists had, of course, broken, related that he had just returned from Hanoi and informed Westmoreland that the North Vietnamese leaders were grim and dejected after TET.

It was an ideal time for the Allies to strike. AGAIN, I want to strongly emphasize I am not making a case for, or against, the Vietnam War. All I know is that we were in it. If and when the President and Congress of the United States make the agonizing, difficult, and drastic decision to send America's young people to serve in an arena of combat, one would hope that victory would be the only goal. Many, perhaps most, who served in Vietnam didn't believe that their leaders who sent them there subscribed to that notion.

Ace Pilot Robin Olds, who was the genius behind Operation Bolo which had wiped out the enemy's MIG 21 fleet, visited President Johnson in the White House in 1968 after his tour in Vietnam had concluded. Olds bluntly told the president: "With all due respect to you as my Commander-in-Chief, get us the hell out of that goddamn war!" When Johnson asked how, Olds replied: "It's simple, Sir, just win it!" A perfect summation.

(Why there has never been a movie made about Robin Olds is anyone's guess. He was an all-American football player at Army – famed sportswriter Grantland Rice named him National Player-of-the-Year; is enshrined in the College Football Hall of Fame; became an Ace (pilot) in WWII; married a beautiful movie star; became an Ace again in Vietnam; and assumed the role of Commandant of Cadets at the Air Force Academy. If the two Top Gun movies can become all-time favorites, Olds' story would be a natural hit. He was truly a "maverick" in every sense of the word, including his non-regulation bushy mustache. I highly recommend the book *Fighter Pilot*, penned by his daughter, Christine.)

A theory persisted that Lyndon Johnson purposely dragged out the war because he owned an extensive amount of stock in Bell Helicopter, which sold helicopters to the U.S. government for the military effort, as well as a large number of shares in other defensive contractors. I sincerely hope that this sickening premise was not true.

At the time, despite Robin Olds' admonition, when victory seemed to be in our grasp, we didn't take advantage of it. Instead, President Johnson called for his bombing halt of Hanoi and Haiphong following the tremendous Allied successes in TET.

The communists learned early on that if they cried out "peace talks" when things were going badly for them, the U.S. would fall for the gambit *every* single time and ramp down military actions instead of going for the throat. There was a total of 16 bombing halts during the war, all largely for that reason. North Vietnamese leaders would actually shed tears in front of the cameras when talking to media members about negotiating an end to the war. They were crocodile tears.

Meanwhile, the NVA and V.C. would use the down time -- compliments of misplaced trust in the communists by U.S. leadership -- to lick their wounds, re-supply, re-build their forces, plan new strategies, and sneak back into South Vietnam. It was always a reprieve that they badly needed, and they consistently exploited the cessations. To constantly allow them those opportunities was madness on the part of the Allies (mainly due to politics in the United States).

In many ways, TET was to the communist forces in Vietnam what the Battle of the Bulge was to the Nazis in WWII. It was an all-out effort to try and break the back of the Allies. Neither worked; it was a decisive victory for the U.S. and its Allied partners in both encounters.

The only difference between the two was that in WWII, the Allies did not let up and instead applied more pressure to a demoralized enemy. They chased the beaten Germans back to their homeland and within half-a-year, the Allied forces could claim victory and an end to the war.

That did not happen following the triumphs over the NVA and V.C. in Vietnam. Failure to follow through to vanquish the communist forces after their TET debacle is reminiscent of Union General George Meade's failure to nip at the heels of the Confederates after the latter's crushing defeat at Gettysburg in the Civil War, which made President Abraham Lincoln furious. However, in the case of TET, it was the President and his cabinet's reluctance, not the general officers, to follow and inflict destruction on an exhausted and disheartened enemy.

Admiral U.S. Grant "Oley" Sharp, Commander-in-Chief, United States Pacific Commander (CINCPAC), said at the time: "We are at a crossroads; either the U.S. uses its military power at full effectiveness with provision of adequate forces, or continues a campaign of gradualism and accepts a long drawn-out contest."

President Johnson, pressured by the anti-war movement, beaten up by the press, held hostage by an antagonistic Congress, and dealing with a wishy-washy cabinet regarding Vietnam, had lost his stomach for the fight. In fact, a tired and bitter LBJ announced that he would not run for re-election at the end of March in 1968.

In my opinion, the impediment in the Johnson Administration (and briefly under Kennedy) was Secretary of Defense Robert McNamara, who was basically the main architect of the American war effort in Vietnam from 1961-1968. It seems that McNamara, a San Francisco native and University of California-Berkely graduate, started having doubts and cooled on the U.S. involvement midway through his tenure.

As later revealed, at a cocktail and dinner party involving Washington D.C. dignitaries held the first week of 1966, McNamara allegedly indicated to those in attendance that in essence, it was impossible for victory to be achieved in Vietnam. His successor in 1968, Clark Clifford, a prominent Washington D.C. attorney, was of the same ilk.

I'll ask again, if that was truly the belief of our Secretaries of Defense and others in Johnson's administration, why did they keep sending more young American boys into the Indochina slaughterhouse? The politicians were seemingly using these soldiers, many of them teenagers, as cannon fodder at that point since there was no blueprint for victory. (This is what my dad meant at the airport when we said our good-byes, when he uttered while shaking his head: "Why do old men always send young boys to war?")

How much respect would you have for a coach who didn't think his team had a chance of winning? Thank goodness the members of our American Armed Forces, who made up the different branches of service in Vietnam, didn't subscribe to that despicable thought process.

Some so-called "experts" were apprehensive that if we embarked upon an all-out final drive to win the war, China and/or the Soviet Union would up the ante and throw their full military might against the U.S. and other Allied forces to protect their North Vietnamese comrades-in-arms. I have my doubts.

If we had made it clear that we had no desire to occupy North Vietnam, even after an invasion by South Vietnamese Armed Forces, and that our only demand was simply for all sides to honor and abide by the original Geneva agreement terms regarding the borders of North and South Vietnam, I believe that this would have been given much consideration by the two communist superpowers. They knew that – at the time – they were backing the losing horse in the race.

At no other time did the United States have such an advantage of negotiating from a position of strength as it did after smashing the communist forces on the battlefield during the '68 TET Offensive. They were reeling and in dire straits.

The Soviet Union and China could have put pressure on North Vietnam to accept an agreement to return to the 17th parallel accord, with a guarantee from the South Vietnamese that it would cease combat operations in the north, pulling out its troops, and an assurance from the U.S. that it would withdraw its forces from the area altogether. All communist troops, of course, would have to settle in the north.

(Similar to the Korean border situation, fortified guard posts could have been built on each side of the DMZ serving as a buffer zone, with perhaps another comparable protective barrier on the "Ho Chi Minh trail." United Nations troops could have provided protection against aggression).

That would allow the South to remain a sovereign state that could control its own destiny without fear of further invasion from the North. In my opinion the Soviets would have definitely been receptive to that, and I believe the Chinese would have seriously contemplated it, too.

The Soviet Union and China were as war weary as the United States; they might have even been relieved to have had an "out" from the mess that was the Vietnam War, especially after the devastating (for communist forces) results of TET, although they would never have admitted it.

The Soviets, and let's face it, we're talking about Russia, had bigger fish to fry at the time, mainly trying to keep their "iron curtain" satellite states in line. Many of those countries, swallowed up by force after WWII, were clamoring for autonomy and freedom. In fact, just five months after the TET Offensive, Russian forces along with soldiers from four other Warsaw Pact nations invaded Czechoslovakia, with some 250,000 troops needed to put down an independent insurrection by the Czech people.

Most importantly the United States had a trump card to play on the Soviet Union at that very moment. During the same period as the TET invasion, the U.S. Central Intelligence Agency (CIA) had honed in on a sunken Soviet submarine that the U.S.S.R. had been unable to locate.

The search and discovery by the U.S. revolved around a Pacific missile sub that had imploded on February 24, 1968, and laid at the bottom of Pacific Ocean. Though the Soviets undertook a thorough search, they were unable to pinpoint where the accident occurred.

However, as early as March 8, 1968, with superior technological advances, the U.S. knew of the general locale of the stricken craft, but the knowledge was kept secret from Russia, with the U.S. keeping the knowledge highly classified.

This connection has never been made in any other publication or reported anywhere else to my knowledge, but perhaps if the United States had been willing to strike a deal with the Soviets, sharing the details on the missing submarine's location and offer to assist in bringing it to the surface, it could have been a major step in getting the U.S.S.R. to work with the Americans to convince North Vietnam to accept the original terms of the 1954 Geneva Accords. The Soviet Union could have informed Hanoi that it would halt the shipment of any further arms and technical aid if it did not comply.

The stricken sub lay approximately five miles deep and was almost impossible to retrieve, but the U.S.S.R. could not take a chance of it ending up in the hands of the United States. The contents of the doomed underwater ship included codebooks and cryptic information, and entry into it would allow American engineers a valuable inside look at Soviet technology.

Thus, the Russians may have been willing to strike a deal with the U.S. to put the reins on the North Vietnamese, especially since the communists were staggering after the TET defeat. Unfortunately, for whatever reason, apparently no thought was ever given to using this valuable bargaining chip and approaching the Soviets on the issue.

(During my year in Vietnam, a specially made drilling ship, tied to eccentric billionaire Howard Hughes, collected site data at the crash site from September 1970 to January, 1971. The U.S. did manage to finally bring up a section of the submarine three years later in 1974, although it was less than 12% of the 330-foot submerged wreckage. Nonetheless, it was a treasure trove of intelligence.)

War is expensive, and the Soviets were feeling the financial pinch from the Vietnam encounter, but probably not as much as the Chinese. Just a few years early, nearly 30 million Chinese citizens had died from a deadly famine due to a disastrous economic period.

Like Russia, China had more problematic headaches to deal with than the Vietnam conflict, due to internal discord and turmoil at the time. Mao's 1968 Cultural Revolution was violent and resulted in as many as 20 million additional civilian deaths.

China had lost nearly 200,000 soldiers in the Korean War less than two decades before, and despite the country's claims of non-inclusion in the Vietnam War, unconfirmed reports said that Chinese casualties were rapidly mounting again in the conflict as they were forced to help offset heavy personnel losses sustained by the North Vietnamese Army and the Viet Cong. The monetary cost of continuing to maintain that level of commitment financially-strapped the relatively young Chinese communist government.

The reader might be surprised to know that at least 12 American aircraft, most flying off course with pilots likely confused as to their exact location, were shot down over Chinese territory during the war. Yet possibly because of the problems that the communist giant was facing as mentioned above, the leadership of that country did not choose to publicly exploit the forays of U.S. aircraft into its airspace as much as might have normally been expected.

There was also the fact that at best, China and North Vietnam were uneasy partners-in-arms. The tension between the two neighboring countries, caused mainly by a historical mistrust of each other, was always smoldering just beneath the surface.

It was simply a communist collaboration between the two; they were not friends. Those countries would be in a border war against each other in less than 10 years from that time. And, of course, there was always stress and strain between China and Russia, too.

To add to all that drama, the North Vietnamese Army and Viet Cong guerillas, although communist accomplices in the Vietnam War, were growing more and more leery of each other. The NVA looked at the V.C. as undisciplined disciples.

There was conjecture that the North Vietnamese purposely made the Viet Cong bear the brunt of the fighting during the TET offensive because they knew that it would be a suicide mission. The North Vietnamese Army could then take more control of the depleted V.C. units in South Vietnam, which they ended up doing.

In the end, sadly, none of those things, all positives for the Allied side, mattered. These hypotheses were for naught because there was obviously no thought by our government of going for final victory at the most favorable time of the entire war. For whatever reason, the United States was simply not the same fearless and valiant country that it was in WWII, primarily, in my opinion, because of the difference in political leadership.

In my estimation, a triumphant conclusion, in the least an agreement to honor the Geneva pact of 1954, was in sight in the spring and summer of 1968, but those in power got cold feet at a very ill-chosen time. Simply put, it was a blown opportunity. Seven more years of war and millions of casualties could have been prevented if the decision had been made to put unbearable pressure on the North Vietnamese, forcing that government to finally observe the original Geneva agreement.

Failure to take advantage of the enormous gains made during TET 1968 was the beginning of the end. Though losing badly on the battlefield, the communists had won an unexpected major psychological victory in the U.S., thanks to slanted world media reports and a timid and indecisive U.S. government.

Although American troops would be in Vietnam for another four years, there was never another serious threat, or apparently even a desire by our government leaders, for an Allied victory. It simply became a half-hearted stalemate by those in power, particularly in the U.S. Congress. Such a stance seemed to be the objective of our politicians.

***

Why? Why did they allow almost 30,000 more young men die from that point if there was no intention of doing what it would take to be triumphant?

Still, today, there is no answer. The final shot was never heard.

CHAPTER XII
Promotion Commotion

The TET holiday of 1971, when I was in-country, was relatively quiet. There were rumors and threats of another surprise uprising by the communist forces, but there was little activity in '71. On January 27, the first day of TET that year (the same as the 1968 invasion), I wrote a letter late at night telling Nancy: "Everything is quiet and I'm fine; Charlie hasn't hit us yet anyway." Because of the significant number of American troop reductions the previous year, we were expecting the communists to take advantage of that and stage another full-scale attack on South Vietnam.

For a few days I had been seeing double and was having severe headaches. I went to a medic and he told me that it was due to eye strain. He gave me the pain-killer Darvon, which I believe has since been outlawed in the U.S., for my headaches. I remember that after taking that stuff, I wasn't seeing double, I think I was seeing pink elephants. I only took two of those pills and threw the rest of them away.

On the first day of February, a buddy of mine, who was dating a Vietnamese girl, invited me to join him to a family dinner with his girlfriend and her parents. It was a ritzy affair at a two-story white colonial-style abode of an affluent Vietnamese family.

I had read that proper manners in the country required that you do not eat until the elders had commenced the meal. The cuisine, distributed by servants, was very good, but I had a hard time with the half-hatched foul embryos (sometimes erroneously termed 1,000-year-old duck eggs). I managed to act as normally as possible as I chewed, or should I say crunched, through bones and probably a beak, not to mention claws. I had to eat it so as not to insult my hosts.

The home-grown fruit was a welcome treat. I enjoyed a fruit cocktail of bananas, apples, pears and oranges. There were also plums, pomegranates, and papayas. If my memory serves me well, I believe our main course was pork.

The head of the family apologized that he was unable to get a delicacy of monkey brains for the occasion. To this day I'm not certain if he was serious, or if he actually wanted to get a chuckle out of seeing the reactions of a good ol' Midwestern American boy at the thought of ingesting such a repugnant item (to me). Whatever, I'm glad the host's food supplier was all out of that "yummy" treat.

On February 3rd, LTC Brash called me into his office. He said: "Starr, get in here and close the door; this is pretty serious!" I entered and saw that Major Mark was also in his office. Both were stern-faced. My commanding officer told me that he had received a call from the Headquarters Commandant who told Brash some very negative things about me.

The colonel called Sergeant Reynolds into the session and asked him how he thought I had performed lately. Sarge said: "He just hasn't been doing well at all, he's been slacking off." To say I was stunned would be an understatement.

Major Mark added to the piling on: "You've really been goofing up lately." Finally I blurted out: "Sir, I've been working so hard and I'm devastated. What have I been doing wrong?" LTC Brash replied: "Well, for one thing, you are out of uniform." I was baffled; I was wearing my regular fatigues. He continued: "When you are an E-5, you're required to wear E-5 insignia!"

Then they all burst out laughing heartily, including the rest of the staff which had entered the Colonel's office by then. That's how I found out that I had been promoted to Specialist 5 (better known as Spec 5), the equivalency in rank to a sergeant. I was usually the jokester of our unit, but they had beaten me at my own game; I had been played.

Major Mark said: "I have never been so happy to see someone promoted, you really deserve it." Captain Gaines added: "It couldn't happen to a nicer guy."

I was elated and told them I felt very lucky. Sergeant Chargualof waved that off and said: "Don't say that. You have worked hard and deserve it. There's no luck involved." It's no wonder why I liked my Project Hieu staff so much!

Although it had taken two months to get the promotion after finishing number one in the rankings in December, it was still extremely gratifying. I had been promoted four times in one year, and it was my understanding that special orders for E5 rankings and above had to come from the Pentagon. I was now officially a Non-Commissioned Officer. (The bonus was a much-needed bigger paycheck.) Westmoreland called non-commissioned officers "the backbone of the Army."

LTC Brash had a succinct way of putting it: "You earned it, Starr. In life, just always make sure your 'attaboys' outnumber your 'aw shits' and you will do just fine, and you have."

Shortly following the promotion, I was getting pressure to go to Officer Candidate School (OCS) again, both from the officers in my Crypto meetings and from MACV. It was hard to keep holding them at arm's length on the matter, but the truth was, I did not want to wait any longer than needed to start my career in the field of intercollegiate athletic administration. Had I gone to OCS, I would have had to sign up for an extended period of time.

Colonel Brash said that with my new rank, my first order had to go out to my wife: She was required to send more pumpkin bread to the office!

Nancy's letter of February 4 said that Iowa was undergoing a terrible blizzard again, with snow as high as street signs. The temperature had dipped to -15 degrees. But she was consoled by the fact that just over four weeks later, the two of us would be sitting on the beach in Waikiki. Our Hawaiian R&R (Rest and Recuperation) – although soldiers crudely termed it I&I – was to begin March 1. I had already reserved our hotel room and it took me a whole $16 to do that.

I woke up with red welts all over my arms on the morning of February 7. They were obviously bug bites. They probably came from spiders. I went back to the medic, and he gave me some lotion to cover the bites. It was ugly but apparently nothing serious. Stupid spiders.

The South Vietnamese military carried out an attack on communist forces inside Laos commencing February 8. The United States provided air support but was not allowed to send ground troops into the combat zone due to the Cooper-Church Amendment. (Signs stating: WARNING! NO U.S. PERSONNEL BEYOND THIS POINT were posted on the border of South Vietnam and Laos.)

The purpose of the operation was to interrupt a huge buildup of personnel and munitions by the communist forces on the Ho Chi Minh Trail and stop a possible invasion of the South by the North Vietnamese Army from Laos. I knew this was coming; prior to the attack, this had been the primary talking point of one of the (Immersion in Incursion) meetings that I had attended requiring my Crypto clearance. It was supposed to be a top-secret operation, but somehow the press learned of the mission and ran with the story, thus eliminating any chance of the ARVN forces surprising the enemy.

In a letter dated the 8th of February, Nancy said that a bulletin had just crossed the television screen that said South Vietnamese troops had crossed into Laos. In a letter that I wrote back to her dated the 21st, I said: "The ARVN is really getting hit hard in Laos. The communists have them surrounded. The South Vietnamese have had over 100 killed today; it is really a blood bath."

The initial 17,000 ARVN troops of the invading force had run head-first into a brick wall of up to 60,000 NVA soldiers. The unfortunate leak by the media regarding the desired stealth operation allowed the communists to concentrate their effort at the attack point, stopping the South Vietnamese soldiers in their tracks.

The battle would rage on until March 25 and though it was reported as a draw, in truth it ended in defeat for the ARVN, much to the disappointment of the U.S. High Command. Both the NVA and South Vietnamese suffered heavy losses, and the U.S., providing air cover, lost over 100 helicopters and several fixed wing aircraft to North Vietnamese anti-aircraft fire. Nevertheless, enough American pilots made it through to destroy 88 communist battle tanks.

It was hoped that the aggressiveness would show the strength and strong leadership of the South Vietnamese military, but the confidence of Allied officials was badly shaken after the failed offensive. Over half of the ARVN attackers were killed, captured, wounded or missing in action.

On a more pleasant note, I received a huge card and cookies from Nancy on February 14, Valentine's Day. (She asked me if I was getting tired of all the cookies; I said I hoped that she was being facetious; it was the only decent food we had.) Somehow, I found a way to send her flowers by mail. They were supposed to be roses, but she got orchids and carnations instead. She had to pick them up at the Post Office. A couple of days after receiving the cookies, I got the pumpkin bread that LTC Brash had required after my promotion.

On February 20, I received orders telling me that I would be assigned guard duty with C Company, 3rd Pit, 3rd Squad from March 15 to May 15.

The remainder of February was pretty uneventful in my neck of the woods, with the only tragedy being two U.S. soldiers killed by a booby-trapped Jeep in Saigon. I remember that right after I received that awful news, I heard a song that seemed so appropriate at the time:

> *"Come on people now,*
> *Smile on your brother,*
> *Everybody get together*
> *Try to love one another right now."*

■ Get Together
--The Youngbloods

We didn't have catchy songs in Vietnam similar to ones the U.S. troops had in WWI and WWII, classics such as "Over There," "Boogie Woogie Bugle Boy," and "Praise the Lord and Pass the Ammunition." The popular songs with military themes during the Vietnam conflict were pretty much of the ani-war variety, including "*War*" by Edwin Starr. No relation!

CHAPTER XIII
Paradise Found

March was finally at hand, and my Rest and Recuperation vacation to Hawaii was in my sights! The most important preparation I made was to have a friend, who was just returning from his R&R to Hong Kong, bring me some Jade East After Shave and Canoe Cologne! I wasn't sure whether or not I had a certain "scent" after the seven months that I had just endured.

I had finalized all of my Hawaii R&R paperwork and plans in mid-January. I sent Nancy two copies each of MACV Form 439-R, Permissive Orders for Out-of-Country Travel, and Department of Defense Form 1580, Military Standby Authorization for Commercial Air Travel, so that she could get a discount on a flight to Honolulu. Those were proof that she had a spouse in Vietnam. She was able to get a round-trip ticket on United Airlines from Des Moines through Los Angeles on March 1 for a grand total of $325.85.

My flight plans were not as concise. Because of the uncertainties of everyday life in Vietnam, G.I.'s leaving for Hawaii were on standby. I had a Military Assistance Command Airline Passenger Ticket, Baggage Check, and Boarding Pass, Mission #207. As it turned out, I couldn't leave until March 2.

While I agonized through the 1st, waiting for a flight, I was told that a bomb had exploded in the U.S. Capitol Building in Washington D.C. early that morning. Thank goodness nobody was killed but there was extensive damage. The radical anti-war group, Weather Underground, took credit for the horrible act. How depressing for our country.

The Weather Underground, an offshoot of the Students for a Democratic Society (SDS) went on to plant bombs at the Pentagon and at the U.S. Department of State, in addition to several other government buildings, campus buildings, and banks.

I could never wrap my head around the logic of "peace" groups using such detestable violence, killing innocent everyday working people, to make their platforms known.

My Honolulu hotel reservation was for Denny's Imperial Hawaii Hotel on Lewers Street. We had a room that was rated Superior, and I paid a whopping $16 per night with the R&R discount. The hotel guaranteed us a room that was on an upper floor, with a private lanai and an ocean view. We could have stayed for free at Fort DeRussy, not far away from our hotel. No way! I wanted to divorce myself from military life for a week.

As mentioned, Nancy flew into Honolulu on March 1, but I wasn't able to get there until the next day. She learned of my delay through a phone call from General Creighton Abram's office. My buddy Chopper, who worked on Abram's staff, contacted her after I had called him knowing that he would have the wherewithal to notify Hawaii. I guess she thought the general, himself, was calling.

She had a busy day in my absence. The wife of another soldier, who was also delayed, injured her ankle and Nancy accompanied her to Tripler Army Medical Center in Honolulu.

I caught a flight from Tan Son Nhut and flew nearly 600 miles to Da Nang in the northern part of Vietnam on the first leg of my journey. From there, I was able to go directly to Honolulu. I was on Flight M212 and landed in Honolulu at 3:30 p.m. My fellow military passengers and I had to process through public health (showing our shot records), immigration, and customs.

We were then transported to Fort DeRussy by military bus. I had to smile because there was no wire window protection necessary unlike the last military bus in which I had ridden on my first day in Vietnam.

At Fort DeRussy, we finally re-united with our loved ones who were gathered there to welcome us at the Maluhia Service Club. Obviously, it was a very emotional time for everyone. Nancy and I had not seen each other for over seven months. Coincidentally, March 2 was the same date that I had seen Nancy for the first time in months following the conclusion of basic training the previous year.

At first it was rather orderly as we all entered in somewhat of a line where our family members were located, but after all soldiers were adorned with leis from island girls dressed in grass skirts, all heck broke loose when the G.I.'s and wives/girlfriends rushed towards each other, engaging in crushing hugs that lasted for at least 15 minutes. It was a surrealistic scene with nobody wanting to let go, for fear that it was really just a dream. Finally, we had to listen to a brief orientation and fill out emergency locator forms.

We were informed that "serious violations such as boisterous conduct, excessive public drinking, political agitation, and disturbances will result in your immediate return to Vietnam." No problem there, General! (Oh, one question…. what is considered "excessive" drinking?)

Still another of my high school classmates was involved in my Vietnam experience. Linda Ziegeler was meeting her husband at Fort DeRussy the day after Nancy and I were there. (Linda barely beat me out for Salutatorian of my high school class. Well, perhaps barely might not be the correct word. Academically she was ahead of me along with a couple of other classmates... perhaps dozens....probably hundreds.)

I had rented a white Dodge Challenger convertible to have available for our stay in Hawaii. When we got to the hotel, I quickly saw the stunning panoramic viewpoint from our deck. Nancy had already checked into our room the day before. We were right on Waikiki Beach and the view of the ocean and of Honolulu were picturesque, especially for a couple of small-town Iowa kids.

It goes without saying that it was a magical week. It's hard to explain what it's like going from where I had been to a place that was absolute paradise. That is not a slam on Vietnam, which is a beautiful country; I was just not there at a good time in its history.

On our first full day, Nancy and I just enjoyed being together again, walking along and sitting on Waikiki Beach, and then taking a stroll downtown. We then retired back to our room and ordered a pizza from a chain we had never heard of, which turned out to be a mistake.

After the delivery man had dropped it off, we both sat down to have our first bite and both of us made sour faces. It was terrible! We both said "yuck" and then started to giggle. We didn't even want the smell of it in our room. I took it out to find a trash can in the hall, but after a futile search, instead, I put it in an empty elevator and sent it to the first floor. Maybe somebody else had different taste buds and could enjoy it.

On day two, Nancy and I went to the huge Ala Moana Shopping Center to do some power shopping; well, what our small budget could afford anyway. When in

Hawaii, dress as the Hawaiians do, so we bought some clothes to blend in just a tad better. I was SO glad to get out of my fatigues for a week.

The following day we drove our convertible, top down, of course, around the entire island of Oahu, staying as close to water as possible. We stopped for a while to enjoy the exploits of some excellent surfers and then continued around, periodically pausing at other awe-inspiring sites. Our timing was perfect as we pulled into our hotel just as the sun was going down. We sped up to our room and were observers to a spectacular sunset.

Another foray outside of the hotel took us to the U.S.S. Arizona Memorial, which had only opened eight years before our visit. The somber setting honored the dead from the Japanese attack on Pearl Harbor, which prompted America's entry into World War II.

I was surprised to see that bubbles were still rising from the bottom of the ill-fated ship after 29 years. A total of 2,403 U.S. military personnel and 68 civilians lost their lives on that December 7, 1941, date, with thousands of others badly injured.

There were 353 Japanese planes used in the raid, with 29 of them being shot down. They came in two waves, with 183 aircraft (mostly Mitsubishi Zeroes) in the first and 170 in the second after taking off from a 33-ship task force. All but one destroyer of that 33-ship Imperial Navy armada was eventually sunk by the Americans and their Allies later in the war.

On the day of the unexpected assault, there were 94 ships in Pearl Harbor (named because of its fertile pearl-producing oyster beds in the 1800's). Eighteen of the moored warships were damaged or sunk. Fifteen were repaired and returned to action. Three -- Arizona, Utah, and Oklahoma – all battleships, were total losses.

A total of 390 American military aircraft were stationed on Oahu, but only 38 got into the air during the Japanese incursion, and 10 were shot down. Several were destroyed because they were parked close together to avoid sabotage from the ground. They became easy targets from the air.

Coincidentally, the movie Tora, Tora, Tora, an outstanding movie about the surprise Japanese attack on Pearl Harbor, had just been released to theaters, and Nancy and I went to see it on the same day that we had visited the Arizona. It was a great way to get an even better perspective of what had transpired.

(How intelligent is it to leave a place of war to relax at a beautiful paradise, and then go to a movie about war when you get there?)

I picked up and read a newspaper only once during my week in Hawaii, wanting to avoid reading about anything relating to Vietnam. I should have stuck to that practice.

One of the first articles I read regarded a Viet Cong attack on Song Mao, the small camp that I had visited less than two months earlier. I wondered how the 34 Americans stationed there fared in the battle. From what I could ascertain, the outcome was probably not positive.

As the saying goes, all good things must end, and the R&R that Nancy and I had looked forward to for so long drew to a close on March 8. We went to the Oahu airport together and both of us flew out that day, but I had to leave first.

In the letter that she wrote on the day of her return home, Nancy said: "I went to the railing above where I knew you would walk to your plane. I saw you come out and head for it. I wanted to run after you and beg you to stay….to come with me. I stood there and watched that plane leave. It was the loneliest moment of my life."

I felt bad for Nancy when I left and was glad that she had made a new friend at Fort DeRussy when the two of them were waiting for their husbands to arrive a week earlier. Fortunately, the new acquaintance was on the same flight during the first leg (to Los Angeles) of Nancy's journey back home. I was so glad that she did not have to be alone. They talked and vowed not to break down; they were a huge help to each other as they wiled away the time until their flight to L.A. lifted off a few hours later.

It wasn't a bed of roses for me, either. Euphoria morphed into melancholy. It was a needed break, and I'm glad we waited until after I had served seven months. Only five months of my year's tour remained. We were over the hump. Nonetheless I was in the doldrums for a few days after our marvelous vacation.

In Hawaii I had given Nancy a copy of a drawing that was passed out among the soldiers in 'Nam. It was a color-by-numbers piece, with 365 spaces; one to be filled in daily. When it was finished, it was an artist's conception of a smiling girl sitting on her knees, sans clothing. I had one back at MACV and filled it in day-by-day. Nancy did the same after she got back home. She asked me that if she colored it in all at once, would that mean that I could come home immediately?

CHAPTER XIV
A Case of Abduction

When I returned to my base from R&R, I received a notice that there had been reports of some clown in Iowa who was playing a very sick game. He was calling wives and/or parents known to have loved ones in Vietnam, and falsely notifying them that their husband or son had been killed.

We were instructed to tell our families to be aware of this deranged imposter, and to again inform them as to the proper government procedure of notification if we were to meet our demise. Thus, I sent that information along to Nancy and to my Mom and Dad.

Soldiers knew that their loved ones back home worried about them, but what many might not understand is that we were concerned about our folks back in the U.S. to possibly a greater extent, because we knew the stress that they were constantly under. We were obviously aware as to when we were, or were not, in harm's way, but the unknowing was a constant anguish for them.

Unhinged nutcases like this evil person spreading false KIA information only added to the anxiety. Mothers, fathers, wives, girlfriends, children and other beloved individuals in my home state were aware of the reality of what could happen; a total of 855 Iowans lost their lives in the war. Thus, it would have been understandable for a family member to naively believe the erroneous horrible news from a demented individual.

(My little state has paid a terrible price on our nation's battlefields. Iowa suffered over 13,000 killed in action in the Civil War; 6,816 in WWII (including 85 at Pearl Harbor and 68 at Normandy); 2,251 in WWI; 855 in Vietnam; 558 in Korea; 64 in Iraq; and 31 in Afghanistan.)

I noticed a letter from William L. Boyd, President of the University of Iowa, included in my stacked-up mail upon my return. It was dated February 26, and had been delivered when I was in Hawaii. I had corresponded with Dr. Boyd on February 10, requesting that I be allowed to receive my degree without requiring me to finish my final three hours in foreign language (i.e. fourth semester Portuguese). If the university would do so, I could receive my diploma.

President Boyd took my inquiry to the Liberal Arts Adjustment Committee and while they would not release me from the requirement, I was informed that I would be allowed to complete it via a correspondence course. I would also be allowed to enroll for my Masters' Degree with the three hours of credit remaining but would have to take that final course while attending graduate school. In addition to the professional letter, Dr. Boyd included a very nice personal note and closed by saying "the University is proud to be associated with you, Tom."

(Following my service duty, I researched where I could complete my degree requirement and learned that Brigham Young University offered the correspondence course in Portuguese that I would need to finish my undergrad requirement. Thus, I became a parttime BYU Cougar to earn my B.A. from Iowa. It would be years later before I visited that school's beautiful campus in Provo, Utah to attend a football game.)

I caught up on some newspaper reading, including perusing the latest issue of *Stars and Stripes*. Most of the news concerned the ongoing battle between ARVN and NVA troops in Laos, but there were some other articles of interest from back in the states. For example, I read that the ocean liner Queen Mary was being retired to the port of Long Beach, California. Many years later, I would reside in a high-rise apartment that overlooked the fabled ship in that city.

A couple of things that I missed out on when I was on R&R was the arrest of one of our resident mama-sans, who was proven to be a Viet Cong collaborator, and the apprehension of two soldiers who lived in my barracks.

My understanding is that the mama-san was attempting to plant an explosive device in our billet when she was caught in the treacherous act by an American G.I. The two American military men who had been nabbed by M.P.'s were charged with numerous drug offenses.

In a continued de-escalation of the American involvement in the war, the U.S. Army announced that the Green Berets would be leaving Vietnam the second week of March. The 5th Special Forces Group would be returning home to Ft. Bragg in the States. At their peak, there were 80 Green Beret Camps dotting the Cambodian and Laotian borders, with some 2,800 Green Berets working with ethnic groups such as the Montagnard's. A few of the Special Forces soldiers would stay in the country as advisors during the drawdown.

Somebody gave me a March edition of *Newsweek*, which had a cover story titled "The Helicopter War." It featured a photo of both an Apache and a Ranger chopper and it was an interesting read. Nobody had to tell me about it being a helicopter war, though!

I received my official guard duty orders on the 15th of March. This was more intense and serious than my simple one-man guard chores of the previous fall. I would now be on permanent assignment for two months. I had to appear before a battalion staff and be ready to answer questions regarding standard operating procedures (SOP). I was also informed that I would be a squad leader; my recent promotion again translated into more responsibilities.

We were required to know our entire chain of command; our primary line of fire; the meaning of a red star cluster and a green and red star cluster fired simultaneously; and be knowledgeable of what was indicated by an intermittent siren and a steady siren.

Star clusters were only used when radio contact was lost or not readily available. Red star cluster (a flare) meant that there had been enemy contact and assistance was requested; a red star cluster and green star cluster fired together meant "cease fire," usually to indicate that friendly forces were returning and needed to pass through our lines.

An intermittent siren indicated an attack by mortar or artillery fire, while a steady siren indicated that a ground attack was underway.

We would be on duty every fourth night and on standby the three nights in between. We had to be available to be assembled in no less than three hours when we were on standby. Our duty would run from 1830 hours (6:30 p.m.) to 0630 (6:30 a.m.).

According to my orders from the battalion commander, Perimeter Defensive Force duty "has priority over other duty." The regulations went on to say that those who were absent would face disciplinary action, unless they were on leave, on R&R, hospitalized, or had special permission from the C.O. (commanding officer).

My already busy schedule was getting even more intense. I still had to tend to my workload with Project Hieu and be ready on a moment's notice to use my Crypto clearance for meetings requiring top secret information. Now I had my sentry chores, too. (The battalion commander of the Perimeter Defensive Force would have learned differently that the guard duty had "priority over other duty" if I had been called on for my Crypto chores.)

The commencement of my guard duties was delayed one week, so I took an opportunity to accompany a buddy into Saigon on a rare weekend off. When we got into the heart of the city on Friday night, he informed me that he was going to get a "massage" from a local establishment.

We turned off on a side street from Plantation Road to enable him to visit his sought-out establishment. I told him that I was going to find a nearby bar and just have a beer while I waited for him.

I was a little nervous because we were far away from the main traffic area of Saigon, off the beaten path so to speak, and when I entered the bar, I immediately realized that I was the tavern's only customer.

I felt a sense of apprehension because I had not seen any other American G.I.'s around the region we were in, and you always wanted to avoid being caught alone without some of your "brothers" in close proximity. In addition, we had carried no weapons on that trip into Saigon (disallowed for non-official business in the capital city).

A petite Vietnamese waitress came over to my small round table and I ordered a Ba Muoi Ba beer, made in the home country. She brought me the bottle with the famous "33" on the label well known to American troops. Halfway through my second bottle, I started to feel woozy. Something was wrong, the bartender and waitress, the only other inhabitants of the small saloon other than me, seemed to be moving in slow motion and their voices sounded distant, plus my eyes wouldn't focus. I passed out.

I'll make this short. In essence, I was abducted and held for over three days, obviously drugged the entire time. I hesitated to include this in the book because frankly, I don't have any idea what transpired in that time. In what I believe was a brief moment of consciousness during my ordeal, I did see that I was in a small room with cement walls coated with green mold, and I was apparently lying on a bamboo mat. Perhaps I simply imagined all that.

An Air Force Intelligence report just a few months earlier warned about an uptick and emphasis on kidnappings by the Viet Cong. The V.C. had a bounty on American soldiers and when one was captured, he would be turned over to the North Vietnamese Army. I can only surmise that was what happened.

Did it have anything to do with my work with Project Hieu, my Crypto clearance, or even possibly my new guard leadership role? I don't see how that could have been possible; how would my captors have known about my association with any of those unless a villainous person with that knowledge was following me of which I was not aware?

Somehow, I eventually ended up in the back of a U.S. Army deuce-and-a-half truck. How I got there I don't know. I was very groggy and disoriented. Had I been rescued? Did I somehow manage to escape, and this unit found me? That's doubtful. I have to believe that these soldiers had liberated me.

Though my mind was still adrift, I later recalled lying on the floor, propped up against the wooden slats behind the rear of the cab in the middle of GI's sitting on the side benches. I was in and out of consciousness.

After a length of undetermined time, the driver stopped at what was some type of medical facility. I was assisted into the structure and placed on a gurney, a bed or a cot of some sort and was alone in a hallway, I think. I had no idea as to my location.

The Army had 23 hospitals, plus mobile units that could quickly be moved and constructed, in Vietnam (similar to the portable camps featured in the Korean

War television show M*A*S*H). The Navy had one hospital in-country plus two medical ships offshore; and the Air Force had one hospital but airlifted many wounded to facilities in other countries. Heck, as far as I knew, in my confused state, I could have been in a pup tent in Pocatello.

Eventually I started to revive a little bit and, despite nausea and a pounding headache, regaining somewhat of a thought process. I laid there for what seemed to be a rather long spell and finally decided that I wanted to get back to my base. I did not need to take up the precious time of any of the doctors who were required to tend to the wounded. I assumed that someone had given me a quick, cursory checkup and made the determination that I did not need immediate attention, opting to care for those who required prompt treatment in a warzone (rightfully so).

Although I heard a lot of hustle and bustle, I only saw one young PFC scurry past me. I stood up but was extremely dizzy. Finding an exit, I simply walked (wobbled?) out, apparently undetected.

A Spec 4 was jumping into a jeep parked outside, close to the facility, and I waved him down, asking where he was going. He said he had to pick up an individual at the Hotel Continental, which was great news for me because his destination indicated that we were in close confines of Saigon. I could catch a cyclo back to the MACV compound at Pentagon East from the hotel.

I begged him for a ride and after he looked up and down at this scroungy, dirty G.I. (embarrassingly, my bladder did its own thing without my knowledge, probably several times, in my unconscious state), he begrudgingly agreed. I did outrank him, which might have helped.

Frankly, during the ride, I felt awful. I was still nauseous, and my splitting headache was killing me, especially in the bright sunshine. On the positive side I was now starting to think rationally, but I was still trying to figure out what had happened to me.

I told my Jeep driver about my mysterious captivity, hence my grungy look (and distinct scent, I'm sure), but couldn't give him any details regarding my ordeal, simply because I didn't know any. He wanted to take me back to the medical unit, probably because I was still shaky and had asked him a couple of times to stop because I thought I was going to vomit. I convinced him not to turn around because I had to report back to my base pronto and promised that I would visit the infirmary there.

As we approached the Continental Hotel, I needed to bother my new Spec 4 friend for one more favor. My abductors had confiscated my money.

Without any funds, I had to borrow some piasters or MPC's to get back to my outfit. Thank goodness he was a gracious guy and was sympathetic to my plight. He gave me enough to pay a cyclo driver and a little extra to buy a small French baguette and a drink from a nearby sidewalk vendor. I promised to reimburse him by sending him the amount, which I did later (with a nice tip) after getting him to write down his unit's mailing address. I didn't eat much of my "meal" but it did seem to give me a little bit of a boost.

I went into the Continental Hotel and found the nearest restroom. There was security posted in the lobby, but the guard waved me through when I told him I needed to use the restroom. I wanted to at least attempt to clean myself up the best that I could before reporting back to base. I located a sink with a mirror above it. Hardly recognizing the unshaven, red-eyed, unkempt tired-looking person staring back at me, I scrubbed my fatigues and bathed the best I could from that small basin.

When I finally made it back to my compound via my three-wheeled paid transportation, I was still frail and sluggish. I went to LTC Brash's office immediately; I knew that I had to report to my commanding officer ASAP. I must have looked like a fright to those who saw me. Luckily, only two others were in our Project Hieu offices when I arrived.

The colonel and I met behind closed doors, and I tried to tell him what had happened to the best of my recollection. As it turned out, I had been gone for 3 ½ days. Nobody was suspicious of wrong-doing because I had been given a three-day pass prior to the start of my guard duties. However, this was the fourth day, and it was mid-afternoon. Brash thought that I might have been attending another Crypto (Immersion in Incursion) session and I had just forgotten to tell him.

After asking him if he had any aspirin for my headache (he did, and I took three), I explained to my C.O. that I wasn't too worried about having unwittingly divulged any secret information to my abductors because the last Crypto meeting I had attended was rather uneventful. The primary point of discussion during that summit regarded the current state of affairs in Laos, and no concrete decisions had been made at that particular conclave.

Even if I had been unknowingly interrogated, Charlie couldn't have learned anything of importance. What puzzled me was how they could keep me incapacitated as long as they did. Obviously, I was drugged. Were they giving me injections? I did have some black and blue marks on my arms and legs, were they syringe tracks? Or were they perhaps forcing liquid or pills down my throat? Who knows?

I wasn't physically abused at all, except for a few bumps, scrapes, and bruises, probably from dragging me into my designated captive quarters, and really didn't have any pain other than the effects of the apparent drugging and confinement, causing the headache and nausea. I had sustained several bug bites. Surprisingly,

I wasn't particularly thirsty or hungry; had I been given sustenance during my captivity? Perhaps the soldiers on my rescue truck had helped me drink water.

I asked the Colonel if we could just keep this between us. In fact, I pleaded with him. If I had to make an official report about the incident, I was worried that I would have to go before various committees, fill out an after-action report, and be grilled by investigators because of my Crypto clearance. But frankly, I told LTC Brash, I didn't have anything to report because I had absolutely no memory of my time away, so it wouldn't be of any value.

I had built up a close relationship with Brash and after considering it, following more begging on my part, he respected my request. I was greatly relieved. For one thing, I was worried that I might have my Crypto clearance taken away from me.

My C.O. did tell me that he was going to report the location of the bar to a high-ranking officer friend of his in the 716th Military Police Battalion, which oversaw security and law enforcement in the Saigon region. I was fine with that. One thing I did recall was the name of the side street my buddy and I had taken that fateful night, so I gave that to the Colonel. I could not, however, remember the name of the establishment where I was captured.

Brash theorized that I had been taken by V.C. collaborators, seeking a reward, to a holding camp to be picked up by NVA interrogators enroute to a prisoner of war (POW) facility. He further speculated that the U.S. Army unit that rescued me had the way station where I was being held under surveillance for various criminal and villainous activities (possibly including abductions) and extracted me from my cell.

Was I the only soldier being held there? I'm pretty certain I was the only rescued captive on the Army truck that I was riding in, but there may have been other such vehicles in a caravan.

For several seconds, LTC Brash quietly stared at me intently, studying me, through squinted eyes and sporting a worried expression. It was more of a fatherly concern than a commanding officer's concern. He wanted to know if I was really all right after my kidnapping and forced confinement. I wanted to relieve his anxiety about the situation, so I grinned and told him: "Well, Colonel, it wasn't the Waldorf-Astoria, but I obviously slept well."

After meeting with Brash I asked permission to go have some chow and then head "home" to really clean up. He mockingly held his nose and said that I might want to reverse that order! Though I was getting my hunger back, I took his advice and went back to my barracks to take a nice, long shower and put on some clean fatigues. I can't describe how good that felt after what I had been through; it made me feel like a new person. The aspirin had also lowered the level of my headache significantly and my stomach had somewhat settled down.

I found a cook in the mess hall who was nice enough to provide me with some chow during off hours after explaining my situation. Unfortunately, I overdid it. It was stupid of me, and I regretted it later because loading my plate after going almost four days possibly without eating (to my knowledge), plus the effects of any drugs that might have remained in my system, really messed up my gastrointestinal tract for an extended time. One positive was that the food did further ratchet down the pain from my headache.

From there, I proceeded to the base infirmary to get something for the insect bites, nausea, and headache. There was a Spec 5 on duty -- I assume he was a medic -- and he was able to get me the medicine I needed without the necessity of me having to see a doctor and also without having to divulge the reasons for my maladies, which I really didn't want to discuss. He insisted on taking my temperature, and I did have a small fever. He said that it could have been from the bug bites.

Upon reflection, I did the wrong thing. I should have agreed to be hospitalized, which is what my C.O. had urged me to do before he relented to my pleas. There was the possibility that later on I might have had some serious lingering medical problems from whatever had happened to me during my imprisonment. Machismo is part of a young man's makeup, especially in a war zone. My reluctance to be treated stemmed from that, but so did embarrassment, anger, and a desire to get back to normal.

It was also selfish of me because I should have filed an official report to stop the possibility of the same thing happening to another soldier. However, I do take solace in the fact that I had no idea what I would have stated regarding the location of the place where I was imprisoned because I simply did not know.

I also took comfort in the fact that my account regarding the site of the bar that I gave to LTC Brash was passed along to the Military Police. The colonel later told me that he learned that all the bars on that side street were shut down by Saigon Police. Thus, at least the establishment I had chosen couldn't kidnap another G.I. Hopefully the proprietors were arrested.

Despite my stubbornness of not agreeing to a thorough medical evaluation, I was fortunate to be my old self within a week.

I would do anything to know what had transpired in my nearly four "lost" days. It was a surreal experience. Please don't ask, your guess is as good as mine. The thought of having possibly been a prisoner of war, with the chance of summary execution, chilled me to the bone. The inhumane, vicious, and downright disgusting treatment of American captives by the North Vietnamese was well-documented.

The rules of war, particularly regarding captured prisoners, as outlined in the Geneva Convention, meant absolutely nothing to the communists. Instead, regular debilitating torture by sadistic guards was standard operating procedure.

I had my Geneva Convention identification card on me at the time of my capture, but that wouldn't have mattered; it would have been as useless as my Newton library card.

If I was indeed a POW, mine had to be the shortest such tenure of the war. As LTC Brash theorized, my captors, whom I termed the Keystone Kops of Kidnappers, were Viet Cong sympathizers looking for a bounty payday by turning over an American soldier to North Vietnamese forces. My abductors delivered me to a POW "halfway house."

I would still like to know how they kept me sedated for so long. Sitting alone in that bar with nobody around, I was easy pickings for them. I had made myself a target by being isolated from any other U.S. military personnel in a shady area of Saigon; it was pure foolishness on my part. I made certain I was never unaccompanied again during my remaining time in Vietnam.

The worst part about the whole ordeal to me was the fact that I never had the opportunity to thank the guys who saved me from God-only-knows-what my fate could have been.

My friend whom I had escorted to Saigon on the previous Friday evening simply thought that I had blown him off since the bar I had gone to was closed after he had finished his business. He figured that I had returned to base on my own, and I didn't tell him differently.

However, I did inform him: "Next time, pick a different wing man."

CHAPTER XV
"Highway" Through Hell

On March 28, some 50 Viet Cong sappers infiltrated Fire Support Base Mary Ann of the Americal Division in Quang Tin Province, killing 30 American soldiers and wounding 82. It saddened me when I read the report; these G.I.'s were within days of going back home, with the base being converted to a South Vietnamese Army facility within a couple of weeks. How heart-breaking for the families back in the United States who had probably already made homecoming party arrangements.

There were repercussions. Charges were made that guards around the base had become lax, possibly because they knew they only had a few days remaining in their one-year tours. Several individuals faced dereliction of duty charges. Disciplinary action was taken against the division commander, assistant division commander, and four other officers.

On the topic of disciplinary measures, the Army announced on March 29, 1971 that platoon leader First Lieutenant William Calley, Jr. had been convicted of the murder of "at least" 22 civilians during the evil slaughter at My Lai three years earlier. He was sentenced to dismissal from the service and confinement at hard labor for life. It was reduced to 10 years by Secretary of the Army Howard Callaway. Incredibly (and to me, inappropriately), he ended up only serving 3 ½ years under house arrest, living in his apartment at Fort Benning.

Westmoreland insinuated that the officer corps had been watered down because of the necessity of war, and that Calley should never have been an officer in the U.S. Army; it "exceeded his abilities." The Commanding General went on to say that the Army had lowered its standards to fill the needed number of officers for the war effort.

He may well have been correct. Calley went to four different high schools in four years and flunked out of community college before joining the Army. He attended Officer Candidate School (OCS) and despite having a poor academic record, he graduated one year before the My Lai tragic event, probably to fill the roles of much-needed junior officers in 'Nam.

In addition, it was learned that the unit which carried out the atrocity had been deployed to Vietnam before completing its training because of the rapidly increasing deployment rate mandated by President Johnson at the time.

March had turned to April and for the first time I was starting to feel like a "short-timer," someone who could finally see the end of his tour. I would become a "two-digit midget" (less than 100 days to go) in the middle of the month. We used to say, "I'm so short that I can't have a long conversation." I was jumping the gun just a bit; I still had four months remaining.

In Nancy's first letter of the month, she said that Captain Crump, a former Project Hieu staff member who had completed his year in Vietnam and was back in the states, called her from Baltimore to tell her I was doing fine. That was very thoughtful of him. Nancy also informed me that my friends and high school classmates,

Doug and Tanya Auten, had their baby girl on April 9, missing out on my birth date of April 12.

Non-denominational Easter services were conducted on April 11, and I attended them with my buddies on the MACV compound, with services starting at 8:15 a.m. (I said a special "thank you" for helping me escape my recent forced confinement!)

Nancy sent a decorated cake to me for my birthday on the 12th. Well, I should say TRIED to send me a cake! It hardly resembled one when it finally got to me on April 15. Somewhere between Newton, Iowa and Saigon, Vietnam, it had apparently been used as a soccer ball, run over by a steamroller, and dropped from an airplane. What a mess. Despite being a bit dry from being in transit for six days, it still tasted great!

My mom's birthday card was touching. She said: "I'll never forget the day you were born and how happy I was that I had another son. Only at the time of my happiness, I never dreamed of you having to go to war. I keep praying for your safety and for the time to go fast."

I received somewhat of another birthday gift on April 14 from Uncle Sam. I got my special orders for my DEROS (Date Eligible for Return from Overseas). It was for July 30, which was no surprise, but it still warmed my heart just to see it!

On the 16th I received a letter from University of Iowa Head Basketball Coach Dick Shultz, responding to a note I had sent him a couple of weeks earlier. He had just completed his first year after replacing legendary Ralph Miller.

Dick, who would eventually go on to become the executive director of the NCAA, had a rough start following an icon like Miller, who developed three national powerhouses at Wichita State and Oregon State in addition to his nationally-ranked teams at Iowa, and only had three losing seasons in 38 years of coaching. Coach Shultz's first Hawkeye team finished 9-15 overall.

In his note to me, Schultz said: "Of course we had hoped that the season would have been much better. We lost 9 games by a total of 22 points. I am sure that you heard about the situation with Jim Speed, and this had a great effect on our season. He was looking like a super player and probably would have given us 15-20 points a game from an area where we were not getting anything from. With him, we probably would have been the surprise team of the league."

Speed, a 6-7 junior college transfer who was an elite recruit for Iowa -- spurning some 85 other scholarship offers -- tragically went blind from a serious sinus infection caused by meningitis prior to the season. He never played a game for the Hawks.

I received a letter from U. of I. Sports Information Director George Wine on the same day. I had learned that his assistant, Tim Simmons, was leaving, and I informed George of my interest in the open position by mail. Wine was very receptive until he learned that my tour of duty ran another three months; he needed someone immediately. George tabbed my classmate, Phil Haddy, who went on to have a long and illustrious career for the Hawkeyes, including a lengthy stint as the head S.I.D. Simmons and Haddy remain buddies to this day.

It seems that I had been having my share of unique adventures and experiences since the beginning of the new year (i.e. kidnapping, helicopter crashes, near drowning, Hawaiian vacation, etc.), and I added another in April.

Sergeant Chargualof and I had to take a trip to Long Binh, Bien Hoa, and Xuan Loc (zwan lock) in mid-May. Instead of jumping on a chopper, we took a Jeep. Our assignment was to deliver unmarked (for security reasons) bags of Military Payment Certificates to bases in those three areas. Perhaps it was in preparation for a secret "C" Day, when G.I.'s had to exchange their existing MPC's for newer bills to help stop merchants from hoarding the military currency for the purpose of trading them for American dollars.

I have no idea how we drew that duty because it was totally out of our realm; maybe it was because nobody would have suspected us doing such a chore. We had to wear sidearms as well as carry our M16's on the expedition. Sometimes you just scratched your head; shouldn't that have been an assignment for the Military Police or payroll officers or some similar entity?

Again, I guess the decision was to have someone inconspicuous deliver the goods, and I was given permission to miss out on my guard activities for a couple of days. (Trying to figure out the ways of the Army would have driven me bonkers if I had dwelled on it.)

On our return trip, we received a report that the Viet Cong had cut off part of the main route that we would normally have taken back to our base. Chargualof, who was in his third tour in 'Nam, knew the area well and said: "No sweat, I know some back roads we can take."

We dipped down south, and our detour primarily consisted of dirt roads. After a short while, we came upon a hamlet that seemed to have more churches than residential huts. Sergeant told me that it was a settlement of Vietnamese citizens who erected the numerous places of worship to celebrate their freedom of religion. I simply referred to it as the "Village of Churches." I have no idea as to the location's actual name.

Our trip continued and we were soon pretty much in the countryside featuring thick vegetation, which was always a little disconcerting when you don't know if the area was controlled by friend or foe (and it could always change at a moment's notice).

The sound of small automatic weapons fire and explosions, which could be from one of many sources, plus the occasional sight of bellowing smoke rising to the sky, were not uncommon in the rural areas and we experienced them all on our drive, albeit they all seemed to be a good distance away.

I had faith in Antonio's knowledge of the landscape. I really liked the sergeant; he was an interesting guy who, among other talents, was an excellent guitar player. During our ride, I asked him to tell me all about Guam, his home. I worried about him, though, because he had a bad stomach. He would constantly chew Rolaids as if they were candy.

In a strange way our side trip was kind of fun. I enjoyed being away from the rigors of work back at Pentagon East; it was as if we were simply out on a Sunday drive in a convertible with the top down!

Several minutes after going through the Village of Churches, in the distance, I could make out something quite dark ahead of us. Was it a tunnel of some sort? Possibly a cave? As we drew near, much to my utter horror, I could see what was partially blacking out the light…. spiders! Zillions of them!

For several yards, there were multitudes of the creepy critters spaced out on each side of the road, with their webbing starting on wires strung between telephone pole-like structures spaced at intervals (there might have been some netting, too) and going all the way to the ground. Here we were, in our olive drab Army Jeep with no top, ready to drive on this narrow dirt path between these freaks.

Approaching this purgatory on earth, I said: "Crap, Sarge, let's turn back. We've got our M-16's and 45's; I would rather take on Charlie blocking the highway than I would these monsters!" They seemed much more sinister than the bad guys did at that point. "Heck," I continued, " I would rather take on the entire North Vietnamese Army rather than going through this!" I was being facetious. Sort of.

Later, it was explained to me that these spiders were purposely kept by Vietnamese farmers, who would place mason-like jars on the ground to catch the webbing as it would eventually fall. The contents were then sent to Japan and used in making microscopic lenses. From my understanding, they were probably golden silk orb spiders although they looked black to me, and their webbing was also used for making fishing line and nets.

Now, if there are any entomologists reading this, I am the first to admit that I don't know if any of these details are factual, but what I DO know is that we had to drive through the middle of what seemed like thousands of spiders on each side of what was no more than a thin trail in a completely open vehicle.

I was frozen at the thought of a strong wind blowing these hideous creatures on to us. I had so many chills down my spine that it turned into an icicle. Each of those pests appeared to be the size of a small sports car to me. That's probably why I hadn't seen any of the elephants that were supposedly in Vietnam; these eight-legged mutants had probably eaten them all.

Okay, maybe they weren't *quite* that big, but that five-minute ride through the gauntlet of arachnids was the most nerve-wracking of my life. I called this "Village of the Spiders," but deep in the recesses of my brain, it was "Village of the Damned." You might have guessed by now that I don't like spiders.

(Yes, I am aware that spiders control insects and without them, our food supply would be in danger, but they are still stupid, and I personally think they come from outer space.)

When we had finally passed the last poles and were back in the clear and spider-free, I said: "Hey Sarge…." He looked at me and responded: "Yeah?" Looking straight ahead, I blurted out: "Pass me those fucking Rolaids!"

CHAPTER XVI
Paranormal Encounter

The anti-war movement was in full swing back home. I understood: The Vietnam War was extremely controversial and unpopular. I am 100% behind protesting; it's the right of every American. Thank goodness we live in a country with those kinds of freedoms.

However, what I read in 1971 regarding a protest in our nation's capital made me sick. On April 23, some half-a-million protesters marched through the streets of Washington D.C. That part was fine, what was not fine was this: Some were carrying and waving the flag of North Vietnam in addition to photos of Ho Chi Minh, and were chanting, "Ho, Ho, Ho Chi Minh, NLF is gonna win!"

Ho Chi Minh, of course, had been the leader of our enemy forces – the communists – and NLF were the initials of National Liberation Front, a.k.a. the Viet Cong. In other words, these "Americans" in our capital were cheering *against* their own native sons on the battlefield. They wanted the United States and its Allies to lose, and they wanted the communist forces who were invading a sovereign nation (South Vietnam) to win.

Stunned, dispirited, and disillusioned would be adjectives to describe the feelings of me and my buddies. It was one thing to be against a war, but it was something far different to be cheering for the enemy. It was hard enough being in Vietnam, but to have your fellow countrymen rooting against you, hoping the U.S. would lose the war, was devastating. Furthermore, captured secret COSVN documents accentuated that this and other protest marches were huge morale boosters for the communist forces. That was a blow to those of us representing our nation.

> "It wasn't me that started that old crazy Asian War,
> But I was proud to go and do my patriotic chore."
>
> ■ Ruby, Don't Take Your Love to Town
> --Kenny Rogers

I often wondered what would have happened to protesters in the early 1940's if they had marched down any street in America, let alone in our nation's capital, carrying Nazi Swastika and Imperial Japan rising sun flags in addition to pictures of Hitler and Hirohito, chanting: "Adolf Hitler's gonna win."

The FBI issued a report that Chinese agents were secretly fostering the anti-war movement in the U.S. Another report stated that they would help instigate protests and then slowly and silently slip into the background and leave the premises altogether undetected once the revolt had blossomed with local dissidents.

In addition to these pep rallies for the communists in our own country, we also had to swallow hard when we learned that church groups from the United States were sending large sums of money (a good source indicated a total of $10 million) to the NVA and V.C. for "humanitarian purposes." The cash didn't go for that, of course, unless you consider bullets "humanitarian."

As an added slap in the face, actress Jane Fonda later spent two weeks in North Vietnam, broadcasting multiple times on Hanoi Radio, denouncing American prisoners of war (POW's) as criminals. She said that "they should be tried and probably executed."

Many have seen the famous picture of the movie star sitting on an anti-aircraft gun, surrounded by North Vietnamese Army soldiers, that had shot down American planes. In all fairness, Ms. Fonda did regret her actions and later apologized.

I blame much of this negative sentiment on the continuous misrepresentation of the Vietnam War by many media outlets.

During the conflict, a lot of what U.S. citizens saw was taken out of context. There were two quintessential pictures that would become the face of the Vietnam War.

One of the most famous photos showed the Chief of the South Vietnam Police, Nguyen Ngoc Loan, executing a plain-clothed Viet Cong lieutenant by shooting him in the head with the pistol close to the man's temple. The ugly picture, taken at the point of impact, flashed around the world and intensified the anti-war movement.

The photographer who captured the shot was Eddie Adams of the Associated Press. Adams said years later that he felt unsettled about the photo and thought the criticism of Loan was unfair. The picture was taken at the hectic and frantic opening of the V.C. attack on Saigon during the TET Offensive, and the communists had just murdered a close friend of Loan, one of his officers, plus the man's wife and children, in addition to killing scores of other citizens in the city.

As famous as that photo became, four years later the horrifying and sickening picture of a naked 9-year-old Vietnamese girl suffering from burns, crying with arms outstretched running down a road towards the camera, was just as prominent. A South Vietnamese pilot had dropped napalm on a village, Trang Bang, which had been overrun by the North Vietnamese Army.

The girl, Phan Thi Kim Phuc, suffered through a 14-month hospital stay and 17 agonizing surgeries, and there was a concern at the time that she might not survive. Thankfully, as of this writing, she is a healthy and happy grown woman residing with her family in Canada. She works with the United Nations for the protection of orphans and innocent victims of war and is a peace activist. The photograph, taken by Nick Ut, won a Pulitzer Prize.

War is horrid, grotesque, loathsome, and any other similar word found in the dictionary. Those two photos are proof of that. Nonetheless, it was disingenuous by media outlets to imply that U.S. forces had anything to do with either one of the two incidents depicted in the pictures. In fact, there were not even any American combat troops remaining in Vietnam when the June 8, 1972, tragedy involving Phan Thi Kim Phuc occurred.

I had several R&R days remaining and I selected Sydney, Australia as my destination, commencing on May 5. This was just a "getaway" on my own. Nancy and I could not afford to have her join me for another vacation just two months after our Hawaii trip, and I couldn't go back to the U.S. until my tour was complete. My buddy, Chopper, was supposed to go with me to Australia, but last-minute duties in the office of General Abrams required him to postpone his holiday with me.

I worked throughout the night prior to my early morning flight, originating out of Ton Son Nhut Air Base. Upon checking in, we were all herded into a building where, among other things, we exchanged our currency. My fellow military passengers and I were then told to proceed out of a side door and directly up the portable stairs leading to the aircraft.

There was no assigned seating. Since I was traveling alone, I didn't care where I sat; a lot of buddies were flying together so I wanted them to be able to grab seating next to each other. Thus, I waited until the room was totally empty before heading out. Immediately after passing through the door of the building as the final passenger to head to the plane, it was locked behind me.

I scanned the cabin of the aircraft from the front after I had climbed the stairs and noticed that there were several seats remaining, all centers, with no window seats and just one aisle seat left, which was about halfway down on the left side of the plane. Obviously, I selected the lone remaining aisle seat and after storing my tote bag, I sat back and relaxed after I had met the person sitting next to the window.

As I was enjoying the comfort of the cushioned seat just prior to takeoff, I looked down the aisle and here came another soldier. I couldn't figure out how that was possible since I was the last one out of the building. He came to the row I was in and for whatever reason, he wanted that particular middle seat although there were probably at least 10 empty middle seats in the rows ahead. I introduced myself after he had settled in. He reciprocated and said his name was Paul.

The first leg of our flight took us from Tan Son Nhut Air Base to Darwin, Australia in the northern part of the country, a journey of approximately 2,300 miles. I slept most of the way. We were allowed off the plane to walk around the airport a bit. I bought some gum and candy bars before settling back on the second and final leg of our flight of just over four hours to Sydney.

Paul and I made small talk for a few minutes before I decided I wanted to take another nap prior to landing in Sydney. (I had stayed up working almost 48 straight hours before my trip.) After we touched down and taxied to the terminal, we exited the plane and had to go through immigration. I was surprised that they confiscated my gum and candy bars since I had bought them in the same country. I was informed that it was a required cautionary measure.

After immigration, it was time to pick up our bags. I gathered my luggage, but Paul didn't have any, saying he was going to go shopping for what he needed in Sydney. He stayed by my side, actually latched on to me (apparently, we were pals now) as we headed for an area where hotel assignments were being made for those who didn't yet have any. There was a line specifically for officers and a line for enlisted men. Two things struck me; (1) there were only a few officers; and (2) the check-in system was pretty lax.

As I carefully watched and listened to the first officer who reached the desk in his designated line, I noticed that he wasn't asked his rank. We were all in civilian clothes, and he wasn't required to show any proof of his status. I don't know if that was SOP (standard operating procedure) or if they were just being sloppy because of the few numbers in that line.

Thinking that the officers were probably being offered the best hotels, a light bulb went off in my head. I asked Paul: "Have you heard of Battlefield Commissions?" I continued: "Well, I'm giving us an Airfield Commission. We are now 1st lieutenants; come on!" He reluctantly followed me, and my plan worked. We were able to secure rooms at the Texas Tavern, a popular American lodging facility. Our R&R rate was $8 per night.

Impersonating an officer is serious stuff; it goes against the Military Code of Conduct and I'm pretty sure there's some rule against it in the Geneva Convention. The penalties are very stiff. However, I was pretty sure that the United States Army had never executed a soldier for trying to get a better hotel room.

Some of the guys getting off the plane wanted to go into the bush and explore the outback. There were Australian families who graciously opened their ranches to such outdoor lovers, offering free lodging. Not me! I wanted life in the big city.

Once we had finished all our chores, we started walking through the terminal and we were all flabbergasted at how many young attractive girls were there to cheer us on. Apparently, some had come to reunite with soldiers that they had met before during a previous R&R, and there were those who, I guess, wanted to become acquainted with their own American soldier boy or airman. I was a good (married) boy and walked past the gaggle of Australian honeys, who were nicknamed "Sheila's."

Outside the terminal, we caught a bus that was provided for our transportation to our home for the week. Texas Tavern was located near the trendy King's Cross section of Sydney. It was the center of nightlife and was only 15 minutes from the beach by taxi. I checked in and waited for Paul to finish. The clerk gave him a room next to mine at his request.

On the way up the elevator, I told Paul: "Let's throw our bags in the room and head out." He hummed and hawed and finally lamely said, without conviction in my mind, that he was going to meet a girl he knew. If it was true, he was a fast worker; we had only been in the country for two hours!

I wasn't going to be held back, I wanted to enjoy some good ol' civilian nocturnal entertainment. I headed for the elevator and when the doors opened, I saw one lone male passenger. He said hello and I could tell right away that he was another military member on R&R. As it turned out, he was in the Air Force and was from either Grundy Center or Guthrie Center, Iowa, I can't remember which one. This was the fourth day of his R&R.

He asked me what plans I had for the night, and I told him that I had just landed and had none. He said: "Come with me; I think you'll be glad you did." After getting off the lift on the bottom floor, I followed him into The Red Garter bar. It was rather large and had a dance floor. Following my leader, we walked up to a table with six girls and joined them. My new buddy had made these new friends on the first night of his vacation, and they had partied together one other time.

It was a very enjoyable occasion; they were a fun group, and of course I loved listening to their accents. I remember to this day that one of the young ladies who sat beside me was named Nola Warfield. I don't know why, but I thought that was a tad ironic considering where I had been the previous 10 months.

There was another gal who could best be described as a real-life Kelly Bundy (from the TV show *Married with Children*). She was drop-dead gorgeous, but her brain fluid was a couple of quarts low. She knew that both my newly-found elevator friend and I had just come from the Vietnam War, but when she learned that I was in the Army and he was in the Air Force, she inquired: "Are you on the same side?" I wish I could tell you that I made that up as a joke, but I didn't. Poor thing.

(Having said that, before being in the service, I never realized that the rivalry between the different branches in the U.S. military – Army, Navy, Air Force, Marines, Coast Guard – was so competitive and sometimes intense. Each one told jokes about the others and sometimes there was even outright antagonism between the groups. However, make no mistake about it; all Americans, no matter the branch, are united and are close teammates and brothers in wartime.)

Our group of new "girlfriends" insisted on paying for everything, including picking up the tab for all the drinks and dinner. Admittedly, that was awkward for me, and I argued until I realized that they genuinely wanted to do it. I was a bit uncomfortable because I had always picked up the tab when I was in the company of females; I simply wasn't used to it.

Texas Tavern Hotel had three other bars – the El Camino Real, the San Antonio Bar, and The Barn, and we supported them all. (They each played a different genre of music. One featured rock, another had country and western, and still another spotlighted easy listening artists such as Frank Sinatra and Dean Martin.) If I thought the Australian soldiers that I had met in Vung Tau could hold their Foster Beer, they were rookies compared to these ladies!

The adrenalin of being a regular human in civilization was wearing off, thanks to my lack of sleep the previous two days. Plus, I'm certain I was more relaxed than I had been in quite a spell. I excused myself, repeatedly thanked my wonderful new Aussie friends and my new Iowa pal and headed for bed.

The rest of the week was a blur. If you had looked up "site-seer" in the dictionary at that time, you would have seen my picture. First of all, I needed clothes. My current civilian garb was badly outdated. The current style was "mod," and I needed to catch up with the latest fads.

I first visited the Phillip Monsour's Shirt Shop and re-supplied; my favorite was a turquoise paisley long-sleeve shirt. My next stop was to the J&J Men's Clothing Store where I bought some slacks -- bell-bottomed of course -- a wide leather belt with a big buckle, and shoes. (Hey, it was the 70's!)

So, there I was, Mr. Tourist, with my sunglasses, new duds, and a camera around my neck, visiting every corner of that lovely city. The shipyards piqued my interest and the beaches were scenic, but my most fascinating experience was watching the construction of the famous Sydney Opera House.

One of the true wonders of the world, the Sydney Opera House had been in the works for 12 years, with construction having startedin 1959 (with completion in 1973). When I was there, they were putting final touches on the outer shell. To say the least, it is a unique design.

From one angle, the giant cement structure reminded me of three sharks with layered mouths opened wide ready to devour you! Australia is famous for Great Whites, correct?

The Australians were awesome and so congenial. Sydney had an R&R Hospitality Service that would help assist a soldier with any questions or problems. That organization sponsored "Mixer" parties for American service members on Tuesday and Friday nights. Over 200 single young ladies (Sheila's) attended them. I stayed away from those get-togethers, again mindful of my wedding ring (and the possibility of temptation ruling the night).

I had the opportunity to call Nancy on May 8 and that was a much-needed joy for both of us. We hadn't spoken, of course, since leaving Hawaii over two months earlier. It was expensive: $10.80 for the first three minutes and $3.60 for each additional minute. I believe we easily ran up over a $50 phone bill on that one.

I didn't see much of Paul during the week, although he did accompany me when I went shopping one day. There was just something different, and a bit eerie, about him. He had sad eyes and rarely smiled, even at my incredibly funny jokes! When he did manage a grin, I had a strong feeling that it was forced as the rest of his face remained solemn.

Paul did not buy one thing when we ventured out, and he didn't have a camera to take any pictures. When I would try to broach anything about personal matters (where he was from, how old he was, how long he had been in Vietnam, etc.), he was evasive and quickly changed the subject. I did know his unit, however, because I had seen him list it when we signed up for housing at the airport.

He always insisted on being back to his room before dark, and he never went out in the evenings with me even though I invited him to dinner and/or a nightcap on a couple of occasions. I thought it was odd, but I just figured that he wasn't into the night scene and simply wanted to stay in his room to read or watch television.

On the day before we had to leave, I talked Paul into tagging along with me on a tour around the city one last time, because I didn't think I had taken enough pictures of the Sydney scenery. We got back to the hotel at 5:00 p.m. Our side-by-side rooms were in the middle of a long hallway, equidistant from elevators at both ends if I recall.

His room was directly next door and knowing I had one remaining frame to take on my film roll of 24, as he was fishing in his pocket for his key, I said: "Paul!" and took an unexpected "candid camera" photo of him as he looked at me with what can only be termed a startled expression.

A couple of minutes after I had entered my room, I heard a knock on the door. I opened it and Paul walked in, carrying a book. He went over and sat in a large overstuffed black leather chair with wide wooden armrests. I had immediately turned on the TV after setting foot in my living quarters, and a re-run of "I Love Lucy" was playing. It was turned on to the only station that didn't have static.

Paul and I made small talk and then he proceeded to get up to leave after only five minutes or so. I reminded him that we had to be down in the lobby at 6:30 a.m. to catch our bus back to the airport. I told him I would tap on his door, and we could go down to the lobby together at that time.

After he departed, I packed my suitcase while Lucy and Ethel were stomping grapes (yes, it was that famous episode). After turning off the tube, I read the Sydney newspaper until I drifted off to sleep. My 5:00 a.m. wake-up call came too soon. I phoned Paul right away, but he didn't answer. I then shaved, brushed my teeth, hopped into the shower, and got dressed. I called Paul again, and still did not get a response. I went over and knocked on his door, but to no avail. I just figured that he had decided to go down to the lobby and would meet me there.

I went back into my room and just as I was picking up my suitcase, I noticed that Paul had left the black hard-covered book that he had brought into my room the night before on top of one of the wooden armrests on the living room chair. I grabbed it, unzipped my suitcase, and tossed the publication into my bag before closing it again.

Paul was nowhere to be seen in the lobby. I tried to call him again from a phone from there, but again, he did not answer. I waited until the last possible moment to board the bus, hoping that I would see him running towards us at the last minute. It didn't happen.

On my way to the airport, I then theorized that Paul had decided to take a taxi in order to get to the terminal early. When we arrived at Sydney International, I went directly to the gate and realized that such was not the case. He was not there.

On command, we walked up the stairs to our plane for the trip back to Vietnam. The doors closed and as we were taxiing for takeoff, I looked around in case I had overlooked him in the terminal area, but there was no Paul. Missing your return flight from R&R was a cardinal sin and all I could think about was the amount of trouble my new friend was going to be in when he got back to his command.

A month or so after returning from Australia, I knew I would be traveling in the vicinity of Paul's unit, so I took his book with me. I walked into his base of operations and asked the company clerk where I could find Paul. (Note: I do not wish to divulge his surname.)

The clerk asked me his name again and when I replied, he responded that there was nobody by that name stationed there and that he had never heard of him. He told me that he had been with that outfit for 11 months and there had never been anybody close to that moniker in that time frame.

I told him emphatically that this was Paul's unit and that I had written it down so I wouldn't forget. It was my hope that maybe the clerk was wrong or that Paul was new and/or just transferred and this guy simply didn't know him yet.

I didn't know what else to do with Paul's book, so I asked the clerk if he would hold it for safe keeping in case our mystery man did show up. He shrugged his shoulders and said: "Yeah, that's fine." I had never really noticed that there was no writing on the outside of the book that I could see when handing it over. I was just glad that the book was now out of my hands and would hopefully find its way to the owner.

A couple of months later when I had returned home, Nancy and I, in addition to her sisters, were looking at photos of Australia that Nancy had just had developed. After looking at pictures of the Sydney Opera House, downtown shots of the city, photos of the shipyards and a few others taken around King's Cross, one showed a shot of an empty hallway. I was stunned, because I knew that was the last-minute surprise picture that I had taken of a startled Paul as he was digging into his pocket for his room key. Only there was no Paul in the photo. I said nothing.

Five years later, when I was well entrenched in my career as an athletic administrator, I was visiting the home of a sport announcer friend of mine. That night, he had a date who was also there, and over cocktails the three of us carried on a conversation involving many topics, but mostly pertaining to the world of college athletics.

My buddy's phone rang halfway through the evening and after answering it, he informed his lady friend and me that it was a prominent coach that he had been trying to get in touch with and excused himself to take the call in another room.

His companion and I made small talk, and during the course of our chat, she mentioned that she was a medium. (Though I knew what she meant, I had to bite my tongue to quell the urge of saying that I was a large, sometimes an XL.) Anyway, it was obvious that this woman truly believed that she had psychic powers.

Up to that time, I had never talked to anybody about my experience in Australia regarding my mysterious acquaintance named Paul, other than to Nancy, my wife, who promised not to divulge it to anyone. There was a feeling among some Americans that all Vietnam Veterans were crazy, so I never broached the subject to a soul. I thought that this was as good of an opportunity as any to discuss the matter, especially since she was a stranger and a person whom I would probably never see again.

I told her about everything; the puzzling nature of how Paul boarded the plane when I was the last to leave the disembarking building in Saigon; his refusal to go out after dark in Sydney; the inexplicable nature of the photo I had taken of him, when his image was not in the developed picture; his absence on our scheduled flight back to 'Nam; the clerk at Paul's unit in Vietnam telling me he had never heard of him; and the black book he had left in my room on the night before our departure.

It goes without saying that my new clairvoyant friend was intrigued. Her focal point was the black book. She asked me what the title was and wanted to know if I had looked inside for a message. Unfortunately, I had thrown it into my baggage at the last minute when I was on the run to catch my plane in Sydney and didn't give it any thought.

I said that I had not seen any writing on the outside of the book when I handed it to the clerk, and I had not opened it to check to see if there was some type of note inside. (And, yes, I know what you are thinking, and later I thought the same thing and could have kicked myself: Why hadn't I been curious enough to at least peek inside the publication? I guess I just had way too many other things occupying my mind at the time.)

She was convinced that he had purposely left the book in my room and departed knowing that he would never see me again. The book, had I browsed through it, would have provided the answer to the mystery, in her mind. She urged me to check with the National Archives to see if there had ever been a soldier with the name of my phantom friend.

I took her advice and started my investigation shortly thereafter. After extensively researching the matter, sure enough I did find a Paul with his very unusual last name who had served in the U.S. Army.

In World War II.

CHAPTER XVII
The Final Countdown

After returning from Sydney in mid-May, the rest of the month went by quickly. My two-month guard duty had ended. Someone had learned about my journalism background, and I was asked to write an article for a Vietnamese magazine, *Thong Cam* (with a readership of one million) explaining the sport of baseball. The game was relatively unknown in the country at the time.

Where does one start on such a project? How do you describe a home run….a sacrifice….strikes and balls….stealing….errors….or a fielder's choice?

(In his parody of baseball nomenclature, the late, gifted *Los Angeles Times* sportswriter Jim Murray, one of my personal favorites, said that a fielder's choice is "usually a tipsy blond in the hotel bar at 2:00 a.m." Some other great lines by Murray: Regarding Sandy Koufax --"Sandy's fastball was so fast, batters would start swinging as he was on his way to the mound." Discussing the Indianapolis 500 – "Gentlemen, start your coffins!" Describing UCLA basketball straight arrow coaching legend John Wooden – "He's so square he is divisible by four." On his golfing game – "The only time I ever took out my one iron was to kill a tarantula, and I took a 7 to do that.")

To assist me with the baseball article I corresponded back and forth with Monte Irvin, the Hall of Fame player who starred for the Giants after spending 10 years as a standout in the Negro Leagues. Mr. Irvin was an assistant to Major League Baseball Commissioner Bowie Kuhn at this juncture. He was nice enough to send me some photos and pertinent information for the piece I wrote.

I did my best to teach the South Vietnamese the ins and outs of baseball; in the first couple of paragraphs, I explained the origination of the sport and discussed the advancement to the point of its immense popularity in the U.S.

In the most recent World Series, I explained that Coach Earl Weaver's Baltimore Orioles, featuring such greats as Jim Palmer, Frank Robinson, and Brooks Robinson, topped the Sparky Anderson-mentored Cincinnati Reds and their superstars, including Johnny Bench, Pete Rose, and Tony Perez, in the World Series.

I then proceeded with the basics, explaining it this way: "Baseball is played between two teams, with nine players on each side. The object of the game is to score the most points, or 'runs' as they are called." From that point, I talked about the different positions, tried to elucidate baseball terminology, and went on to point out different strategies.

I ended my Vietnamese sports writing career with my final two words being "choi bong" to close out the article. That loosely translates to "play ball," or at least that is what Lt. Cau told me! Actually, the entire article was translated into Vietnamese for obvious reasons.

In a letter Nancy had written on May 12, among other things she discussed, was a hike in the cost of postage stamps. "It seems like eight cents is a lot for just one letter," she lamented.

She continued sending sweets such as brownies, cupcakes, chocolate drop cookies, and new goodies called "buckaroo" cookies, which were simply chocolate chip cookies with oats, I think. Whatever the case, they were all Godsends.

I had to keep those snack items at my workplace because we were losing the battle against the rats, mice, spiders and cockroaches where we lived. It's no wonder why we had to have so many plague shots.

The heavy monsoon season started in May. The weather in Vietnam certainly had an effect on our guys in the field. They were sometimes overcome by heat stroke and heat exhaustion on search and destroy missions, especially early in the war. The heavy rains just added to the agony. Humid, warm air also sometimes made it difficult for the helicopters to get the proper lift that was required, and many times prevented hovering. That put pilots and troops trying to get out of a hot LZ (landing zone under fire) into additional danger.

June was upon us, and I was looking forward to going home within 60 days. Troop withdrawals were accelerating; 50,000 had left since the first of the year. We were down to about 60% from the number of soldiers that we had had at our zenith in Vietnam. Morale among the those of us still in country was getting lower and lower for several reasons.

Our government leaders were in a constant state of turmoil as to what course of action to take in 'Nam, causing a lot of foot-dragging on their part; we were being called "baby killers" back in the States (no doubt a result of the recent trials for those who participated in the horrible My Lai civilian massacre three years earlier); and it seems as if American troops were getting killed for a nation that didn't care.

A couple of buddies received "Dear John" letters from their wives, with the apathy and anger in our country possibly adding to the reasoning process of their spouses. Two of my friends were obviously crushed at the devastating news from home, and both went into severe depression, feeling hopeless as to what they could do. There's not much to say to someone in that condition but you try to do whatever you can. Throughout the war, those heart-breaking letters caused some soldiers to either go berserk, endangering their fellow G.I.'s, or resort to suicide.

On a personal note, I was battling exhaustion; could it have been a lingering effect from whatever I was given during my forced confinement? I underwent another series of shots, including plague, tetanus, and typhoid. For the first time, my arm really got sore from all those needles.

One of my bunkmates came down with Cholera and was hospitalized. He wasn't the only one who required medical treatment. LTC Brash became very ill and was taken to a hospital and eventually flown out of the country. I would never see him again and I was saddened because he had been so good to me.

Despite all of that, I tried my best to keep a positive outlook on things, which is my natural state.

Nancy's letter of June 18 said that she had received the Koala Bear that I had sent her from Australia. He was a little feisty when I tried to put him in that box to mail him, but I threw in some eucalyptus leaves to keep him calm. No, I really didn't do that of course! It was a stuffed animal.

In the same correspondence, Nancy told me that she had picked out her favorite pattern of China dishes from a Noritake catalogue I had sent her, offering a great military discount. We also selected a Magnavox console stereo from a different booklet, also offering a cut rate to soldiers. Both would be delivered to Nancy at her parents' house.

A hometown pal of one of my cohorts was going to be visiting our compound on June 20, and my friend wanted me to meet him. After he had introduced the two of us to each other, our trio sat down for a beverage on some outside stairs of a building on base. I learned that the visitor was a sniper and had been out in the bush for the previous six months.

After some light and humorous banter, mainly regarding their days growing up in the same neighborhood, our guest began to shake and then burst into tears. Soon the crying turned into sobbing, and he mumbled: "I can't go back....I just can't take it anymore!" My friend and I were stunned, to say the least, and we tried our best to console the guy. He started to become incoherent, and I thought he was going to hyperventilate.

Finally, after 15 or 20 minutes we were able to calm him down, but he was still in deep distress. My friend and I were at a loss as to what to do or say, so we thought it best to take him over to the infirmary. I had to leave to attend an important briefing, but my friend escorted him to see a doctor.

Later, he told me that our stricken companion had been transported up to the 95th Evacuation Hospital in Da Nang and flown to a military hospital in Okinawa shortly thereafter. The bottom line was that his nerves were shot. The life of a sniper was a lonely existence and he had obviously snapped under the unbearable pressure.

On June 22, I received glorious news; my date for leaving Vietnam had been moved up from July 30 to July 6 thanks to the rapidly expanding troop withdrawals!! I called Nancy – I believe it was the only time I had an opportunity to call her from Vietnam and I had to pull some strings to get it done. She was beside herself when I told her about it and could hardly talk. We were both so excited. We only had two more weeks remaining of this torturous year.

A bonus for me was that I had learned that I still had four additional days of R&R that I hadn't taken. I considered Thailand or Taiwan, but finally decided to go to

Hong Kong. I would only have one more week of duty when I returned to Vietnam.

I flew to Hong Kong on June 27. At that time, it was still a British Crown Colony and a free port known for its bargain shopping.

We were required to fly in our dress greens to and from Hong Kong, but we had to wear civilian clothing while there. Thus, one of my first orders of business was to buy more civilian clothes to add to those that I had purchased in Australia and also some items I would need when I returned home. I found a nice shop named Maxwell's Clothiers, where a purchased a tailored three-piece suit for $38.00; one sports jacket for $22.00; and three pairs of tailored slacks for $38.00. Total bill: $98.00.

I stayed at the Astor Hotel on Carnarvon Road in Kowloon but visited all five of the major districts of the city. My highlights were going up on a tram to a vantage point where I could overlook downtown Hong Kong and surrounding areas; visiting -- simply for site-seeing purposes -- the "World of Susie Wong" red-light district; and viewing the hundreds of old Chinese sampan boats as I took a ferry ride on one of the city's many water outlets.

The latter experience was an eye opener. The word sampan literally means "three boards" or planks. Some were very, very small and didn't look sea-worthy to me. These were fishermen who earned their livelihood on these tiny floating boats, with family members being constant companions.

Some of the sampans were tied together with the ability to walk from one to another, with several clusters attached to each other. I was told that some of these people, who were quite poor, never left the water; they were born on such a boat and never touched terra firma, good ol' Mother Earth's land.

On one evening, I was transported by a water taxi to a beautiful floating restaurant, named the Tai Pak in Aberdeen, featuring spectacular decorations and a striking Chinese décor. The cuisine was, of course, scrumptious. I had my very first Chinese beer, Tsingtao, while there.

I spent a very relaxing four days in Hong Kong. I would get up, go to breakfast, and read the *South China Morning Post* (an English newspaper). Following that, I would normally go out, take a walk, and enjoy the sunshine and warm weather. This magnificent city was certainly a unique experience for a small-town boy.

On one of my late afternoon strolls, I was doing some window shopping and while peering into an antique shop, I heard this sweet and demure voice say: "Hello, G.I." (Obviously my short stylish Army haircut was a giveaway as to my identity.)

I turned and saw a very striking young Chinese girl. With her beautiful long dark hair, a bright yellow summer dress, and oversized sunglasses, she was quite elegant and classy. She was a Chinese version of Audrey Hepburn.

She stuck out her hand and said in broken English: "My name is Tiger, what's yours?" I replied: "Millard Fillmore." Don't ask me why that name came into my weird mind; all I knew was that I was a lone American soldier just a few miles from the Chinese border. During that period of time China was a North Vietnamese ally and a closed, hostile and mysterious nation similar to North Korea today. Thus, I didn't think it was wise to reveal my true identity.

I wasn't sure of her intent. I mean, I didn't think she was a Hong Kong version of a Mata Hari or anything, but I couldn't take the chance. And I was also pretty certain that "Tiger" wasn't up on her U.S. presidential history, so my pseudonym wouldn't ring any bells.

She asked: "Do you want to party?" Now I understood what business she was in; her freshness and charm had belied the fact that she was in the world's oldest profession. I was a bit surprised because we were far from the red-light "Wan Chai" district of the city (aka the "World of Suzie Wong" after the movie of the same name).

I answered: "How much?" She responded: "Fifty U.S. Dollah." I agreed to her terms and then asked her where there was a good restaurant within walking distance. She led me to a nice little cozy café and as we sat down, she looked at me with a puzzled expression. After taking off her huge-framed sunglasses, I viewed a stunning Asian goddess.

After we had ordered dinner, I asked her where she was from and learned that her homeland was in mainland China, where all of her family still resided. She was simply in Hong Kong to make money to send home to them, and this was the best way she could do it. She looked down and couldn't look me in the eye when she told me this; it was obviously not a preferred career choice. This delicate young thing should not have had to live such a lifestyle. I wanted to hear everything about her up-bringing and she was just as curious to hear about mine.

Soon, the different roles that we played in life melted away. We both let our guard down and simply enjoyed each other's company. She giggled at my clumsiness with chopsticks, especially while I was eating my rice. We talked and laughed the afternoon away as if we were two long-time friends, which was amazing since we were from two very different cultures and had grown up under far different circumstances.

"I could escape the feeling
With my China girl;
I could pretend that nothing really meant too much
With my China girl."

■ China Girl
--David Bowie

She told me that she wanted to learn how to write her name in English and I showed her how. I then asked her to write mine in Chinese and she reciprocated. Before we knew it, we had staked our claim to that little bistro table for over three hours!

Grinning at my companion, I finally told her I had to return to my hotel to pack my bags as my flight back to Vietnam was leaving early in the morning, so I bid her adieu. She smiled back and I believe she wondered if I had anything further in mind. I did not; that was never my intention. I was simply a lonely soldier boy who wanted to talk with someone for a while. I paid the dinner tab and then slipped her the $50, telling her to take care of her family, and herself.

I got up to walk out, but she remained seated. I turned around when I was outside and waved good-bye through the window; she waved back with a radiance that lit up her porcelain face. I had made a special friend from the other side of the world, but somewhat sadly, it would be an acquaintance whom I knew that I would never see again.

It wasn't a total loss; somewhere, I still have a piece of paper with Millard Fillmore written in Mandarin Chinese.

My return trip to Tan Son Nhut Air Base on July 1, 1971, went smoothly. I proceeded immediately to the Project Hieu office where a great guy named James D. Spencer had been training to take my place. His nickname was "Rat," and that's what this Mississippi lad wanted to be called. He even signed the letters that he later wrote to me with that unique moniker. I wish we could have spent more time together because we became good friends in a very short time.

One day, Spencer and I sat down and had a deep conversation about, well….pretty much about life! I asked him if things were tough on him as a black man growing up in the South, asking him if some of the things I had read were true.

He responded with a smile – which he always seemed to have – saying that he thought we had more problems in the North than the South did about such matters.

Waxing philosophically, James added, with absolutely no bitterness in his voice: "As a black person, there are places I probably wouldn't want to go back home, but if you ever visited me, there are places I wouldn't want you, as my white friend, to go, either." Both ways saddened me.

I had two major problems staring me in the face upon my return from R&R. One, my booking flight had been moved up to July 2, which was the very next day, while I was gone! I wouldn't even be able to get my stuff together and do everything that needed to be done in that short amount of time.

However, I had a bigger concern: If you returned to the U.S. from Vietnam with five months or less on your two-year draftee status, you could get an "early-out." I wanted to make certain that I didn't get back to the States with one or two days *over* that five-month cut-off and then have to stay in the service until December. My plans were to go back to college in the fall.

Luckily, I knew the guys at Pentagon East who were in charge of flights back to the U.S., and I told them to rebook me and find a seat on a plane two days later and they did. Officially, I was "persona non grata" in Vietnam after the 2nd. I had to check in all of my gear and move out of my barracks. For a couple of nights, I hid out at a friend's billet.

I had another serious issue; I came down with an excruciating toothache after I returned from Hong Kong. It came in the night, and it was debilitating. I went to a military dentist the next day, but his electricity had been knocked out in an explosion, apparently in an act of sabotage. Thus, he accomplished all that he could do for me manually. He was sympathetic but said his only solution was to give me some pain killers to get me through my upcoming flight. I made it clear, no Darvon!

I found a poem with the title, "The Word From 'Nam." I wrote it on the back of the envelope of the final letter I sent to my parents:

"Call the butcher, order steaks three inches thick!

Call the beer man and order three cases quick!

Fill the car and polish the phone,

Then batten the hatches, 'cause the kid's comin' home!"

CHAPTER XVIII
My Farewell to Arms

On the 4th of July, 1971, I was leaving the Vietnam War for good. How appropriate; I had the honor of celebrating our nation's birthday on a plane filled with soldiers who, indeed, had earned the right to be called America's best. It was a year of many trials and tribulations, but it was now over.

> *"So long boys, you can take my place,*
> *Got my papers, I've got my pay*
> *So pack my bags and I'll be on my way....*
>
> *Put my gun down, the war is won,*
> *Fill my glass high, the time has come,*
> *I'm going back to the place that I love...."*
>
> ■   Yellow River
> --Christie

Soldiers leaving 'Nam would say that they were going back to "the World" on a "Freedom Bird," and that's what I was now doing. My flight was on a chartered Pan American 707 aircraft, filled with guys like me who hadn't seen home for a year. As we lifted off, the pilot came on and said: "Gentlemen, look down, this may be your last glimpse ever of Vietnam." It was a muted response of low-level cheering.

As I looked around, there wasn't as much joy or jubilation as you might have expected. It was pretty quiet and subdued. No backslapping, grab-assing or yelling. Some of that could have been caused by some hard partying the previous night, but more so, I believe it was a planeload of mentally and physically exhausted men lost in the reflections of what had transpired over the past 12 months.

We were forced to age at a far greater rate than the one year that took us away from our previous lives. It was as if we had defied the principle of time. One could feel, however, a sense of relief by all. We were the fortunate ones who had won the life lottery of war.

The flight attendants tried to lift our spirits, too. When they demonstrated the flotation devices on their backs, they turned around and when the release straps were pulled, out tumbled three-page foldouts of *Playboy* Playmates attached to the innertube safety apparatuses each one was wearing.

The flight from Vietnam to the USA was far different than the one we had taken a year earlier going the other direction. We simply wanted to get home. We were not filled with anticipation and giddiness at the different stops as we had been the year before. The pain pills that the dentist had given me kept me sedated. We re-fueled at both Yokota Air Base in Japan and in Honolulu, but I honestly cannot remember getting off the plane at either place, although I'm sure we did.

We finally touched down at Travis Air Force Base in Oakland. As we taxied, I looked out the window deep in thought remembering 12 months prior when I had last viewed this same scenery, wondering at that time what the future would hold for me and if I would ever see this landscape again.

In the end, all things considered, the year had been good to me. Although I had lost 26 pounds (despite all those cookies!); came home with a 13-foot tapeworm as I would eventually learn; was unknowingly a bearer of a later diagnosed peptic ulcer; had jungle rot on both sides of my nose; suffered some partial hearing loss which led to tinnitus; and had a bad tooth that later came out in 11 pieces, I was one of the lucky ones. I had no complaints.

I had obviously had a guardian angel looking over me in some pretty traumatic and chilling situations during my tour in the small Asian country; specifically, the near drowning; the helicopter crashes which included hostile fire; and the kidnapping.

And that doesn't include the near tragedy on the hand grenade pad in basic training when a quick-thinking sergeant kicked a dropped live grenade into a cement bunker, which would have put a world of hurt on me and others.

I wondered how many of my fellow soldiers on my flight to the war one year earlier had returned instead to Dover, CT in those metal military coffins. I grimaced while remembering that I had been the one to force some of those guys away from loved ones to get on the plane to Vietnam. Over 8,000 Americans had been killed in 'Nam during my year there; God forbid that some of them were among that number.

When we disembarked from our aircraft on that late Monday afternoon, we were taken to a building for a long-awaited meal. We walked down a long hallway and at the end just before we made a right turn to enter the dining hall, there was a life-size cut-out of Uncle Sam. Complete with a star-spangled stovepipe hat and flowing white beard, he had his arms extended with a caption saying something to the effect: "Welcome Home, I'm Proud of You." I don't know how anyone else reacted, but personally it touched me, in fact my eyes got misty. I'm a little corny that way.

Entering the large chow hall, we were seated and served a steak dinner with all the trimmings by high-ranking officers, which had become a tradition with returnees.

We were confined for three days, sleeping on bunk beds, to do our out-processing. It was rather boring, but we had some pool tables to help pass the time. I was able to call home, which was wonderful.

Nobody on base gave us any crap; they knew where we had been. In fact, I was walking outdoors without any type of head covering, which is verboten in the military, and an officer walked by me and didn't say a word; he knew that I was part of the group that had just come back.

There was a lot of paperwork involved in the switch from soldier to civilian. I was called into a side office at one point where a Captain informed me that because of my Crypto clearance and the meetings I had attended, I was not allowed to leave the United States for at least six months.

We had to pass physical and mental status reports before being discharged. I think the Army was cautious about releasing any returnees whom they deemed a little unstable from their year's experience. I passed all tests and received my DD (Department of Defense) Form 1811, the approval needed to show that I didn't have any debilitating physical or mental problems, necessary for release from active duty.

Next was a meeting with a therapist/counselor, who cautioned me that I could very well lapse into depression, which could last from one week to several years. I thought: "Yeah, right! I'm going home, how could I possibly get depressed!" At a later date, unfortunately that prognostication would become a reality for me and most others who served in Vietnam.

The medical part of the process was the final step, other than picking up our dress greens for the trip home. With that, I received my DD 214 listing my honorable discharge from the United States Army. Picking up a final paycheck was the highlight of the time spent there. From that point forward, I would be a proud Veteran for life.

I had to take a bus from Oakland to San Francisco. I wondered whose bright idea it was to dump Vietnam Veterans into the Bay Area upon our return, undoubtedly the largest anti-war and anti-military region of the country. It was not a pleasant experience because my attire clearly showed that I was a soldier; I had to wear my Army dress uniform to get an airline discount.

The bus I was on stopped at a transfer point, where I had to disembark and board a different one headed to the airport. So here I was, in my military greens, holding a souvenir rifle and my duffle bag; I was an obvious target for those who were upset with the war.

A group of young people gave me some verbal abuse, and one boy attempted to spit at me. I informed him that he was lousy at it and proceeded to show him how to spit through his teeth. He couldn't help but break out in a little smile and hopefully this teenager thought that I was an okay dude, and that maybe we had more in common rather than being vastly dissimilar. I wasn't that much older than them.

I finally made it to San Francisco International Airport for my morning flight. I was able to get a special cost of $55 for a one-way ticket on United Airlines to Des Moines, changing planes in Denver.

It wasn't quite as mortifying to wear my dress uniform as it had been the previous year when I was traveling from Seattle to Newark during my break from basic training; I had acquired six medals in 'Nam so the ribbons from those medallions dressed up my formal military outfit a bit more; it didn't look quite as stark.

I brought back two war keepsakes, a ChiCom (Chinese Communist) version of the Russian semi-automatic SKS rifle (officially a ChiCom Carbine Type 54), and a Chinese version of a 45 pistol and knockoff of a Soviet TT-33 (ChiCom Pistol Type 54).

The ChiCom Carbine Type 54 used by the communist forces was illegal because it featured an attached 12" thin bayonet that folded up under the barrel when not in use. The bayonet had "blood groves," which were not allowed under Geneva Convention rules. The entry point caused by such a sharp instrument was small and would belie serious internal injuries to a wounded soldier by an unsuspecting medic who was doing a quick check.

I was carrying the official paperwork from the South Vietnamese Government allowing me to take those items out of that country. Both weapons had been disabled as required. I was given permission to take them onto the airplane but had to check in with the crew, at which time a flight attendant secured them in the front storage closet.

After releasing those two items, I found my seat, stowed my tote bag, and sank back with a big smile; the realization had hit me that I was really out of Vietnam. I couldn't believe it. The jet bridge was pulled back from the aircraft, the pilot backed away from the gate, took our place in the line of ground traffic, taxied to our runway, and sped down the cement strip before finally lifting off.

I was going home.

After the safety demonstration by the flight attendants, one of them, whom I had worked with to store the two weapons, said on the intercom: "Ladies and gentlemen, we have a returning soldier on board who is coming home for the first time after a year in Vietnam." I was shocked because there was resounding applause. Though embarrassed, it gave me a warm feeling because I realized we weren't quite as despised as I had feared.

And yes, this returning G.I. had to hide his tears at the response.

While back in Oakland, the anticipation of going home offset any chance of getting much sleep when we were confined, even though all of us were very tired and I was still taking the pain medication. On my final night, I did finally fall into a deep slumber and woke up with just enough time to jump in the shower and head for San Fran the day of my departure. However, I didn't have the opportunity to shave, so I took the time to do so in one of those tiny airplane lavatories on the first leg of my flight.

I didn't want to "hog" one of the bathrooms, so I knew that I had to be quick. I grabbed my dopp kit and headed towards the back. I squeezed into one of the petite aircraft restrooms and laid out my razor, shaving cream, and after shave lotion. Do you realize how hard it is to find an area to place your suit coat, dress shirt, tee shirt, and tie in such tight quarters? I somehow managed to avoid slitting a carotid artery during the shave; I was thankful for the lack of turbulence.

After exiting the "latrine," two of the flight attendants who were sitting on their designated jump seats adjacent to the tiny lavatory said they wanted to hear about Vietnam. The attractive young women, one white and one ebony, were curious because they both had relatives who were draft age. The duo, who were roommates, asked me if they could take me to dinner, apparently thinking that Denver was my final destination. I told them I was very appreciative but that I was catching a connecting flight to Des Moines where my family awaited my arrival.

I was sitting by the window nearly a third of the way back in the aircraft on the first leg, and after we had landed, the normal herding of the passengers towards the front exit took a while as everyone collected their bags from the overhead bins.

When I finally made it up to the front closet, I looked in to retrieve my two souvenir weapons. The pistol, which was in a holster, was hanging there, but the SKS, which was in a rifle cover, was missing. I called over one of the First-Class flight attendants, but she had no clue what could have happened.

Somebody had obviously taken it. I was determined to do my best to track down the SKS, which was enclosed in an imitation black leather carrying case that I had purchased in Saigon with the word "Vietnam" emblazoned on the side. Luckily, I had a couple of hours before my connecting flight.

I raced through the terminal, looking here and there, knowing it would be like finding a needle in a haystack. However, fortune smiled upon me. After several minutes I spotted the black rifle carrying case at a gate leaning up against a bag at the end a row of interconnected airport lounge chairs. Sitting next to it was an Army major in his dress greens.

There was no fear of this man, militarily speaking, because I was no longer in the Army. But since I was wearing my uniform, I maintained military courtesy. I went up to him and said: "Sir, I believe you must have taken this weapon by mistake; here is my paperwork from the South Vietnamese Government. The serial numbers on the rifle will match this document."

He was shocked that I had caught him because we were far from the gate at Stapleton Field, where we had landed. I scanned his row of medal ribbons and noticed that he had neither the Vietnam Service Medal nor the Vietnam Campaign Medal, therefore I knew that he couldn't have "mistaken" this rifle from another; he had never even been in Vietnam. He had flat out stolen it and was trying to get away, plain and simple. I knew that, and he knew that, but I had given him an easy way out.

The Major responded as he picked up the weapon: "Well let me see here; you're absolutely correct, I grabbed the wrong one!" Of course, he was lying because mine was the only rifle that was secured in that closet on our San Francisco to Denver flight. Plus, the fact that he had never been in Vietnam was a key giveaway. It was sad that a man with such questionable principles had such a high ranking in our military. Perhaps General Westmorland was correct regarding the lowering of the bar for officer qualification due to the need for personnel in Vietnam. Whatever; I was just happy that I was able to get back my prized possession.

I boarded my flight from Denver to Des Moines and had to again check in the two souvenir weapons with the new crew. Therefore, some of the flight attendants and the two pilots, who were standing at the front of the plane when I entered, knew that I was just coming back from overseas because of the requirement to relinquish my weapons to them.

Sitting in my assigned seat, knowing I was coming home for the first time in a year, I was trying to figure out how one analyzes his feelings at that time? Relief? Nervousness? Anxiety? Anticipation? A guilty feeling that you were coming home and so many others weren't? Was I a changed person? I had two hours to wrestle with all of those emotions.

Finally, on July 7, 1971, I was on my home soil again as the tires screeched upon touching down at Des Moines International Airport.

As a courtesy, in a very nice gesture, the flight attendant on the P.A. asked the passengers on the plane to allow me to disembark first, explaining that I was returning from Vietnam and that my family was anxiously waiting. With the eye strain that I had experienced, I had been given a couple of pairs of both regular prescription glasses and prescription sunglasses in 'Nam. My eyes weren't that bad, and I didn't wear them all the time, but nonetheless, I had managed to break all of the glasses I had been given other than one set of sunglasses. Thus, those were the ones I had to wear off the plane to make certain I recognized everyone from a distance.

So, there I was, wearing sunglasses, probably disheveled by this time, carrying my travel bag, a 45 pistol, and a rifle….and wearing a big grin! When I reached the end of the jetway, I saw them all. My family. I have never experienced as much joy as I did at that moment. After a million hugs, kisses, and tears, our herd of relatives walked through the long hallway, descended down the escalator, picked up my checked duffle bag, and formed a caravan to drive the 30 miles to the farm where Nancy grew up.

When we reached our destination between Newton and Reasnor and turned down the path to the farm, I saw a huge "Welcome Home, Tom" written on a giant cloth bedsheet attached to the barn straight ahead. We went into the house for a feast of drinks and snacks, featuring patriotic plates and glasses adorned with the American flag. There was also a red, white, and blue cake. Conversation flowed for hours; after all, we were a year behind. I think Nancy would have preferred for just the two of us to be alone, but she understood how important this reuniting time was for everyone.

The next day, after sleeping in until Noon, among other things we gathered around to look at the pictures I had taken in Australia. (I hadn't had time to develop my Hong Kong film rolls yet.)

That is when everyone saw the empty hallway, in which Paul evidently did his Houdini act. He was not in the picture. Everyone just thought I had taken a photo of the hallway to show how long it was.

I didn't tell them differently.

CHAPTER XIX
Vietnam: Good Intentions, Bad Decisions

The Vietnam War would rage on for another four years, but the final chapter had pretty much been written by the time I left. It was obvious that the U.S. was simply looking for a way out; the desire for victory wasn't even on the menu anymore, if it ever truly was. President Nixon did try to stay in the fight, but a hostile Congress fought him at every step.

Government leaders had always tried to conduct the war from Washington D.C. President Johnson once proudly proclaimed: "They can't even bomb an outhouse without my approval."

Why didn't he, and our other government leaders, depend and trust our West Point, Annapolis, Quantico and Air Force Academy trained commanders, who could better decide on immediate correct courses of action while they were on the ground in the combat zone, on the other side of the world? Westmoreland called it "the folly of running the minute details of a war by a committee of presidential advisors thousands of miles away."

Any planning and/or operations groundwork often had to go through a ridiculous number of levels, causing such projected actions to proceed excruciatingly slow and sometimes making them outdated and useless. Many times, items had to first be forwarded to the U.S. Ambassador in Vietnam…. through CINCPAC (Commander in Chief, Pacific)….then to the Department of Defense….from there passed on to the Joint Chiefs of Staff….forwarded to the Department of State….on to the Senate….through the House of Representatives…. to a foreign intelligence board….to the presidential advisors….and finally into the hands of the president. (I might have had a step or two out of order, but hopefully you have a picture of the futility of it all.)

It was extremely frustrating to Generals Harkins, Westmoreland, Abrams, and Weyand, the four commanding officers of U.S. and Allied Forces during the war.

In addition, limited rules of engagement edicts greatly hampered our forces throughout the conflict. A good example was not allowing our military to take the fight to where the enemy could be found in his sanctuaries in Cambodia and Laos, or even in North Vietnam itself. The communists knew that they were protected, by United States governmental rules no less, in those areas. We also weren't allowed to bomb enemy airbases, where we could have destroyed all of their fighter jets while they were on the ground. Haiphong Harbor, where Russians unloaded war machinery, was off limits, too.

From the start of the war, the North Vietnamese Army (NVA) learned that it was able to advance and probe deeply into South Vietnam on forays of military operations and destruction, knowing full well that its forces could then dash back to the north, crossing the Demilitarized Zone to safety completely unfettered, or cross the borders of Laos and Cambodia to be equally safe. The U.S. government would not allow the Allies to pursue the communists in those areas. It was another one-sided absurdity of the war.

There were other mandates that hindered our progress. On one occasion when I was flying on a Huey, we started taking fire from the ground. I shouted to the door gunner, asking why he wasn't firing back. He told me that there could be "friendlies" in the area and that we would be far away from that area by the time it would take to seek permission from his HQ, which would have to go up an additional level of command to receive approval.

While riding in a Jeep on another occasion, we zoomed past a rubber plantation because I was told that "Charlie" was aware that we had rules not to fire into such protected trees; thus, the V.C. would hide behind them and take potshots at Allied soldiers whenever they had the opportunity.

Still other U.S. governmental regulations, in some instances, didn't allow our troops to fire on the enemy unless they were fired upon first. The unilateral directives that our forces had to follow were seemingly endless.

Another advantage of a one-sided nature, the communists never had to contend with a confrontational press or a dissatisfied citizenry. There were no anti-war rallies or criticism from the media. Those types of "nuisances" simply weren't allowed under a communist dictatorship. That, of course, was the opposite of what leaders in the United States had to face on a daily basis. Don't get me wrong, I wouldn't have it any other way.

In short, American forces and their Allies had to "play by rules," while the enemy had no such constraints.

I fully understand the necessity of civilian control of the military and am one hundred percent behind it, but sometimes the thought process of our white-collar leaders bordered on lunacy.

General Westmoreland, in his autobiography, related that when he and Lt. General Joseph H. Moore, MACV Deputy Commander of Air Operations, tried to get authority to destroy Russian SAM (surface-to-air missile) sites being constructed in North Vietnam early in the war, Asst. Secretary of Defense John McNaughton asked, incredulously: "You don't think the North Vietnamese are going to use them?" While denying the request, he added: "Putting them in is just a political ploy by the Russians to appease Hanoi."

Some ploy. A multitude of American aircraft, including B-52 bombers, were shot down directly by the supersonic telephone pole-sized projectiles that Secretary McNaughton wasn't concerned with. (We learned that hundreds of Soviet engineers were sent to assist in the utilization of the SAM's.)

Westmoreland was quoted as saying: "What special audacity prompted civilian bureaucrats to deem they know better how to run a military campaign than did military professionals?" He added: "Is no special knowledge or experience needed?"

All of these regulations and denial of requests were very exasperating to our combat arms people. That is why it seemed that the Vietnam War dragged on endlessly.

Sun Tzu, in his disquisition *The Art of War*, said: "There has never been a protracted war from which a country has benefited." Every historical military leader on earth worth his salt over the past couple of centuries has studied this essay, written some 2,500 years ago by Tzu, an ancient Chinese combat strategist. I'm sure our generals and admirals during the Vietnam conflict wanted to adhere to Tzu's design for victory; unfortunately, our political leaders did not.

One might ponder whether or not the war would have been conducted differently, and more effectively, under John F. Kennedy had he not been tragically assassinated. A WWII hero, JFK had a vested interest in Vietnam, and I believe he would have been a far better wartime president than Lyndon Johnson.

In my opinion, the popular Kennedy may have been more aggressive and may have espoused a policy of securing victory instead of being satisfied with a deadlock, which seemed to become the U.S. stance under the Johnson administration. In the least, he probably wouldn't have stymied our military leadership with so many ludicrous restrictions.

(Perhaps the Soviet Union believed that Kennedy would have been a tougher foe, too. At the risk of adding to the vast number of conspiracy theories regarding JFK's death, it's conceivable that the Russians, utilizing one of its former citizens, Lee Harvey Oswald, ended the possibility of John Kennedy remaining as the Commander of Chief of U.S. forces in Vietnam by having him eliminated.)

The Vietnam conflict was supposed to have been over in January of 1973 when the Paris "Peace" Accord was signed. I believe it should have been termed the Paris Capitulation Accord. The talks started in May of 1968. Remember, this was shortly after Allied forces had routed the communists following the failed TET Offensive. From the start, the North Vietnamese consistently made demands, sometimes almost comical, and the United States gave in every time to the communist requirements. For example:

- The communists demanded a U.S. bombing halt, but they were allowed to continue their clandestine attacks in the south. We acquiesced.
- The communists rejected several locations where the U.S. had proposed to conduct peace talks (Geneva, Djakarta, New Delhi, Rangoon, Vientienne) while the North Vietnamese demanded Paris. We acquiesced.
- South Vietnamese President Nguyen Van Thieu proposed internationally supervised open and

free elections with communist participation in his country to end the fighting, but North Vietnam rejected the generous offer. We acquiesced.

- The communists refused to recognize the government of South Vietnam and said that they would not attend the talks unless it was only North Vietnam and the U.S. being the primary parties at the table. We acquiesced.

- North Vietnam demanded that the U. S. withdraw all of its forces from South Vietnam, but that all 219,000 Communist troops (illegally) operating in South Vietnam at the time be allowed to stay in place in that country. We acquiesced.

- The communists rejected a rectangular table at the talks, demanding a round one. We acquiesced.

Thomas Jefferson once stated: "Establish the eternal truth that acquiescence under insult is not the way to escape war."

The United States, which did not lose one major military encounter to the NVA or V.C. in the entire war in Vietnam, was now letting the communists dictate ridiculous "peace" agreement terms. On January 27, 1973, the ill-fated document was signed at the Hotel Majestic in Paris, which, ironically, was the headquarters for the Nazi Gestapo during the WWII occupation of France.

Although the unfavorable terms should not be blamed wholly on U.S. Secretary of State Henry Kissinger, who led the American delegation in Paris, there are those who didn't think he was as tough as he could have been while representing the Allies' side.

President Richard Nixon and Kissinger were close, but the war was starting to show a schism between the two. Nixon and South Vietnam President Nguyen Van Thieu wanted a reluctant Kissinger to amend a "peace" proposal from the North Vietnamese, particularly demanding that all communist forces leave the south upon the signing of any agreement.

Kissinger, anxious to reach some kind of an accord, didn't think that the North Vietnamese would agree and was against such an amendment. He had grown exhausted and exasperated, and in an interview, said that he always "acted alone." That made Nixon furious, and the president refused to see him for months and considered replacing him.

The only positive to come out of the end of the five-year talks for the U.S. was the release of American prisoners of war. The Department of Defense listed 687 returned P.O.W.'s. At least 62 died in captivity in the inhumane communist prisons.

There were those in the U.S. who did not believe that the North Vietnamese had released all of our captured military members as required. Over 2,646 Americans were missing in action (MIA) at the time. Were they still being held in secret?

The ink was hardly dry on the new "peace" agreement when the communists resumed their attacks against South Vietnam. Why *anybody* would have been under the illusion that North Vietnam was going to abide by the terms of the Paris treaty, essentially the same rules that were put into effect during the Geneva Conference and violated by that country 19 years earlier, staggers the imagination.

Perhaps that is why the principal party at the Paris talks for the North Vietnamese, Le Duc Tho, refused to accept the Nobel Peace Prize. He knew there was never any intention of implementing "peace." Or maybe his lying at the conference table gave him a guilty conscience.

The communist North wasted little time in quadrupling their number of troops to a total of 400,000 in the beleaguered South. Now fighting alone, the South Vietnamese Army, with 13 Divisions, would be facing an overwhelming 20-Division force of the communists.

The Paris pact was supposed to be internationally supervised to stop such an incursion by the North, but that was one last farcical piece of the ridiculous Paris "Peace" Agreement, which also read, by the way, that the "South Vietnamese will have the right to determine their own future without outside interference."

For all practical purposes, ground combat operations by American troops had ended in early 1972, (although bombing runs did continue). There were only 24,000 U.S. troops remaining in Vietnam at the end of '72, all in roles such as protecting our Embassy and other secure locations as well as serving as advisors.

All other Allied countries departed South Vietnam after the Paris agreement in January of 1973, too, leaving the South Vietnamese military to fend for itself against the NVA and V.C.

With everything considered, it had been time to pull our combat troops out of Vietnam, which we did in the spring of 1972. The real shame of the United States government was substantially reducing, by our Congress, the necessary military aid and materials required by the South Vietnamese Army to continue defending itself from the communist aggression.

The cutting off of supplies guaranteed defeat for the South Vietnamese and victory for the North Vietnamese Army and the Viet Cong in 1975.

At the time of the signing of the "peace" treaty in Paris in January of 1973, President Nixon told the South Vietnamese government and citizens: "You have my assurance that we will respond with full force should the settlement be violated by North Vietnam." Unfortunately for our ally in Southeast Asia, timing was not on their side; Watergate soon consumed Nixon's attention, and Vietnam slid to the back burner.

In addition, the Secretary of Defense at the time, Melvin Laird, did not endear himself to either the Joint Chiefs of Staff or Creighton Abrams, Commander of

U.S. Forces in Vietnam. They were of the opinion that Laird simply wanted to make himself and the administration look good by ignoring the top military officers' opinions on troop withdrawals, demanding a more exhilarated pullback of troops without an understanding of what was happening on the battlefield at the time. That put some remaining units in danger.

Congress would likely have forbidden a response by the Nixon Administration in the event of an NVA invasion anyway. Furthermore, the Senate and House, as mentioned, took the cruel step of drastically cutting aid to our Ally to a trickle, spelling South Vietnam's demise. It proved to be devastating.

(In my mind, it equaled the shame of the United States' failure at the last minute to supply guaranteed air support to the 1,400 Cuban exiles who were trying to overthrow Castro's Cuban communist regime at the Bay of Pigs in 1961. Right or wrong, that commitment had been made and we did not live up to our end of the bargain, and the anti-communist rebels became sitting ducks on Cuban shores.)

Yes, we had already done a lot for South Vietnam, but since our country was a signatory to two agreements to assist a nation defending itself from aggression (SEATO and the Geneva Accords), it was disgraceful for our government to cut off military aid virtually cold turkey. In the final months of the war, the Army of the Republic of Vietnam (ARVN) had to actually ration its last few bullets that it had because of the near cessation of aid from the U.S.

South Vietnam President Thieu was forced to mandate that each of his soldiers be limited to one hand grenade and 85 bullets *PER MONTH!* He said that it was "like filling up the ocean with stones."

It doesn't take a military genius to understand that you cannot long sustain successful combat operations against a well-equipped enemy that way. The North Vietnamese Army continued to get whatever it needed from China and the Soviet Union, who quadrupled their aid. The two communist behemoths were still cash-strapped, but they could see that the end was near and continued supporting North Vietnam in its conquest of South Vietnam, which met that another country on the world map would be under the hammer and cycle of communism, with the "Domino Theory" becoming a reality, meaning neighboring countries were in even in greater peril.

Possibly the one thing that will infuriate many Vietnam veterans and make their blood boil is reading or hearing that "the United States lost the Vietnam War." How is it possible to lose a war when you aren't even there? The conflict in Vietnam went on for over three years, from early-1972 to mid-1975 without any American combat troops in the country.

Only 50 Americans remained in South Vietnam by the end of '73 and they were there primarily to protect our Embassy. The last Marine detachments and Green Beret Special Forces left in 1971, and the last Army combat units left in March of 1972. The Vietnam War did not end until May of 1975.

The U.S. certainly did not win (as alluded to, we blew that chance when it was in our grasp after TET 1968), but when at full strength, American troops and our Allies controlled South Vietnam.

The communists did not come close to sniffing victory in those years. They never won a major engagement against forces from the United States. I guess if one is searching for a silver lining to all the madness, the fact that U.S. forces dominated on the battleground during the war would be it.

No, despite what you may have heard or seen written, America did not lose the Vietnam War. Although some gleefully proclaimed otherwise, "little men in black pajamas" did not defeat the greatest military in the world.

THEY NEVER HEARD THE FINAL SHOT

The truth of the matter, of course, is that the United States Government simply wanted to get out of Vietnam and was willing to do whatever it took to disengage. North Vietnam's elite General Vo Nguyen Giap had predicted early on in the war that patience would have a short lifespan in the U.S. and the American will to win would falter if the NVA and V.C. could just drag it out.

General Giap was absolutely correct. It is in our DNA as Americans, for the most part, to initially be patriotic when our military is called into combat. However, it has also been proven that such fervor does not last long, and our citizens quickly grow weary of war, as Giap indicated. This has continued to be true in our country.

I had no problem with the withdrawal of our forces from 'Nam, but the ending was pathetic. Everybody who was alive at the time saw the frantic chaos and frenzy on top of our Embassy in Saigon in April of 1975 as the last remnants of Americans were lifted by helicopter to American ships offshore.

Amazingly, in the Paris Accord, we did not even demand (request?) that the communists allow our personnel at the Embassy to leave peacefully when the time was appropriate. With *all* the concessions we had made to the communists in Paris, we didn't even require them to assure safe passage to the few remaining Americans left in the country after our troops had been long gone.

The helicopter pilot who flew U.S. Ambassador Graham Martin from the roof of the Embassy to the safety of a Navy ship on one of the final flights of that hectic period of April 29-30, 1975, was Iowa native Marine Colonel Gerry Berry from Indianola, an acquaintance of my brother, Dick.

Prior to that, Berry had flown 14 missions from the Embassy to the safety of ships at sea in his CH46 Sea Knight (precursor to the Chinook "Jolly Green Giant"), loaded with Americans and families of South Vietnamese citizens who had worked closely with U.S. Armed Forces.

Throughout a non-stop two-day period, Col. Berry and nearly 100 other Marine, Navy, and Air America (CIA) pilots would fly over 7,000 individuals away to safety.

Those courageous pilots did a marvelous job, but it should never have come to such a frantic ending. It was a shameful and inglorious exit for the world's number one military power, badly mishandled from a diplomatic standpoint by our government officials.

The original plan was to have a fleet of C-130 transport planes land at Tan Son Nhut Air Base and take Americans and tens of thousands of South Vietnamese, whom had been close associates of our efforts, to safety.

However, communist rocket and artillery fire on the air base made that impossible. Thus, officials had to scramble and use the rooftop of the Embassy for helicopter rescues. Oft used military acronyms FUBAR and SNAFU would both seem to apply to our evacuation plans.

Army Master Sgt. Max Beilke, who was assigned to help military personnel with the final exit, is credited with being the last American soldier to leave Vietnam. Tragically, Beilke was killed 26 years later while in the Pentagon Building during the terrorist attacks of September 11, 2001.

The bloodbath that we all feared might transpire when the communists took over South Vietnam did, unfortunately, take place. It is estimated that over 700,000 South Vietnamese became, or at least tried to become, "boat people," anxious to find a new place to call home away from the perils of the vindictive conquerors. Some have guessed that as many as 400,000 may have perished in the attempt to flee the ruthless new dictatorship.

Many South Vietnamese who were trapped and who couldn't get out of the country in time were executed, imprisoned, or sent to "re-education camps" and classified as war criminals by the new communist regime. Over 30,000 South Vietnamese were reported to have been executed immediately after the takeover.

Estimates range from 300,000 to 1 ½ million as to the number who were sent to the communist camps (some would call them concentration camps), where they endured torture, starvation, disease and hard labor. A total of over 150,000 reportedly died at the hands of the North Vietnamese and Viet Cong while in such confinement.

Due to my Crypto clearance, I received a copy of a Top Secret COSVYN (Viet Cong) document that had been captured in 1971. It included a list of those who would be executed if and when the communists took control.

Some of those on the list scheduled for killing by the V.C. were: *All South Vietnamese government administrative personnel; all government (ARVN) soldiers; South Vietnamese policemen and their families and relatives; students from South Vietnam whom had studied abroad; key personnel of religious sects; persons working for "disguised organizations" such as malaria prevention or land survey; persons who had corresponded with anyone in France or Japan; South Vietnamese citizens who had worked with the United States military;* and persons listed in 16 other categories.

When the war ended, I was dumbfounded to read accounts in publications in our own country calling the North Vietnamese and Viet Cong "liberators." I wonder if all of those people and families of those who were murdered, died trying to escape, imprisoned or "re-educated" thought of them as liberators?

Insulting the former citizens of South Vietnam by calling the Vietnam conflict a "civil war" is equally distasteful. It was never remotely a civil war; it was one country invading another, pure and simple.

Every American should have been livid with Hollywood director Bert Schneider praising the communist victory at the 1975 Academy Awards (aka Oscars) celebration. Schneider said: "It's ironic that we're here at a time just before Vietnam is about to be liberated." He then read a telegram "of greetings" from a communist Viet Cong official, Dinh Ba Thi.

Liberated. Wow.

I couldn't help but feel ill and shuddered to think what happened to my mama-san, my orphans, the wonderful South Vietnamese friends and co-workers I had known during my year in that country, the Montagnard tribesmen who were so loyal to us, the Hoi Chanh conscripts (those V.C. who had come over to our side), and millions of others who had been faithful to the United States. Many took their own lives rather than await their fate at the hands of the new brutal rulers.

I was heartened to learn that some 2,700 orphans had been successfully evacuated and prayed that those in my small group had made it. I was especially concerned for the Amer-Asian children.

The citizens of the "new" Vietnam under communist control suffered mightily in other ways. In 1983, Vietnam was named the "most repressive government in the world." It was an economic disaster for several years after the takeover; inflation had gone over 100% by the late 1980's.

Starvation was rampant. Over a million city-dwellers were forced into the countryside to clear the jungle and grow crops. The nightmare scenario that the population of South Vietnam had feared if overtaken by the communists, had come true.

If South Vietnam had prevailed, instead of wallowing in the misery of the oppressive victorious invaders, it would most likely have turned into an economic success story like Japan after WWII and South Korea (following its fight against the North Koreans).

Former South Vietnam Premier and Vice President Nguyen Cao Ky was bitter after the war, and rightfully so. He had no problem with sending the American forces home, but he begged for military aid from our nation which was necessary to continue the protection of his country and was rebuffed by the U.S. Congress at the time.

He was sympathetic to the American generals who had been forced to oversee a limited war that was run by the politicians. Ky said: "(General William) Westmoreland fought with his hands tied. How can you win a war if you are restricted politically? It was like fighting in handcuffs. If the Americans had gone all out in an attack on the North earlier, nothing could have prevented victory. They had the air power, the fire power, and the manpower to smash Hanoi to its knees, but this was never permitted."

Ky's frank and forthright statement couldn't have been more truthful. The United States has the wherewithal, technology, and the most modern of weaponry to enter into any theater of operations to put down a foe quickly, decisively, and with overwhelming odds, but to a great degree, since WWII, we have been reluctant to do so, mainly because of indecisive and hesitant politicians.

I truly hope to God that our country never has to go to war again, but, unfortunately, it's a dangerous world and we had better make up our mind to go full tilt if we find ourselves ever forced onto a battlefield again. I understand that it is a more dangerous world now with nuclear arsenals dotting the globe, but that's even more reason to be decisive.

Though both had often been ridiculed in some circles regarding their "domino theory," former presidents Eisenhower and Kennedy proved to be correct regarding their early predictions: Once South Vietnam had been overrun by the communists, they didn't stop there; Cambodia and Laos soon fell as well.

Eventually, a large contingent of South Vietnamese would re-settle in the U.S. They have prospered and have proven to be excellent citizens. In his book, *The Politically Incorrect Guide to the Vietnam War*, author Phillip Jennings pointed out that in 2005, "the combined income of the two million Vietnamese (who were then living in the U.S.) equaled the entire national income of communist Vietnam, a country of 80 million people." (The population in Vietnam has since grown to over 90 million.)

Vietnam today is still ruled by a one-party totalitarian communist government, but like China, it has finally realized the benefits of capitalism and has gradually opened up to the world to attract trade and tourism. It is becoming a competitive manufacturing sector.

I have a friend, Kris, whose husband. T.J., worked for Proctor & Gamble and was transferred to Vietnam in 1995. P&G was the second American company, behind Coca-Cola, to start doing business there. They resided in a suburb of Saigon (Ho Chi Minh City) for five years.

If you are a person who loves freedom of choice in all aspects of life, Vietnam might not be a place for you. Peaceful assembly, religion, unrestricted movement (especially leaving the country), right of expression, some forms of modern technology, and the use of the internet are tightly controlled and monitored.

Kris said that anything related to the war (books, newspaper articles, etc.) was strictly forbidden. If they wanted to have a party, the names of all attendees had to be submitted to proper officials, and it had to be a limited number. (Humorously, Kris said that it became a joke and said that you could have put down names like Mickey Mouse and Mickey Mantle, and they would have never known the difference.)

There are no freely elected officials, and corruption (called Party Rule violations) has been rampant among the communist leadership. Old-time zealots are becoming uneasy about the rapidly growing free enterprise, prompting the Communist Party to recently commence a "Blazing Furnace" anti-corruption campaign.

The country has gone through a major purge in leadership ranks. In recent months, two presidents and the head of the parliament were forced out; a deputy prime minister and eight members of the powerful Politburo were removed, and thousands of other communist party officials, including provincial party chiefs, have been "disciplined."

The roundup has hit the citizenry, too. A woman has recently been sentenced to death after being found guilty of bank fraud, and a man was sentenced to 21 years for stock fraud. Trumped up charges have been leveled against would-be opponents of the regime.

Powerful Communist Party General Secretary Nguyen Phu Trong, a Marxist-Leninist who ruled with an iron fist for the past decade, died in July of 2024, and observers are waiting to see if the hard-liners or younger and more moderate candidates will eventually take over the reins of government.

Vietnam made a bid with both the United States and the European Union to officially be designated as a "free market economy" in 2024, but both the U.S. and EU rejected the plea because the communists still oversee pricing and all trade. Both consider Vietnam to be a "non-market economy."

The government remains under the thumb of big brother Russia, which still supplies the country with its military hardware.

Almost half of the population (45%) is under 25 years of age, and I have been told that those young people have little animosity towards the United States; the war is as ancient as the Roman Empire is to them. In fact, many have affection for the U.S. while maintaining a strong inherent mistrust of the Chinese. Hopefully they will take Vietnam on a path to a free and prosperous future.

CHAPTER XX
Sorrowful Statistics

The final two American military men to die in Vietnam were Marines Darwin Lee Judge of Marshalltown, Iowa (so close to my hometown that it was in my high school's same athletic conference), and Charles McMahon of Woburn, Massachusetts. Both men had been in the country less than two months and were killed in a rocket attack while on guard duty at Tan Son Nhut, probably getting ready for the proposed evacuation from the air base on the C-130's which never materialized. Judge was 19 and McMahon 21.

They would be the last of 58,220 Americans to die in the small country of South Vietnam during the war. Of those, National Archive Records indicate that 40,934 were killed in combat; 9,107 died in accidents; 5,299 eventually died of wounds suffered in the war; 1,201 were declared dead; 938 died from illness; 382 committed suicide; 236 were murdered; 32 were presumed dead with bodies eventually recovered; and 91 were presumed dead but bodies were not recovered. To this day, there are still over 1,500 POW-MIA unaccounted for; you are not forgotten. A total of 303,644 Americans were wounded in the Indochina theater.

Eight women in the U.S. Armed Forces died in Vietnam. All were assigned to medical units. One died from shrapnel wounds suffered in an enemy attack in Chu Lai, five died in helicopter or plane crashes, and two passed away from illnesses.

Regarding the respective services, 38,224 of the total deaths were U.S. Army members; 14,844 were Marines; 2,586 were from the Air Force; 2,559 were Navy personnel; and 7 served in the Coast Guard. Thirty (30) percent of KIA were draftees.

The unit which suffered the most casualties because of its tenacious mentality, mobility, and willingness to go anywhere, was the Army's 1st Cavalry Division (and its elite reconnaissance element, 1st squadron, 9th Cavalry).

Continuing with this morbid numbers list, sadly 497 Americans were killed on their very first day in Vietnam while 1,448 met their fate on what would have been their final day in the country. Both are horribly tragic. I don't know which one would be worse for family members.

South Vietnamese military losses were put at between 200,000 and 250,000. Other countries allied with U.S. and South Vietnam forces reported the following numbers of killed in action: South Korea – 5,099; Australia – 521; Thailand – 351; Canada (serving with U.S. forces) – 134; New Zealand – 37; Taiwan – 25; and the Philippines – 9.

The number of communist soldiers, including the North Vietnamese Army (People's Army of Vietnam), Viet Cong (National Liberation Front), Peoples' Republic of China, Soviet Union, and North Koreans who were killed in action is murky, but is known to be over one million, with as many as 1.4 million KIA's being a possibility.

Fewer than 25% of those Americans who served in the Indochina theater and survived the war are still alive. Sadly, I have lost contact with many of my friends from back then. I did visit the Vietnam Wall in Washington D.C. once but simply couldn't handle it. I will probably never go back.

It may be hard to believe, but there were fewer Vietnam Vets who suffered psychiatric problems as there were in either WWII or Korea, and also fewer incidents of individuals going AWOL.

If I could be allowed to borrow the phrase of Admiral Chester Nimitz describing the brave men who lived through the hell of Iwo Jima in WWII -- "uncommon valor was a common virtue" -- I believe it could be applied to those men who were in combat arms in 'Nam as well.

Vietnam Veterans are a unique group. We were not exactly welcomed or well-respected when we returned home; in fact, we were downright detested in many quarters.

Through no fault of our own, we had participated in the most unpopular war in American history. Thus, we probably bonded more closely than veterans of our nation's other conflicts. We knew that we at least had each other. That is why, to this day, you'll often hear two Vets from 'Nam still say "welcome home" to each other.

> *"Perhaps the most dramatic difference*
> *Between World War II and Vietnam*
> *Was Coming home....*
> *None of them received a hero's welcome."*

■ 19
--Paul Hardcastle

CHAPTER XXI
The Search for Normalcy

Contrary to what I had believed, settling back into civilian life was not all smooth sailing. Shortly after my return to Newton, Nancy and I decided to try out a new pizza place. Sitting across from each other in a booth with high wooden backs serving as a divider between cubicles, we were enjoying a pleasant evening of talking, laughing and dining, in other words just the enjoyment of being together after our one-year separation, when suddenly, my wife lurched forward.

This happened a couple of more times and we realized that there were two boys in the booth behind her. One of them sitting on the other side of the tall common barrier separating our booth from theirs, was rocking back and forth on his seat, slamming his back against the partition between the two booths, causing Nancy to be jolted forward each time.

I got up and walked over to the two young men, thinking that they probably weren't aware of the disturbance they were causing. I politely asked the teenager who was banging the back of his seat to please stop because it was disturbing my wife's and my dinner. I was very courteous.

After I sat back down, I heard the two boys laughing, and the pounding became even more pronounced and more frequent. It had become a game to them. I became enraged. I jumped up, went over to the instigator, grabbed him by his shirt lapels with both hands and literally picked him up and dragged him out of his bench seat. Seething, I glared at him with a snarling face, which was just inches from his. I finally let him touch the ground and shoved him in the direction of Nancy, demanding that he apologize, which he did in a scared, high-pitched voice.

I don't know who was frightened the most; the teenage boys; my wife, who had never seen that side of me; or me, for demonstrating a temper that had never been unleashed, certainly to that extent. I shocked myself, and I wasn't proud of it. Who was this angry person inside my body?

It was the precursor of a three-month period of being a totally different individual. I went into a funk, which as you have probably ascertained by now, is the complete antithesis of my normal demeanor. I was on the cusp of depression, but at least it wasn't debilitating.

I had given little credence to the Army counselors in Oakland who told us that that we might become despondent. Unfortunately, it apparently had come to fruition for me. It's a psychological thing, and the emotional stress is termed "Survivor's Guilt."

In other words, why was I able to come home to my loved ones and friends, when over 8,000 other guys who served during my same year in Vietnam did not? Why did I have the right to forge ahead with a career and start a family when they would never experience those opportunities? Why couldn't I have done more for those orphans? Were any of those young soldiers whom I had ordered away from their loved ones and forced to board our plane to 'Nam been killed? The previous year, and everything that happened in it, came back to haunt me.

*"The changing, of sunlight to moonlight,
Reflections of my life....
All my sorrow, sad tomorrow,
Take me back to my old home...."*

- Refections of My Life
  --Marmalade

It is certainly an underlying condition, and one that is hard to explain. I was fortunate that my spell of such negative thinking only lasted a couple of months; many soldiers lived with that despair for years, and for others it became a life sentence.

When one finally rids himself of such gloomy feelings, it does not mean that he has become cold-hearted, he has finally come to the realization that the unfortunate demise of individuals in the war was not of his doing.

***

Those G.I.'s who did not live through the conflict would want those who did survive to make the most of their "borrowed" time. Following my brief despair, I did take advantage of my "second chance" and was able to have a long and satisfying career in college athletic administration after my discharge.

I do have lingering thoughts and memories, but none affect my daily life. I did have heartbreak, though. My marriage to Nancy eventually broke apart; was it partially a casualty of war? I will always hold her in the highest regard and my only thoughts regarding her are kind and positive. She was instrumental in helping me through some of the roughest patches of my life. We remain friends to this day.

Though devastated at the time of our split, years later good fortune would open the door for my marriage to Cathy, whom I've now been with for over three decades. She is the most amazing human being I have ever known; perfect in every way and I am grateful for her every day. She is the flight attendant whom I guess I was destined to meet since that time when I was first spellbound by the "stewardesses" on my flight to Seattle for basic training.

A lasting reminder of Vietnam is my mustache. I served with a friend who had the ugliest mustache I ever saw, and I razzed him about it. He was fearful that he was going to die in 'Nam, and I brushed aside his consternation, trying to assure him that it wasn't going to happen. I kiddingly said that I was so confident that he would survive that I would grow a mustache in his honor if he met his maker. Sadly, and shockingly, he did die, so I kept my word and have had my upper lip hair ever since.

For a while, the Army kept contacting me to see if I had an interest in joining the Reserves, and while the monthly stipend that was offered was much needed, I wanted to concentrate on graduate school and hopefully an opportunity to serve as an intern in a college athletic department. Though I regularly received correspondence from the Department of the Army 372D Engineer Group located in Des Moines, I kept respectfully declining.

My one regret is that I never did get to fly in a jet fighter, long a dream of mine. In the future, when I would serve as the executive director of the Armed Forces Bowl in Fort Worth, we hosted the Air Force Academy in our game, and it seemed that it might finally happen. Officials in the Falcon athletic department tried to make my desire a reality, but the wars in Iraq and Afghanistan at that time had the Department of Defense in serious mode and such frivolous activities were curtailed. I still keep this fantasy on my bucket list. (However, listed number one on my bucket list is not to kick it!)

One thing that did upset me long after I had returned home was the loss of several mementos from my time in Vietnam. During one of my many moves in later years, a couple of boxes containing personal items were lost in transit by the moving van company. One carton included such items as my dog tags, several photos that I had taken throughout the year, my Bronze Star Medal citation, and two Joint Service Commendation Medal citations. Though demanding extensive tracking by the moving company to find the items, they were never recovered.

The dog tags were my biggest loss. I had worn them around my neck for two years and I considered them to be my good luck charm during some very distressing times. (As Steve Carell, playing Michael Scott in the TV show, The Office, said: "I'm not SUPERstitious, but I am a little stitious.") Fortunately, I had packed my military medals in a suitcase during that particular move, so I did retain those.

As a Veteran, I would like to address an issue of importance: I believe that our government should provide, free of charge, a new house and automobile for any war Veteran who suffered a catastrophic injury (i.e. blindness, loss of a limb, severe head trauma, etc.) in combat (i.e. *only* injuries resulting from hostile action). Perhaps a national home builder could work with Washington D.C. to provide the living quarters at cost to the government, and perhaps the automobile industry could provide cars at no expense.

Houses could be built to cater to a particular handicap. In the case of a blind Vet, the car could be utilized by his or her spouse, a relative, or friend who could transport the Vet to places he or she needs to go. I also believe that grievously wounded combat Vets should be free of all federal and state income taxes and property taxes for the remainder of their lives.

It's the least we can do, especially with the money that our government spends on millions and millions of welfare recipients, legal and illegal, in addition to the vast foreign aid we give to other nations. Who deserves government assistance more than those who were badly wounded while being willing to lay down their lives for the United States of America? This should be applied to war widows or widowers, too. Relatively speaking, in a country of over 345 million, we are not talking about a large number of those needing such consideration.

I am grateful that there are already organizations who do provide housing and other benefits. That is fantastic, as long as EVERY incapacitated war Vet who so valiantly served our country receives complimentary lodging. If not, the government needs to be the provider. It is my sincerest wish for some Senator or House of Representatives member to introduce such legislation and make it happen.

In addition to Creighton Abrams, William Westmoreland, and Fred Weyand, who were all the top Commanders of American forces in Vietnam, over the past several years I have been extremely fortunate to have met some of our nation's other top military leaders of the past century, including WWII icon Omar Bradley.

We honored General Bradley at my first Sun Bowl College Football Game after I became executive director of that El Paso-based post-season contest in 1979. I had a chance to visit with him in our press box club level seating, and later he was nice enough to present me with an autographed copy of his book: *Bradley, A Soldier's Story*. The movie, "Patton," was based on that publication.

The Army was in charge of producing Bradley's presentation at halftime of the contest featuring Texas and Washington, and I was soon to regret not attending any of the planning sessions regarding the ceremonial show.

I was incensed when I saw that this great man was being rolled out in a wheelchair to midfield.

Had I sat in on the pre-activity meetings, I would have insisted that the 86-year old Army legend be driven in a WWII Jeep to the center point of the football field. That would have been much more fitting for this hero.

It was also an honor to meet Generals Tommy Franks and David Petreus. Both Franks and Petreus served tenures as Commander of the United States Central Command, overseeing all operations in Afghanistan and Iraq. Petreus later became Director of the Central Intelligence Agency (CIA).

The first time I met General Petreus (when I was serving as executive director of the Armed Forces Bowl College Football Game), I told him that I wore a lapel pin of my Military Assistant Command Vietnam (MACV) logo just for him. He smiled and said: "Well, that was a little before my time." Ouch! Here was a 3-star (later to become a 4-star) who was younger than me!

A good friend, Alex Powers, had served under Petreus and it was his idea to invite him to our bowl festivities, which was facilitated by Brant Ringler, the present-day executive director of the Lockheed Martin Armed Forces Bowl. During an e-mail to Petreus when he was stationed in Iraq, I kidded him by asking if he, as a West Point grad, could cheer for the Air Force Academy, who was playing in our game that year. He would be in attendance for the Fort Worth-based contest involving the Falcons. In his response, he assured me that he always rooted for our nation's service academies unless Navy or Air Force was playing Army!

Highly decorated and respected, Petreus, who received his Ph.D. from West Point, was the consummate soldier and patriotic American, having served in many command positions in addition to holding the prestigious title of Director of the CIA.

The General was also extremely tough! He was accidently shot in the chest during a live fire exercise when a young G.I. tripped, at which time his M-16 discharged, hitting Petreus. Future United States Senator Bill Frist performed surgery on Petreus to treat the wound, but that barely slowed down the exemplary warrior. Just a few days after undergoing the serious operation, Petreus was spotted doing 50 pushups without stopping!

General Franks, another much admired military leader, would have recognized my MACV pin, because he had served in Vietnam with great distinction. As an artillery forward observer, both from the ground and later from the air while serving out of Binh Phuoc in the Mekong Delta, he was injured numerous times as he continuously put himself in peril to protect his troops.

The good General had an interesting story as told in his autobiography, *American Soldier*, regarding the time he was calling in artillery strikes from a single-engine Cessna (O-1 Bird Dog). He was paired with a pilot nicknamed "Lizard," who sat in front while Franks, then a lieutenant, was seated behind him. Such pilots in 'Nam had the same daredevil DNA as the crop-dusters found in the Midwest back home.

Lizard appreciated the efforts of WWI pilots who simply threw bombs out of their cockpits; thus, he adopted that rather crude strategy in Vietnam. He would jam a hand grenade into a small Mason Jar, making certain that the handle (or "spoon") was tight against the side of the glass, and then he pulled the pin before securing the rubber-seal lid. Flying low, he had Franks toss out the Mason Jars at enemy troop concentrations on the ground while he kept the right wing tilted. It wasn't exactly high tech, but it was effective!

I met General Franks at the 2004 Independence Bowl (won by the Iowa State Cyclones, by the way). We were both guests of the game and sat next to each other on high bar-type stools in a luxury box.

We chatted and I eventually asked him where he had been stationed in Vietnam. He told me, and I casually responded: "Down in the Delta, huh?" Surprised that I knew of the location, he asked me if I had been in Vietnam. When I replied in the affirmative, he stood up and said: "Welcome home, Tom" and shook my hand. I think he even gave me a quick salute.

I was stunned. In the 33 years that I had been back at that point, nobody had ever said that to me. So, what was my reaction? I cried! Freakin' tears started flowing from my eyes in front of a 4-star General! Why do I do that? I turned my head as if I was looking out on the field and hoped that he hadn't seen my reaction. Thank you, General Franks; you have no idea how much that meant to me.

I have met 11 Congressional Medal of Honor recipients. One was fellow Vietnam Vet Harvey C. Barnum, Jr., who had a guided missile destroyer named in his honor. I was fortunate to attend the christening of the ship in Bath, Maine, with another 'Nam Vet, Purple Heart awardee Wayne Hickman, a Marine who recovered from a shot to the head during his service, and Paul Koenig, a friend who knew Barnum and made the trip possible.

Another individual awarded the Medal of Honor whom I met was David Bellavia, a hero in the second battle for Fallujah in Iraq. He touched me when he signed a copy of his book, *Remember the Ramrods*, for me, which I'm certain he meant as a tribute to all Vietnam Vets: "*Tom, Thank you for protecting my generation from what you endured. Welcome home. Thank you. You are loved. DB*

In addition to meeting those distinguished gentlemen, I have also had the distinct privilege of attending the annual Medal of Honor Banquet. I am always humbled in the presence of those courageous men who went far beyond the call of duty for their country. If you ever have an opportunity, google what some of these heroes did on the battlefield; it staggers the mind how fearless they were. (I'm proud to say that 60 Iowans have been so honored.)

One of my most cherished experiences was attending the Pentagon Memorial Dedication on September 11, 2008, exactly seven years after the insidious attack on our country by Islamic terrorists, when they killed 2,996 Americans as the result of hijacking four planes (that figure does not include the 19 repulsive instigators who died).

I remember very well that horrendous day in 2001. I was having breakfast with retired Colonel Jack Lee, who had served as a Chief of Staff and as Commander of a combat support group at Barksdale Air Force Base in Shreveport, Louisiana, and Glen Krupica, the executive director of Independence Bowl in the same city.

There was a television located close to our table with the sound on mute, and we witnessed the first plane crash into the World Trade Center. Like many viewers, we assumed that it was a horrible accident. We didn't recognize the building initially, thinking that the tragedy had taken place overseas. When the second plane hit the Trade Center, we recognized the towers, and it became obvious that a terrorist attack was underway.

When I saw that one of the planes was an American Airlines aircraft, I was horrified. My wife, Cathy, was an American Airlines flight attendant. I knew that she was on a trip in the East, but I wasn't certain where she was flying that day. I called her immediately and was GREATLY relieved when I heard her voice. In fact, I had awakened her; she was on a layover in Hartford, Connecticut and was not yet aware of the attacks.

Colonel Lee had a daughter stationed at the Pentagon and was equally panicked that morning. He was not as fortunate to reach his loved one as I was. It took him three days to learn that she had not been harmed.

It was a bizarre day. Later when I was driving towards downtown Shreveport on Airline Boulevard, I looked over to my left and saw Air Force One on approach to land at Barksdale AFB escorted by two fighter jets. President George W. Bush had been in Florida and was heading back to Washington D.C. when his plane was diverted to Shreveport. The Secret Service and his staff warned him to stay away from the Capitol due to continuing threats. It was decided to send him to the air base for protection.

All flights were grounded, and it took Cathy three days to get home. With no knowledge of how long the waiting would take, some members of the crew, including her, had contemplated renting a car and driving home. However, they were assigned to work a trip back to DFW on Friday, the 14th.

American Airlines flight #77 was one of the planes that was kidnapped on 9/11, 2001. The Boeing 757 had taken off at 8:20 out of Washington Dulles Airport on its way to Los Angeles on September 11, 2001. At 9:37 a.m., five Islamic skyjackers took control of the aircraft and purposely crashed it into the west wall of the Pentagon, causing a partial collapse of the famous military power center, which ironically, was built on September 11, 60 years prior to the attack (with construction finished in 1941). Six American Airlines crew members, 53 passengers, and 125 individuals in the building perished, including Max Beilke, the last U.S. soldier to leave Vietnam. Fortuitously, Colonel Lee's daughter was not in that part of the structure.

On that solemn day in 2008 to dedicate the renovation to the Pentagon, I was a front-row guest. I could have touched the VIP's who stood in front of me on the stage, they were so close. The distinguished group included President George W. Bush; U.S. Secretary of Defense Robert M. Gates; former Secretary of Defense Donald H. Rumsfeld; Chairman of the Joint Chiefs of Staff Admiral Michael C. Mullin; and Chairman of the Board of the Pentagon Memorial Fund, James J. Laychak.

Sitting close to the stage, I also had to move my knees sideways so that other dignitaries, including Henry Kissinger and several members of Congress, could get past me on their way to their seats.

There were several rows of chairs on the ground in front of the stage, with two large bleacher sections behind that. Obviously, security was of the utmost importance and all those in attendance were required to go through two different stations of thorough searching and scrutiny.

Opening remarks were made by Gordon R. England, Deputy Secretary of Defense and two-time Secretary of the Navy. I knew Mr. England, who has ties to the city in which I reside, Fort Worth, due to the fact that he received a master's degree from TCU and later served on its Board. He attended our Armed Forces Bowl when I served as that game's executive director.

Next, there was a tribute to those who were lost on that tragic day. Wreaths were laid by U.S. Air Force General Richard B. Myers, former Chairman of the Joint Chiefs of Staff; Lieutenant David Webster, Pentagon Force Protection Agency officer; and American Airlines flight attendant Deborah Maitland Roland. Following that, "TAPS" was played, followed by "Amazing Grace."

U.S. Army Chief of Chaplains Major General Douglas L. Carver gave the invocation, with a moment of silence observed after the prayer. Next, the president and others on the stage addressed the crowd, with patriotic military music interludes highlighting the speeches. Navy Rear Admiral Barry C. Black, retired chaplain of the United States Senate, gave the benediction. That was followed by the singing of "God Bless America" to end the ceremonies.

I was free to walk around the unveiling of the memorial park that was established next to the refurbished section of the Pentagon building. It features stream-lined benches, slanted down on one end to provide anchoring. A single bench is dedicated to each individual who died in the horrific attack, with their names engraved on the ends of the top "seating" area. Benches are arranged by age, and sadly, the youngest is 3-year-old Dana Falkenberg, who was on the ill-fated flight. Each memorial has a water reservoir underneath to reflect light in the evening. It was a sobering experience, to say the least.

Back to those of you who served in Vietnam, welcome home, and thank you for your service. It is my sincerest hope that every reader of this literary work will have a better understanding of the intricacies, puzzling government policies, and vitriol that 'Nam Vets experienced and endured. Perhaps, then, that understanding among the American populace will help the Veterans of that war find peace without the need to hear that long-elusive "final shot."

> *"Though we never thought that we could lose,*
> *There's no regrets;*
> *If I had to do the same again,*
> *I would my friend....."*

■   Fernando
    --Abba

ACKNOWLEDGMENTS

Ernest Hemingway once said: "There is nothing to writing; all you do is sit down at a typewriter and bleed." Well, things are a bit easier now with a computer, but it can still be an interesting and sometimes trying ordeal. One quickly learns that he or she needs a great supporting cast to produce the final product.

It would have been impossible to complete this project without the support and patience of my amazing wife, Cathy. My grandson, Colton Calovich, also played a major role in making this work come to fruition. He served as my IT specialist and without him, I would have been lost. I am grateful for his much-needed assistance.

Katrina Brandle, too, played an instrumental role, bringing her marketing skills to the publication. Others who contributed and to whom I owe a big "thank you" are Kris Tjaden, Nancy Smith, and a host of other friends and relatives, who were instrumental in the realization of the book. And, of course, I want to give a shout-out for the great assistance of Alexandra Lapointe and Cassie Arendec and the other good folks at Palmetto Publishing.

I drew inspiration from several published works on the topic of Vietnam, including "American Soldier" by General Tommy Franks; "A Soldier Reports" by General William Westmoreland; "Fighter Pilot: The Memoirs of Legendary Ace Robin Olds" by Christina Olds; "How We Lost the Vietnam War" by former South Vietnamese Vice President General Nguyen Cao Ky; "The Politically Incorrect Guide to the Vietnam War by Phillip Jennings; and "The TET Offensive" by LTC James H. Wilbanks. Wikipedia was an excellent source when I sometimes found myself needing to double-check my notes regarding a wealth of personal data emanating from my collection of letters, daily journal entries, official papers, tape cassette recordings, and items from memory.

Finally, I would be remiss if I forgot to thank Paris, our beautiful Samoyed, who kept me calm and collected throughout the whole process!

ABOUT THE AUTHOR

Tom Starr, a Vietnam veteran, has been an avid researcher and self-scholar regarding the conflict since his time spent in the Southeast Asian nation. With a Top Secret Crypto clearance during his stint in South Vietnam and a thorough knowledge of that theater of operations, he has unique insight into American history's most controversial military action.

Starr was the recipient of the Bronze Star Medal and two Joint Service Commendation Medals, in addition to the Vietnam Service Medal and Vietnam Campaign Medal (awarded by the South Vietnamese Government) among other honors.

As a civilian, he has maintained close ties to veterans' organizations and is a member of Roll Call. The author was instrumental in founding the Armed Forces Bowl (college football post-season game owned by ESPN), and its Most Valuable Player Award (Starr MVP) is named in his honor.

In addition to the Armed Forces Bowl, Starr served as the Executive Director of the Sun Bowl (El Paso, TX); the Freedom Bowl (Anaheim, CA); and the First Responders' Bowl (Dallas, TX); and was the Sr. Associate Executive Director of the Independence Bowl (Shreveport, LA). He also held the titles of Director of the Service Bureau for the Big Eight (presently Big 12) Conference, and Sports Information Director at Iowa State University.

Starr received a B.A. Degree in Mass Communications from the University of Iowa; completed his course work for a master's degree in public relations at Iowa State University; and graduated from both the U.S. Army Adjutant General School and the ESPN School of Business.

He and his wife, Cathy, reside in Fort Worth, Texas. They have a daughter, Cherish, and a son, Carter.

Milton Keynes UK
Ingram Content Group UK Ltd.
UKHW042115111124
451073UK00020B/420/J